ANALYTICAL METHODS FOR SUCCESSFUL SPECULATION

THE COMPLETE BOOK OF TRADING SYSTEMS

Comprising all major technical and fundamental analytical methods applied to gold from 1975 to 1985.

Including:

- Secrets of Trading
Graphically Depicted and Simply Explained

- Computer Drawn Charts and Studies

- Fundamental and Political Analyses

- Correlation Analysis Including CPI
and Money Supply Analysis

- Technical Analysis of Major Methods

- Psychological Explanation
of Bull and Bear Markets

- Astrological Analysis

JAMES E. SCHILDGEN

ANALYTICAL METHODS FOR SUCCESSFUL SPECULATION

The Complete Book of Trading Systems

By James E. Schildgen

Published by: Capital Futures Associates, Ltd.
P. O. Box 2618
Chicago, Illinois 60690

Printed in the United States of America.

Library of Congress Catalog Card Number: 86-71700

ISBN: 0-939397-00-5

About The Author

James E. Schildgen is an 18 year veteran of numerous investment markets; specializing in the areas of equity, debt, interest rates, precious metals, foreign currencies, the traditional futures, and their cash equivalents. He monitored over 170 precious metal mining stocks and became a quoted authority on futures trading, gold, inflation, currencies, and numismatics.

As an investment broker, he advised hundreds of individuals over the years and developed a thorough knowledge of money management principles demanded by the markets to survive and prosper.

Jim has been fully registered with the National Association of Securities Dealers, the New York Stock Exchange, the Chicago Board of Trade, Chicago Mercantile Exchange, the Commodity Futures Trading Commission, and the National Futures Association.

He has been quoted in such leading financial publications as the New York Times, The Business Week Letter, the Chicago Tribune, and Commodity News Service. He is listed in the 1980/81 edition of Who's Who in Hard Money Economics by Matlock, and appeared for over two years on Chicago's Channel 26, "Ask An Expert" television program as a guest expert.

As an author, he has written numerous articles and commentary in the investment area, including the ACLI Weekly Letter, the Technical Signal, Intermarket, and contributed to the Business Week Letter, all standard newswire services, and various publications of the Dow Jones Publishing Co.

Jim's market experience began as a runner at the Chicago Board of Trade, working his way up to margin clerk, error clerk, order clerk, researcher, retail broker, market letter writer, and advanced market specialist. He developed his own series of analytical data for studying money flows in the futures area.

His fascination with markets enabled him to create a personal financial library greater than many brokerage houses based in the Chicago area. This library includes over 1000 books; 19 years of Wall Street Journal futures prices; 13 years of CRB Computer Trend Analyzer pages; over 2200 daily bar charts done by hand with numerous statistical analyses; and hundreds of commodity fund prospectuses. Also CBOT, CME, and Commodity Research Bureau yearbook collections dating from 1877, 1948, and 1951 respectively. By 1968, he developed a chart library for the third largest brokerage house in Chicago.

During 1969, he taught two courses on commodity futures trading through the sponsorship of the Chicago Commodity Educational Club. This was the very first college accredited courses in the country.

Acknowledgement

I would like to express my appreciation to: Astro Computing Services, Bank Credit Analyst, Mr. John Booth, The Chicago Board of Trade, Mr. Michael Cohen, The Commodity Exchange of New York, Commodity Quote Graphics, Consolidated Gold Fields, Mr. Ed Durell, The Federal Reserve System, Foundation for the Study of Cycles, Institute for Social Research, Ms. Phyllis Kahn, Lambert-Gann Publications, Mr. Richard Ney, Mr. William Ohama, and the U.S. Department of Commerce, for their invaluable assistance and courtesy extended in allowing me to reproduce certain research and statistics contained herein.

You will notice the term "we" has been used throughout this book. Although my name appears as sole author, I did not do all the writing without help. I would like to thank my co-author, who chose to remain anonymous.

James E. Schildgen

Cover by Luis Ramirez

Table of Contents

Disclaimer

Although the information contained herein has been obtained from sources believed to be reliable, accuracy is not guaranteed. Information may be incomplete or condensed. Any judgments, opinions and estimates herein constitute our opinion as of the date of writing and are subject to change without notice.

This book is for educational and informational purposes only and should not be construed as an offer nor solicitation for purchase or sale of any security, commodity, or investment. Nor should it be assumed that any chart, theory, or philosophy can guarantee profits or will equal past performance in any way.

Capital Futures Associates, Ltd. and/or individual officers thereof, and/or members of their families may have positions in the investments mentioned herein.

"There are two times in a man's life when he should not speculate:
when he can't afford it, and when he can."
---Mark Twain

PART I

*"An investment in knowledge
pays the best interest."
---Benjamin Franklin*

Introduction

After many years of research and talking to many people involved in commodity futures markets, we came to the conclusion there is no single publication presenting all the various methods of analyzing price data to predict future prices.

Volumes have been published on single analyses and all the variances and modifications thereof, but we could not find a publication referencing all the different approaches in a simple graphic format.

In an attempt to alleviate this apparent lack of reference information, we compiled over 40 different trend analysis methods.

We also noted that most publications apply only one method of analysis to several different commodities. We felt in order to be more objective, all the analyses should be applied to only one commodity over a bull and bear cycle. We picked gold. Gold is the most controversial of all commodities because of its historical use as currency, mining production, and huge above-ground hoards and, therefore, the most interesting.

Our objective in writing this book was to broaden your knowledge of all the methods by which people attempt to predict and profit from future price moves.

The following analyses have been greatly condensed. Because of computer capabilities, many price analysis methods have been proven unreliable and unprofitable. Computer software is now available that enables you to adjust the parameters of an analysis or combine analyses to shift with market fluctuations.

No single approach to market analysis can totally explain previous trends, nor reliably predict future ones. However, increasing your awareness of the variety of methods people use in an attempt to predict future trends may give you a new investment outlook. At the very least, we know it will increase your knowledge and, hopefully, your profits.

"Dictum Meum Pactum: My Word Is My Bond."
                        ---London Stock Exchange motto

Master Gold Chart

The chart on the following page will be utilized as the primary example throughout this book.

The purpose of this book is to present as many as possible of the various interpretations derived from different quantitative and subjective analytical methods of studying gold price fluctuations.

Rather than presenting one interpretation or numerous interpretations on many unrelated commodities, we have presented a single commodity to which we will apply many different analytical methods.

We have decided to concentrate on the most controversial of all commodities - **GOLD.** Gold is controversial because the usual methods of surveying a commodity's production and consumption simply cannot be applied.

U.S. financial politics separate the banking interests from the interest of the general public by allowing banks to create "money" and its prodigy, credit, thereby creating price inflation. Banking gain is the public's loss through the fractional reserve monetary system. Inflation becomes the indirect tax destroying the value of all money savings, thereby promoting speculation.

In 1971 President Nixon established a two tier gold market. One level for central bank dealings and one for foreign commercial investment activity. This action fully evidences gold market manipulation by central banks which, at best, is artificial and benefits select few.

In December 1971, the official U.S. Treasury gold price was raised from $35.00 to $38.00 per ounce and then, on February 12, 1973, was raised to $42.22, where it remains today - but not for your benefit. The free price of gold is approximately 800% higher, fluctuating around $300.00 to $350.00 per ounce.

A close study of the significant highs and lows of the free gold price shows constant intertwining with major industrial country currencies, interest rates, inflation, and governmental legislation, as well as manipulation.

Master Gold Chart

The following chart is the free gold price used worldwide, quoted in U.S. dollars per ounce, plotted on a futures continuation basis, which best shows the spot price.

On the following pages, sixteen important prices are listed with exact dates of high or low from 1975 through 1985.

Commodity Quote-Graphics   TQ-20/20

Important Prices and Dates for Gold

Descriptions of all major economic, financial, and legal activity coincidental to all major highs and lows from 1975 through 1985.

1. $199.50   <u>December 31, 1974</u> - Due to severe populist demand, legislation is enacted legalizing the possession of gold in all forms by U.S. citizens. This is accomplished by an amendment to a bill raising social security taxes.   Since 1933, the possession of gold by U.S. citizens was illegal. President Franklin Delano Roosevelt demanded all gold held by U.S. citizens be confiscated by the government.   Gold increases 500% in four years after being freed from U.S. price fixing in 1971.   This week is also the last of the credit squeeze by the Fed pushing treasury bill rates to 12%.

    The first week of 1975, money and credit is made fully available to member banks of the Federal Reserve System, thereby collapsing interest rates and dropping gold prices in the process.

2. $127.40   <u>September 23, 1977</u> - New lows are made as foreigners remove buying support which was keeping gold above the $160.00 to $165.00 level.   U.S. citizens are little involved with gold at this time, having only two generations' experience with paper money, a fixed gold price, and shallow price inflation.

3. $99.70   <u>August 30, 1976</u> - By hindsight we see this is the bottom of an eighteen month bear move, after a sharp upturn. This corrects over 50% of the prior four year bull market. From labor day week forward, strength in foreign currencies and higher interest rates continue to maintain bull trends in league with gold. Europeans still dominate the trading action as U.S. citizens are grossly ignorant of the 5,000 year history of gold and its relationship to civilizations.

4. $249.40   <u>October 31, 1978</u> - After a 26 month upmove taking prices approximately $50.00 (25%) above the 1974 highs, President Carter is forced to curb the exodus of funds out of the U.S. into foreign currency debt obligations as well as into precious metals. Funds are also being withdrawn from U.S. banks and savings and loan associations en masse; illiquifying the economy and scaring top banking interests.   The President delivers his famous "Trick or Treat" Halloween speech, offering specific legal actions and constraints in an attempt to defend the U.S. dollar. Foreign currencies, gold and U.S. debt obligations react sharply.   Gold drops for two limit downmoves on futures exchanges as massive profits are taken.

5. $191.20   <u>November 29, 1978</u> - The panic ends after four weeks of continual selling. Interest rates ignore the bulk of this reaction and continue higher as the Federal Reserve Board Chairman, Paul Volker, squeezes credit institutions for liquidity. Gold resumes its bullishness with a steeper rate of climb to new highs.

6. $873.00   <u>January 21, 1980</u> - One of the greatest bull markets in history ends in an emotional buying panic. Gold and silver explode to levels unimaginable just a few years before. The Commodity Exchange of New York changes the legal rules of its silver contract to liquidation only for long positions. What was a buying panic by short hedgers becomes a forced selling panic of long positions, held mostly by speculators. Gold, platinum and even copper, which were dragged into the stratosphere price levels reached by silver, all collapse.

A Prince of The House of Saud and Bunker Hunt, Jr. were primary in the accumulation of physical silver and a majority of long futures contracts (estimated at 280 million ounces by some sources). This has been termed a technical squeeze. They were not attempting to force their positions onto others but rather trying to escape the depreciating U.S. dollar by being in silver, which is often thought of as a substitute for gold.

Foreign currencies, interest rates, inflation levels, commodity prices, and real estate all seem to end their panic activity this year, almost in a bubble fashion similar to the 1700's and 1800's financial panics. Short term interest rates hit 21% in 1980 - a level **double** that of the U.S. Civil War.

7. $453.00   <u>March 25 through 27, 1980</u> - The panic selloff from the $800.00+ level collapses prices into late March. "Black Tuesday", "Black Wednesday", and "Black Thursday" are ingrained into the memory of silver traders' minds as silver falls from a spot price of $50.40 to $10.00 (a loss of 80% of the total value) in only eight weeks. However, gold falls less than 50% in the same time, goes into consolidation, and resumes its up-trend. These three "black" days are created primarily by the forced sale of Bunker Hunt's futures positions as margin calls are presented to him by the Comex's clearing house. Estimates for this week's margin calls range from a minimum of $600 million to $1 billion for Mr. Hunt alone.

8. $727.00   <u>September 22, 1980</u> - The next significant high occurs six months after the "black" week in March. Gold equities top out in tandem with gold. Actually, gold equities made substantially higher prices in September compared to January 1980. This leads students of the market to call this the real final top and the January high an artificial situation, even though higher in absolute terms. The primary 5-1/2 year cycle implied a second or third quarter 1980 high for gold; not January, which would have been a 5-1/10 year peak-to-peak cyclical high.

9. $297.50   <u>June 21, 1982</u> - This 21 month low from the September 1980 high, completes the shortened downmove of the 5-1/2 year cycle in league with interest rates, foreign currencies, and inflation. The projected low that any cycle student could forecast is the second quarter of 1982, which is close enough. The prior upmove is some 40 months long and this down move takes approximately half that time, implying higher highs and lows to come. Foreign interests continue buying U.S. dollar debt obligations as yields here remain higher than comparative foreign government bonds. As the dollar continues to escalate in price, primary foreign demand for gold is token.

10. $501.00   <u>September 8, 1982</u> - From a major cyclical low in June, this is the greatest percentage upmove for gold when compared to the two prior 5-1/2 year cycle upmoves. Two major changes are occurring compared to prior upmoves in the early part of the 5-1/2 year cycle. First, interest rates continue to fall. Second, the U.S. dollar continues to explode upward against foreign currencies. In August 1982, Mexico technically defaults on its foreign debt obligations, creating panic buying of precious metals. Financial institutions begin buying substantial quantities of U.S. industrial stocks this week. Foreign buying of U.S. equities continues as positive returns appear in absolute prices, as well as additional dollar appreciation.

11. $390.00   <u>October 4, 1982</u> - World bankers express extreme nervousness over Third World debt repayment abilities, as most commodity prices continue to fall. The summer's rapid $204.00 gold upmove in ten weeks is corrected by a $111.00 fall in just four weeks.

12. $515.00   <u>February 22, 1983</u> - Gold prices slow appreciably in January and February as Middle Eastern hoards are dumped onto the market to cover the collapsed Kuwaiti stock market bubble (an estimated $95 billion loss). The OPEC Cartel lowers the official crude oil price. Gold drops $110.00 in eight days (20% of total price).

13. $337.80 <u>January 26, 1984</u> - Interest rates, especially long term, have edged slightly higher for over a year but with no apparent effect on gold prices. The U.S. dollar continues to edge higher as foreign interests continue to move cash out of foreign currency holdings. This also has no effect as gold moves constantly lower.

14. $410.50 <u>March 5, 1984</u> - Foreign currencies and gold move up in tandum, but reverse sharply in early March as the Continental Illinois National Bank failure occurs; the biggest single bank run in all history. All financial activity centers on acquiring U.S. dollars at all cost, ignoring the two U.S. deficits and their implications for gold.

15. $282.60 <u>February 26, 1985</u> - The U.S. dollar finally turns sharply down after an extended five year upmove against foreign currencies. Gold goes below 1982's low of $297.50, fails to move lower and retreats into a lateral trend, just after making new five year lows.

16. $345.80 <u>August 19, 1985</u> - Gold rallies to approximately half of its 1984-85 downmove, but falters and continues within its six month trading range.

Master Gold Chart

The following are the actual prices used by Commodity Quote Graphics for the month ended, denoting open, high, low and close to the first decimal.

GC Monthly Bars

Date	Open	High	Low	Close
1/ 1/75	1840	1848	1675	1755
2/ 3/75	1779	1876	1735	1818
3/ 3/75	1833	1836	1750	1771
4/ 1/75	1797	1799	1623	1668
5/ 1/75	1670	1769	1634	1665
6/ 2/75	1645	1685	1624	1678
7/ 1/75	1683	1708	1620	1676
8/ 1/75	1708	1712	1595	1602
9/ 1/75	1502	1539	1274	1405
10/ 1/75	1450	1480	1385	1428
11/ 3/27	1435	1491	1368	1373
12/ 1/75	1388	1479	1367	1410
1/ 1/76	1408	1415	1234	1282
2/ 2/76	1305	1347	1285	1326
3/ 1/76	1325	1353	1273	1291
4/ 1/76	1297	1301	1269	1289
5/ 3/76	1288	1298	1241	1260
6/ 1/76	1278	1325	1235	1239
7/ 1/76	1236	1245	1050	1121
8/ 2/76	1122	1144	997	1028
9/ 1/76	1041	1203	1041	1157
10/ 1/27	1158	1260	1129	1238
11/ 1/76	1228	1410	1228	1315
12/ 1/76	1320	1397	1313	1357
1/ 3/77	1355	1377	1275	1330
2/ 1/77	1340	1454	1328	1446
3/ 1/77	1427	1547	1424	1495
4/ 1/77	1505	1547	1448	1480
5/ 2/77	1479	1497	1420	1435
6/ 1/77	1448	1456	1376	1436
7/ 1/77	1435	1474	1405	1451
8/ 1/77	1455	1488	1425	1467
9/ 1/77	1463	1550	1459	1546
10/ 3/77	1578	1668	1554	1627
11/ 1/77	1638	1699	1547	1602
12/ 1/77	1628	1679	1571	1675
1/ 2/78	1699	1783	1655	1766
2/ 1/78	1794	1858	1736	1844
3/ 1/78	1849	1928	1758	1841
4/ 3/78	1857	1859	1668	1706
5/ 1/78	1703	1857	1692	1843
6/ 1/78	1855	1893	1819	1837
7/ 3/78	1845	2040	1832	2036
8/ 1/78	2110	2180	1985	2076
9/ 1/78	2094	2210	2045	2179
10/ 2/78	2205	2494	2202	2407
11/ 1/78	2307	2307	1912	1932
12/ 1/78	1960	2296	1958	2290
1/ 1/79	2291	2385	2166	2325
2/ 1/79	2350	2588	2320	2529

20

GC Monthly Bars

Date	Open	High	Low	Close
3/ 1/79	2507	2529	2350	2395
4/ 2/79	2438	2507	2318	2492
5/ 1/79	2500	2778	2461	2768
6/ 1/79	2805	2886	2750	2838
7/ 2/79	2843	3078	2823	2869
8/ 1/79	2923	3229	2832	3202
9/ 3/79	3280	3997	3239	3950
10/ 1/79	4165	4445	3730	3857
11/ 1/79	3815	4210	3650	4191
12/ 3/79	4400	5430	4330	5410
1/ 1/80	5660	8730	5660	6815
2/ 1/80	7000	7425	6170	6400
3/ 3/80	6430	6600	4530	5015
4/ 1/80	5250	5700	4830	5070
5/ 1/80	5000	5520	4820	5452
6/ 2/80	5800	6760	5600	6540
7/ 1/80	6700	6960	6040	6197
8/ 1/80	6300	6590	6098	6418
9/ 1/80	6430	7290	6410	6715
10/ 1/80	6990	7085	6270	6420
11/ 3/80	6400	6650	5930	6246
12/ 1/80	6560	6570	5580	5995
1/ 1/81	5935	6120	4850	5017
2/ 2/81	5050	5305	4850	4865
3/ 2/81	4710	5540	4530	5138
4/ 1/81	5240	5455	4760	4890
5/ 1/81	4880	5030	4640	4794
6/ 1/81	4955	4998	4270	4285
7/ 1/81	4265	4315	3970	4035
8/ 3/81	4020	4510	3955	4311
9/ 1/81	4290	4700	4175	4327
10/ 1/81	4460	4690	4265	4312
11/ 2/81	4320	4360	3925	4083
12/ 1/81	4070	4370	3965	4028
1/ 1/82	3990	4110	3690	3846
2/ 1/82	3870	3944	3627	3645
3/ 1/82	3625	3665	3125	3275
4/ 1/82	3345	3775	3288	3465
5/ 3/82	3510	3510	3215	3222
6/ 1/82	3255	3430	2975	3178
7/ 1/82	3140	3770	3083	3427
8/ 2/82	3580	4340	3340	4118
9/ 1/82	4070	5010	3905	3985
10/ 1/82	4085	4650	3900	4230
11/ 1/82	4310	4435	3980	4426
12/ 1/82	4460	4688	4350	4530
1/ 3/83	4550	5110	4495	5101
2/ 1/83	5175	5200	4237	4237
3/ 1/83	4160	4420	4065	4159
4/ 1/83	4220	4508	4220	4335

GC Monthly Bars

Date	Open	High	Low	Close
5/ 2/83	4310	4525	4100	4120
6/ 1/83	4200	4283	4010	4185
7/ 1/83	4195	4390	4095	4128
8/ 1/83	4190	4337	4115	4177
9/ 1/83	4195	4220	3970	4019
10/ 3/83	3960	4088	3780	3788
11/ 1/83	3778	4088	3730	4030
12/ 1/83	4050	4100	3755	3880
1/ 2/84	3855	3862	3625	3738
2/ 1/84	3800	4018	3378	3958
3/ 1/84	3982	4105	3855	3875
4/ 2/84	3945	3950	3778	3796
5/ 1/84	3798	3905	3700	3868
6/ 1/84	3993	4053	3700	3761
7/ 2/84	3730	3743	3320	3377
8/ 1/84	3437	3625	3420	3512
9/ 3/84	3420	3495	3355	3449
10/ 1/84	3520	3558	3335	3360
11/ 1/84	3357	3535	3250	3291
12/ 3/84	3325	3370	3066	3097
1/ 1/85	3070	3095	2967	3041
2/ 1/85	3060	3085	2826	2887
3/ 1/85	2887	3350	2870	3296
4/ 1/85	3240	3386	3150	3165
5/ 1/85	3173	3298	3086	3162
6/ 3/85	3201	3313	3125	3177
7/ 1/85	3171	3310	3083	3271
8/ 1/85	3290	3458	3225	3354
9/ 2/85	3295	3320	3142	3228
10/ 1/85	3260	3357	3249	3267
11/ 1/85	3257	3334	3221	3229
12/ 2/85	3155	3314	3130	3137

Alternative Gold Chart

A more correct way to show gold's price and its odyssey, is to plot it onto a semi-logarithmic scale chart. This shows percentage movements up or down of gold prices at all levels. Percentage-wise, a move from $35 to $70 is the same as a move from $100 to $200 or even $400 to $800. Unfortunately, most market students care more about recent price history than old price history. Gold's recent bull/bear cycle while having large dollar swings, is not that much different on a percentage basis than the last bull/bear cycle (1971 - 1976). Therefore, we present this semi-log chart as our second choice for the book, with the master gold chart and its arithmetic scale as our more utilitarian choice.

Alternative Gold Chart

1972 - 1985

Semi-logarithmetic Scale, To The Base 10, i. e., Every Cycle Tenfolds. All Price Changes Are Shown As Equal Percent.

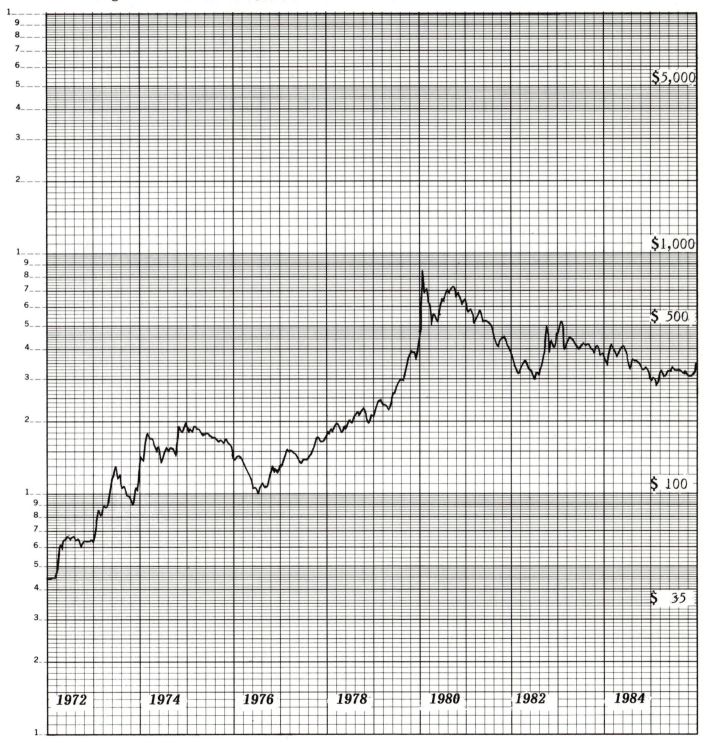

"No lock will hold against the power of gold."
---George Herbert

Gold As An Investment Or Speculation
— Methods to Buy Long and Sell Short Gold —

Bullion:
Accounts (Swiss, Offshore, Broker, Dealer)
Arbitrage
Bars (400 oz., 100 oz., 1 kilo (32.15 oz.) 10 oz., 5 oz., 2 oz. and 1 oz.)
Barter
Bullion Coin (Low Percentage Premium i.e. Krugerrand)
Collateral for a Loan
EFP (Exchange for Physicals)
Gold Clause Contract
London Fixing (Lots of 5, 400 oz. Bars - Approved Banks Only)
Options (On Physicals, Listed, Dealer, and Exchange)
Wafers (1, 5, 10, 20, and 50 gram)
Writing Gold Call Options

Certificates:
Coin (Dealer or Bullion Houses)
Delivery Orders
Free Zone (Swiss Airport Storage)
Holding Account
Loan Investments (Banks, Dealer, or Bullion Houses)
Warehouse Receipts

Coin:
Ancient Coin (High Percentage Premium, Rarity Mainly)
Bullion Coin (Low Percentage Premium)
Commemorative
Counterfeit (Mainly European and Communist)
Medals (Private and Government)
Numismatic Coin (High Percentage Premium - Rarity, Age, Condition, Quantity)
Trade Coin (Medium Percentage Premium - Sovereigns and U.S. $20 Gold Pieces)

Futures:
Contracts
Delivery (Bar Gold)
Options (High Leverage) (Bullion or Dealer - High Leverage)
Spreads

Industrial:
Alloy
Dental
Electronic

Jewelry:
Art & Antiques (Sculptured/Crafted)
Bullion Jewelry (Low to Medium Percentage Premium - Chains, Necklaces, Watches)

Managed Accounts:
Professional Financial Advisor or Broker

Passbook Accounts:
Banks (Foreign and U.S. - Mainly Swiss)
Bullion Houses

Stocks:
Closed End Mutual Funds (Trades Premium or Discount to Asset Value)
Junior Mines
Mining Houses (Holding Companies)
Mining Stocks (Developed - South African and Canadian)
U.S. Mines (Copper/Gold/Silver)
Options (ASA and Canadian)
Open End Mutual Funds
Penny Gold Stocks
Undeveloped Gold Properties

"Knowledge is power."
---Thomas Hobbes

PART II

Fundamental Analysis

Supply/Demand Analysis

U.S. Gold Stock Situation

Political Gold Chart

Gold Viewed Through Three Foreign Currencies

Seasonal Gold Analysis

"Every young man should have a hobby.
Learning how to handle money is the best one."
---Jack Hurley

Fundamental Analysis

Fundamental analysis can be simply defined as the supply versus demand for any product, service or commodity. To apply fundamental analysis to gold, elastic and inelastic supply and demand should be explained.

An elastic supply/demand function is defined as the degree of change in supply to demand in relation to the change in price. As an example, let's look at food. Food is a necessity. Therefore, demand does not fluctuate greatly. If the supply cannot meet the demand, say by 5%, the relative price increase is not 5%, but possibly 50%. If supply exceeds demand by 5%, the price is then reduced by a significant amount. This is an elastic supply/demand function.

As an example of inelastic supply/demand, let's examine gold. Gold is not a necessity for survival. Therefore, demand is somewhat insensitive to supply and price. Should the supply of gold decrease, demand is not greatly affected and could conceivably be reduced. In a hypothetical situation, should the supply of gold decrease and the price increase, actual demand can decrease as other materials, such as platinum, palladium or silver, are substituted for gold.

Of course, the above explanations and examples are based strictly on consumption versus availability. Simple supply/demand factors do not completely influence the price of any given commodity. Variables such as the Mediterranian fruit fly, a floor trader's argument, unusual weather patterns, or a senator's vote, also affect prices.

In relation to gold, only two areas of consideration should be included in any thorough fundamental analysis:

The yearly supply/demand analysis of all known new mine production; scrap and coin reclaimation; and usage by industry; along with estimated investment and hoarding. The same type of analysis applies to other storable and fungible commodities, such as wheat or copper.

A long term approach includes central bank reserves and individual hoards of gold. This is especially true in nations having extremely disasterous financial histories and chaotic price changes, such as panics, crashes, and super-inflation. All these manmade occurances cannot be predicted. Countries with poor economic histories are Germany, France, Italy, Switzerland, and the United States, in the industrialized sector. All semi-industrialized and third world countries have hyper-inflation so frequently that gold hoarding is considered the best form of investment.

In an annual supply/demand analysis, an examination of yearly supply figures shows four catagories to be considered: Noncommunist world mine production, net trade with the communist sector, net official sales, and net official purchases. (See Table 1.) To our knowledge, the best available source of this information is the most recent annual study "Gold 1985" published by Consolidated Gold Fields PLC, London, edited by Louise du Bouley. We sincerely appreciate their allowing us to reproduce the three tables included herein.

An examination of the supply figures in the four columns shows that the major variables to watch are communist trade and official sales or purchases.

Communist gold sales are a by-product of their need for foreign exchange. The Soviet Union needs foreign currency for all noncommunist purchases. The Russian rouble is not convertible in open trade dealings, therefore, completely arbitrary in value.

To examine the supply of gold, we need to also examine gold's history.

The Soviet government has marketed its gold production in an attempt to manipulate prices higher to their advantage. When prices are relatively low, reducing gold sales or entirely withdrawing from the market creates an upward pressure on world market prices.

Official sales are usually forced affairs by the leading monetary institutions of the world to quell very strong demand for gold or very strong dumping of paper currency, usually in response to a panic situation. The joint gold pool between European central banks and the U.S. Treasury (1961 to 1968) saw such demand for gold, that the pool collapsed and the industrialized world was forced off the gold standard in 1968. Paper money is not freely convertible into gold, nor vice versa, in any country. Gold can only be acquired today in a "free trade market" or "aftermarket" at ten times the controlled price of just fifteen years ago.

The years 1977 through 1979 saw both the U.S. Treasury and International Monetary Fund auction bar gold (usually 400 ounce bars) in an attempt to contain feverish buying demand.

From 1981 forward, central banks' selling was due presumably to two distinct actions. The Iran/Iraqi war resulted in selling of gold to raise foreign currency to purchase food and munitions. This is the normal function today of a reserve asset, such as gold.

Secondly, the drop in the price of crude oil began to force OPEC member nations to begin liquidating their gold reserves as oil revenue shrank. The 1982/83 Kuwaiti stock market price rise and bubble collapse in two months created the disappearance of some $95 billion in equity. Gold and silver flooded the market from the Middle East to pay for this bubble; built on predated credit. Further, long term Arabian projects which started in the 1970's needed funds to pay for their completion at the same time that gross oil revenue began collapsing. As a result, gold hoards were dumped by many nations to gain much needed working capital.

Demand is shown by several categories of gold fabrication such as jewelry, electronics, dentistry, decoration, metals and medallions, and official coins. (See Table 3.) A rising or falling price will restrict or expand overall demand as price becomes a consideration in each of these activities.

Another area of demand is gold investment, usually in bar or bullion form. This is done in one of two ways. Either people invest in gold on a constant daily basis or they panic in response to some economic situation or collapse of the local currency.

In most European, Middle Eastern, and Far Eastern countries, gold is purchased in low premium jewelry form as a noncurrency type of savings. Bullion coin purchases as well as small bars are also standard for saving purposes — especially when your nation's currency has disappeared four times within the past 100 years. (See Table 11.)

The largest buyers, hoarders, dealers, and manipulators of gold are the central banks. The U.S. government has an above ground hoard that is equivalent to approximately eight years of newly mined world gold production.

This ready supply or hoard was once used for daily transactions as coin of the realm or "specie" money. Specie money is real money having an intrinsic worth. "Fiat" money or nonredeemable paper currency is money accepted on faith.

The majority of money today is literally electronic blips on computers transferred between financial institutions. Because gold is so tightly held by central banks, is cumbersome to use in commercial transactions, and has been made into an archaic form of doing business, it is rarely used today as a form of exchange. The physical quantity of various paper currencies (or electronic blips) is continually increased by governments thus reducing its value relative to goods and services. This is "money inflation" which results in "price inflation". In 1985, foreign currency transactions between the top ten industrialized countries was estimated at $120 to $150 billion daily.

The potential upward price change for gold by paper money dumping is called a money panic. This is a return to people wanting money (gold) with inherent worth.

In the long run, demand for gold is greatest by central banks, who put a fraction of their money into gold as a reserve asset. Only in extreme situations such as war or economic emergency does gold ever come back onto the market. There will always be demand for gold because of the continual increase in the creation of paper money worldwide.

In conclusion, central banks in the top fifteen industrial countries that deny gold as having any monetary value, have on hand today over 85 times the total yearly world mine production. If one percent of this hoard comes to market in one year, the annual supply of gold would be almost doubled. Therefore, the rules of annual production and consumption cannot be realistically applied to gold because of the erratic nature of hoards and their manipulation by economic events.

Supply/Demand Analysis

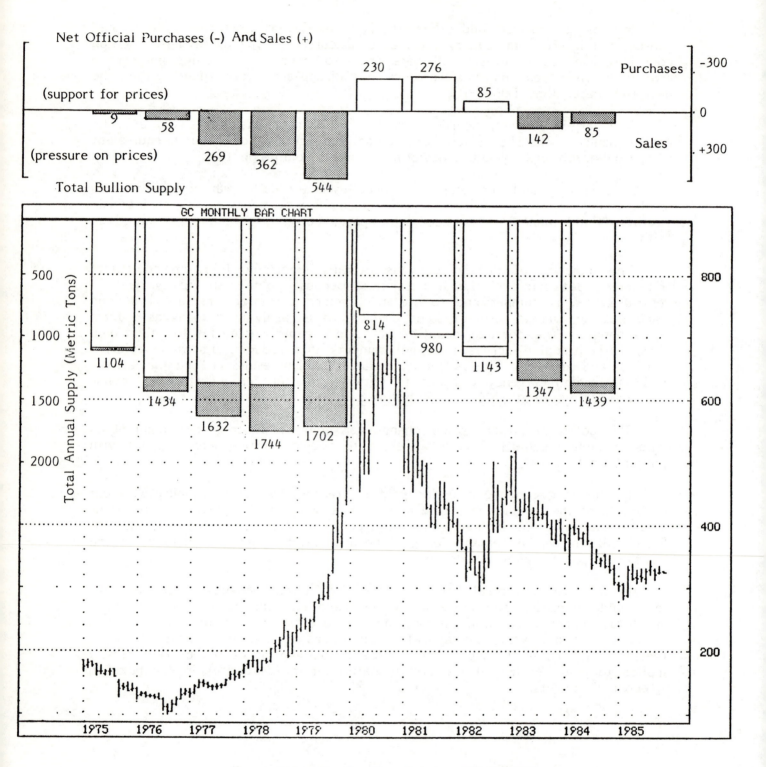

Net Official Purchases (-) And Sales (+)

230 276

(support for prices) 85

Purchases

-300

0

9

58

(pressure on prices) 269

362

142 85

Sales

+300

544

Total Bullion Supply

GC MONTHLY BAR CHART

Total Annual Supply (Metric Tons)

500

1000

1104

1434

1500

1632

1744

1702

814

980

1143

1347

1439

2000

800

600

400

200

1975 1976 1977 1978 1979 1980 1981 1982 1983 1984 1985

Commodity Quote-Graphics   TQ-20/20

Source : Gold 1985, Consolidated Gold Fields PLC, London.

Table 1: Gold bullion supply to the non-communist private sector
Metric tons

	Non-communist world mine production	Net trade with communist sector	Net official sales (+)	Net official purchases (−)	Total
1948	702	—	—	369	333
1949	733	—	—	396	337
1950	755	—	—	288	467
1951	733	—	—	235	498
1952	755	—	—	205	550
1953	755	67	—	404	418
1954	795	67	—	595	267
1955	835	67	—	591	311
1956	871	133	—	435	569
1957	906	231	—	614	523
1958	933	196	—	605	524
1959	1000	266	—	671	595
1960	1049	177	—	262	964
1961	1080	266	—	538	808
1962	1155	178	—	329	1004
1963	1204	489	—	729	964
1964	1249	400	—	631	1018
1965	1280	355	—	196	1439
1966	1285	−67	40	—	1258
1967	1250	−5	1404	—	2649
1968	1245	−29	620	—	1836
1969	1252	−15	—	90	1147
1970	1273	−3	—	236	1034
1971	1233	54	96	—	1383
1972	1177	213	—	151	1239
1973	1111	275	6	—	1392
1974	996	220	20	—	1236
1975	946	149	9	—	1104
1976	964	412	58	—	1434
1977	962	401	269	—	1632
1978	972	410	362	—	1744
1979	959	199	544	—	1702
1980	954	90	—	230	814
1981	976	280	—	276	980
1982	1025	203	—	85	1143
1983	1112	93	142	—	1347
1984	1149	205	85	—	1439

Definition of official sales has been extended from 1974 to include activities of government controlled investment and monetary agencies in addition to central bank operations. This category also includes IMF disposals.

Reprinted by permission: Consolidated Gold Fields plc; GOLD 1985

Table 3: Gold fabrication and net changes in investment holdings

Metric tons

	1974	1975	1976	1977	1978	1979	1980	1981	1982	1983	1984
A. Total gold bullion supply	1236	1104	1434	1632	1744	1702	814	980	1143	1347	1439
Fabricated gold in developed countries:											
Carat jewellery	274	312	477	545	591	546	275	373	421	381	436
Electronics	90	65	73	75	87	97	87	89	83	101	120
Dentistry	56	59	74	82	89	85	62	63	59	52	50
Other industrial/decorative uses	64	54	60	61	68	72	62	61	58	51	50
Medals, medallions and fake coins	11	9	20	22	20	16	18	12	6	22	16
Offical coins	209	221	145	125	255	243	170	141	124	152	124
B. Total	703	720	849	910	1110	1060	673	740	750	759	797
Fabricated gold in developing countries:											
Carat jewellery	−58	204	459	459	413	182	−148	226	292	214	383
Electronics	1	1	1	1	2	2	2	1	2	2	2
Dentistry	2	4	4	4	4	4	2	1	1	1	1
Other industrial/decorative uses	3	4	5	6	7	7	4	4	4	3	3
Medals, medallions and fake coins	−4	12	31	30	30	17	−2	15	16	9	28
Official coins	78	30	37	17	32	48	15	50	7	13	6
C. Total	23	255	537	517	488	259	−127	298	322	242	424
D. Total fabricated gold (B + C)	726	975	1386	1427	1598	1319	546	1038	1072	1001	1221
E. Net changes in bullion holdings (A− D)	510	129	48	205	146	383	268	−58	71	346	218
F. Identified investment holdings (Table 11)	−17	42	185	68	118	191	18	275	303	87	333
G. Net changes in supply (E − F)	527	87	−137	137	28	193	250	−333	−232	260	−115

*Totals may not add due to rounding.

Reprinted by permission: Consolidated Gold Fields plc; GOLD 1985

Table 11: Regional investment holdings

Metric tons

	1974	1975	1976	1977	1978	1979	1980	1981	1982	1983	1984
Europe:											
Greece	5.0	2.0	—	—	—	6.7	−2.5	−2.0	−2.8	1.5	0.4
Spain	—	—	—	—	—	—	—	—	4.5	2.0	—
Total Europe	5.0	2.0	—	—	—	6.7	−2.5	−2.0	1.7	3.5	0.4
Latin America:											
Brazil	2.1	—	—	—	—	4.0	4.0	3.0	8.3	17.5	6.0
Colombia	—	—	—	—	—	—	—	—	—	0.3	—
Argentina	—	−5.0	−3.0	—	—	3.5	5.0	−0.6	—	—	—
Venezuela	0.5	—	—	—	—	—	—	—	—	—	—
Peru	—	—	—	—	—	—	−2.0	—	—	—	—
Other	—	—	—	—	—	—	—	0.5	1.0	—	—
Total Latin America	2.6	−5.0	−3.0	—	—	7.5	7.0	2.9	9.3	17.8	6.0
Middle East:											
Saudi Arabia & Yemen	—	1.0	17.0	13.0	8.0	−4.0	5.0	15.0	33.0	22.0	35.0
Arabian Gulf States	−5.0	—	1.5	—	—	1.4	0.2	3.2	8.0	2.7	7.5
Egypt	—	—	—	—	—	—	−5.0	5.0	2.0	3.0	4.0
Israel	1.6	2.0	1.0	3.0	2.5	9.0	2.0	1.5	—	1.2	2.2
Syria	—	—	—	—	—	0.5	6.0	2.0	10.0	3.0	2.0
Kuwait	1.5	—	—	1.0	1.0	0.6	0.7	3.0	5.0	2.0	2.0
Lebanon	1.0	—	—	0.5	1.0	1.0	2.0	1.0	2.0	1.0	1.0
Jordan	—	1.0	1.0	1.0	—	0.1	—	1.0	1.0	0.3	1.0
Turkey	—	—	—	—	2.0	15.0	−15.0	—	—	2.9	—
Iran	2.0	1.0	—	1.0	8.0	−1.0	−5.0	—	—	—	—
Iraq	—	—	—	1.0	—	0.3	—	—	2.0	—	—
Total Middle East	1.1	5.0	20.5	20.5	22.5	22.9	−9.1	31.7	63.0	38.1	54.7
India	—	15.0	—	—	—	—	−1.0	—	—	2.0	9.0
Pakistan & Afghanistan	—	—	—	—	—	—	—	—	—	—	3.0
Far East:											
Taiwan	—	14.0	55.0	7.0	17.0	68.0	30.0	40.0	38.0	1.5	60.0
Hong Kong	−14.0	−7.5	15.0	4.0	14.0	25.0	17.0	30.0	26.0	−30.0	40.8
Singapore	5.0	2.0	10.0	—	3.0	12.0	6.0	9.0	6.0	6.5	20.8
Indonesia	−13.0	24.0	45.0	25.0	12.0	23.0	−15.0	45.0	71.0	−4.5	13.0
Thailand	—	—	13.0	3.0	5.0	10.0	−2.0	2.0	5.0	1.0	8.0
South Korea	—	6.0	18.0	4.0	8.0	5.7	1.5	2.0	2.0	0.8	8.0
Philippines	—	—	—	—	—	1.0	—	1.0	0.5	1.0	1.0
Malaysia	—	—	—	—	—	—	0.1	0.7	1.4	0.2	0.2
Burma, Laos & Kampuchea	−15.0	−25.0	—	−1.5	−4.0	−4.5	−15.0	−4.0	−3.0	−1.0	−3.0
Total excluding Japan	−37.0	13.5	156.0	41.5	55.0	140.2	22.6	125.7	146.9	−24.5	148.8
Japan	12.3	11.6	10.7	3.2	36.9	10.5	−4.3	113.7	80.2	48.3	110.5
Total Far East	−24.7	25.1	166.7	44.7	91.9	150.7	18.3	239.4	227.1	23.8	259.3
Africa (Morocco)	−0.5	—	0.5	—	—	—	—	—	—	—	—
Australia	—	—	—	3.0	4.0	3.0	5.0	3.5	2.1	1.5	1.2
Total non-communist world	−16.5	42.1	184.7	68.2	118.4	190.8	17.7	275.5	303.2	86.7	333.6

Reprinted by permission: Consolidated Gold Fields plc; GOLD 1985

*"Our great father has a big safe, and so have we.
The hill is our safe . . . We want seventy million dollars
for the Black Hills. Put the money away some place at interest
so we can buy livestock. That is the way the white people do."*
---Spotted Bear

U.S. Gold Stock Situation

While most fundamental (and some technical) analysts study the yearly supply/demand situation of a particular commodity to predict price moves, the gold analyst should consider the above ground stocks and their movement to gain the proper insight. In most of the Western industrialized countries, above ground stocks are 50 to 100 times the annual newly-mined gold production. Since gold is used mainly in reclaimable items, there is little "consumption" or off-take from the available supply. Therefore, the price of gold is dependent on demand changes, best seen in stock changes. The biggest single source of demand is stockpiling by governments; the second, stockpiling by individuals.

To fully understand gold price fluctuations over the long term, you should study the major above ground gold stocks worldwide. Gold is priced or quoted in U.S. dollars due to the U.S. dollar still being accepted as the standard of value to other currencies (similar to the pound sterling prior to the 1930's). The largest gold stockpiles are held in a U.S. bullion depository at Fort Knox, Kentucky, and the New York Federal Reserve Bank in New York. (The Federal Reserve Bank, a private institution, claims certificate title to the over 267 million troy ounces held in U.S. Treasury vaults. Most foreign governments have on deposit in the N.Y. Federal Reserve Bank vaults huge quantities in assigned vault cells. Transfer of physical bars is facilitated by simply moving gold between cells. The largest foreign depositor of gold in the N.Y. Federal Reserve Bank is Russia.)

Regarding U.S. gold stockpiles, some very interesting and explosive information has been published by Mr. Ed Durell in his pamphlet, "Mr. President, Where is Our Gold?" In this pamphlet, Mr. Durell reprints part of a December 11, 1981 news release by the U.S. Treasury. This release was overseen by Donald Regan, then Secretary of the Treasury. (See Table A.)

Essentially, Mr. Durell makes the following points. From 1957 through 1968, the official gold holdings of the U.S. Treasury dropped 52% from 653.1 million troy ounces to 311.2 million; a drop of 341.9 million ounces. At today's free market gold price, that is a loss in currency reserves of $119.6 billion. At the 1980 high level of $800 per ounce, this would have been $273.5 billion. The stock drawdown was large and continual, dominated by one of the four categories specified (see Table A).

To "Official Foreign Monetary Institutions"	-285.4 million ounces
To "Gold Pool"	-45.2 million ounces
Received from "I.M.F."	+10.8 million ounces
To "Domestic Producers & Consumers"	-22.1 million ounces
Net Total	-341.9 million ounces

Table B shows a tally of 18 shipments of gold out of Fort Knox from 1961 to 1971. This information was furnished to Mr. Durell by Mr. H. L. Krieger, Regional Manager, General Accounting Office, Washington, D.C., dated April 11, 1975. The following is a direct quotation from Mr. Krieger's accompanying letter. "The Treasury acknowledged there had been at least two additional big shipments, but has given no explanation as to why these shipments were omitted from the tally."

The final column in Table B shows the average bar gold content. All bars in international gold transactions are approximately 400 troy ounces of at least .995 fineness. From March 1968 on, bar gold quality dropped down to coin gold melt quality of only 80% gold content — not .999 or even .995 fine as normally required for international transactions. Due to penalties and discounts involved in dealing with such impure gold bars, the question arises of whether or not all .995 fine gold is gone and if so, why. According to Treasury tabulations and breakdown of what is still being held, this is not so.

The enormous ten year drawdown evidenced in Table A is not as shocking as the alleged fact that, according to Mr. Durell, the U.S. Treasury legally owns no gold. This implies the U.S. government is operating on a de facto fiat currency basis.

Mr. Durell alleges this because the U.S. Treasury and the Federal Reserve Bank both list 267,000,000 troy ounces of gold on each of their balance sheets. Actually, the Federal Reserve Bank has assets with the U.S. Treasury payable to the Federal Reserve System Board of Governors in ounce denominated gold certificates. These obligations are fully secured by gold held by the U.S. Treasury. We would like to remind you that the Federal Reserve Bank is a private bank and not an extension of the Treasury. It is owned by the 1913 founding banks, of which the top five New York money banks alone own 47% of the stock.

While it is required by Constitutional law that an annual audit be done of the U.S. Treasury's gold, (held as backing for its money) the last official audit occurred in 1953. Secretary of the Treasury, William Simon, assigned a 10 year audit plan in 1974 to be completed and announced in 1985. It has not yet been released, if it has been done at all. The 1974 audit plan was implemented to quell much fear and public outcry over whether or not there was gold in Fort Knox, of what quality it was, and how much really had been used in the 1961-68 gold pool operation.

In August 1971, President Nixon halted U.S. dollar redemption privileges for Treasury gold by foreign entities. Since then, gold's price has escalated from 6 to 25 times the prior "official" price controlled by the U.S. government. Therefore, effective August 1971, the U.S. dollar was no longer backed by gold. There are currently 1,800,000,000,000 U.S. dollars held outside U.S. borders. Foreigners cannot turn in these paper dollars for gold, but must buy gold on the free market. So must you. What was once a citizen's right guaranteed by the U.S. Constitution, written by statesmen who experienced the 1776-1781 hyperinflation, has been taken away by Congress in the past 50 years. What happened to all the bullion confiscated in 1933 when President Franklin D. Roosevelt outlawed possession of gold by U.S. citizens? Who legally owns the above ground gold stockpiles? There appears to be a great deal of confusion surrounding the United States' gold stockpile.

Contrary to those who claim gold is a "barbaric relic", the majority of people worldwide put a great deal of faith in gold as a store of value. With the actual ownership of above ground gold stocks being in question, what happens to the price of gold when everyone wants out of paper dollars? How could anyone reliably predict gold's future price with the above facts and unanswered questions?

If you want to learn more about the discrepancies and controversy surrounding the U.S. Treasury's main gold stockpile, we recommend reading Mr. Durell's publications, "52 Unanswered Questions Regarding Alleged Gold Reserves of the United States" and "Mr. President, Where is Our Gold?". Reprints of these pamphlets are available for $2.00 to cover handling and postage, from Mr. Edward Durell, P. O. Box 586, Berryville, Virginia 22611.

U. S. Gold Stock Situation

Table A

U.S. GOLD STOCK 1944 - NOVEMBER 1981
(millions of fine troy ounces)

Year	Gold Stock Outstanding end of period	Gold Stock Change during period	Foreign[1] Countries	Gold Pool	IMF	Domestic Producers & Consumers
1944	589.5					
1945	573.8	-15.7	-12.9	–	–	-2.8
1946	591.6	+17.8	+20.6	–	–	-2.8
1947	653.4	+61.8	+81.8	–	-19.6	-0.4
1948	697.1	+43.7	+43.1	–	–	+0.6
1949	701.8	+4.7	+5.5	–	–	-0.8
1950	652.0	-49.8	-49.3	–	–	-0.5
1951	653.5	+1.5	+2.2	–	–	-0.7
1952	664.3	+10.8	+11.3	–	–	-0.5
1953	631.2	-33.1	-33.3	–	–	+0.2
1954	622.7	-8.5	-9.3	–	–	+0.8
1955	621.5	-1.1	-1.9	–	–	+0.8
1956	630.2	+8.7	+2.3	–	+5.7	+0.7
1957	653.1	+22.8	+4.9	–	+17.1	+0.8
1958	588.1	-65.0	-65.5	–	–	+0.5
1959	557.3	-30.7	-28.5	–	-1.3	-0.9
1960	508.7	-48.7	-56.3	–	+8.6	-1.0
1961	484.2	-24.5	-27.5	-0.3	+4.3	-1.0
1962	458.8	-25.4	-21.3	-2.5	–	-1.6
1963	445.6	-13.2	-19.2	+8.0	–	-2.0
1964	442.0	-3.6	-12.3	+11.2	–	-2.5
1965	394.5	-47.6	-37.8	–	-6.4	-3.4
1966	378.1	-16.3	-13.9	-3.4	+5.1	-4.1
1967	344.7	-33.4	+2.9	-32.3	+0.6	-4.6
1968	311.2	-33.5	-6.0	-25.9[2]	-0.1	-1.5[2]
1969	338.8	+27.6	+27.3	–	+0.3	–
1970	316.3	-22.5	-18.0	–	-4.5	–
1971	291.6	-24.7	-24.1	–	-0.6	–
1972	276.0	-15.6	-0.1	–	-15.5	–
1973	276.0	–	–	–	–	–
1974	276.0	–	–	–	–	–
1975	274.7	-1.3	–	–	–	-1.3[3]
1976	274.7	–	–	–	–	–
1977	277.6	+2.9	–	–	+2.9	–
1978	274.9	-2.7	–	–	+1.4	-4.1[3]
1979	264.6	-10.3	–	–	+1.4	-11.7[3]
1980	264.3	-0.3	–	–	–	-0.3[4]
1981-Nov.	264.1	-0.2	–	–	–	-0.2[4]
		-325.4	-235.3	-45.2	-0.6	-44.3

1/ Official foreign monetary institutions.
2/ Sales through gold pool and to U.S. consumers ended March 18, 1968.
3/ Gold sold at public auctions.
4/ Gold sold in American Arts Gold Medallion Program.

Sources: Federal Reserve Bulletins, Annual Reports of the Director of the Mint.

U.S. Department of the Treasury, December 1981

U.S. Gold Stock Situation

Table B

GOLD SHIPMENTS FROM U.S. BULLION DEPOSITORY, FORT KNOX, KY.
JANUARY 1, 1961 TO JUNE 30, 1974

Shipment Date	Destination	No. of Bars	Fine Ounces	Value at Time of Shipment ($35/Troy Ounce)	Average of Fine Ounces Per Bar*
5- -61	U.S. Assay Office, N.Y.	24,534	10,005,848.009	350,204,680.33	407.835
2- -62	U.S. Assay Office, N.Y.	35,080	14,402,551.668	504,089,309.07	410.563
8-17-62	U.S. Assay Office, N.Y.	34,987	14,375,277.124	503,134,699.42	410.875
4-26-63	U.S. Assay Office, N.Y.	21,341	8,676,727.819	303,685,473.65	406.575
4-26-63	Federal Reserve Bank, N.Y.	14,192	5,736,753.372	200,786,367.97	404.224
2- 3-65	U.S. Assay Office, N.Y.	25,048	10,308,492.599	360,797,240.90	411.549
3- 9-65	U.S. Assay Office, N.Y.	35,864	14,491,994.910	507,219,821.85	404.081
3-24-65	U.S. Assay Office, N.Y.	36,203	14,455,737.781	505,950,822.32	399.297
7-28-65	U.S. Assay Office, N.Y.	35,236	14,510,428.065	507,864,982.28	411.806
4-26-66	U.S. Assay Office, N.Y.	42,497	17,227,760.267	602,971,609.29	405.388
9- 7-66	U.S. Assay Office, N.Y.	35,644	14,484,435.037	506,955,226.35	406.363
10-18-67	U.S. Assay Office, N.Y.	24,576	9,058,592.688	317,050,743.96	368.595
12-3-67	To London via Federal Reserve Bank, N.Y.	35,991	14,289,517.149	500,133,100.24	397.030
1-29-68	U.S. Assay Office, N.Y.	70,398	28,698,040.664	1,004,431,423.25	407.654
3-22-68	Federal Reserve Bank, N.Y.	11,102	3,558,023.973	124,530,839.04	320.485
3-27-68	U.S. Assay Office, N.Y.	32,646	10,726,843.364	375,439,517.25	328.581
6- 3-68	U.S. Assay Office, N.Y.	45,436	14,424,295.394	504,850,338.78	317.464
7- 9-71	U.S. Assay Office, N.Y.	44,835	14,292,245.793	500,228,602.73	318.774
	Totals	605,610	233,723,565.676	$8,180,324,798.68	385.931

*Column added by Edward Durell to show the wide variance in weight of the bars and the need to weigh one bar in each "melt".

*"You have to chose (as a voter) between trusting to
the natural stability of gold and the honesty
and intelligence of members of our government.
And with due respect for these gentlemen, I advise you,
as long as the capitalist system lasts, to vote for gold."*
---George Bernard Shaw

Political Gold Chart

The historic and legal actions affecting the free gold price are inextricably tied to all the major highs, lows, turning points and violent swings as evidenced below and with the Master Gold Chart. This is due to the fact that gold, currencies, interest rates and all values of debt, equities and commodity prices are interrelated.

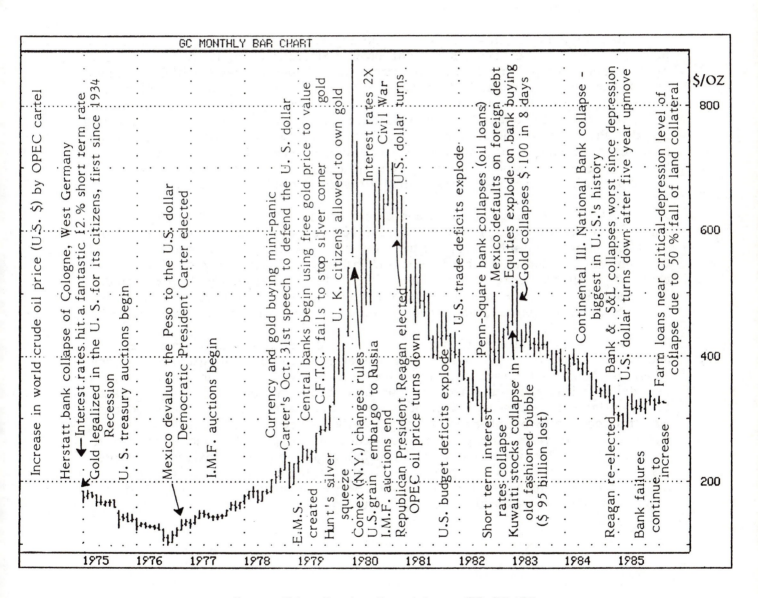

Commodity Quote-Graphics   TQ-20/20

Gold Viewed Through Three Foreign Currencies

The U.S. dollar is the primary denomination for world trade and world financial activity. We must not forget that other nations must use their own currency within their borders for evaluation purposes. Foreign investments must be adjusted for currency differences for valuation and transaction purposes, as well as income tax purposes. Gold is viewed in different countries through different legal constraints, inflation levels, and currency restrictions. To better show these factors, we selected three countries that have an interest in gold for commercial or monetary reasons.

Ironically, South Africa is one of the biggest recent beneficiaries of gold's long term bull market and its current drop. Since 1982 or 1983, the financial rand dropped sharply in U.S. dollar terms, as foreign interests withdrew liquid assets from South Africa. Since South Africa's business is mining and selling raw materials to the world which are mainly priced in dollars, the revenue has been mostly in U.S. dollars. This is a windfall for the government's mine marketing board. Prices in financial rand for gold valuation purposes within South Africa have even extended the lifetime of some mines from 10 to 40 percent. To South Africans, gold held internally and priced in rands per ounce is viewed in a bull market which is close to its high of 1980 in rands (see chart).

West Germany has long been a pro-gold oriented culture, having experienced currency destruction four times in the past 100 years. To control price inflation, West Germany maintains strict controls on the generation of currency. In fact, Germans revere gold as an investment and insurance of final reserve. The central bank of Germany respects German citizens' legal sovereignty to own gold. The Bundesbank tightly maintains its own gold horde as a reserve of last resort. In Deutsche mark terms, gold is near levels close to its benchmark high of 1980.

Mexico as a culture is over 400 years old and has long favored its gold and silver production, but has a very unstable socio-political situation. Since 1954, the Mexican government pegged the peso to the U.S. dollar at 12-1/2 pesos per dollar with free movement of currency between borders. When decades of an inflated money supply were let free to take effect as the unpegged peso was floated, (in September 1976) it promptly halved in dollar terms within a week. In nine years, the peso has succeeded in losing 92% value compared to the U.S. dollar. In other words, the U.S. dollar as seen by a Mexican has appreciated 2200%. Since gold is primarily quoted in the world in U.S. dollars, gold has been an extremely volatile affair but always bullish in price to the Mexicans, regardless of their newfound oil production boom.

Gold Viewed Through Three Foreign Currencies

A gold producer, a gold horder and an inflationary oil producer - pro-gold.

······ Peso (Mexico - pro-gold & silver producer, oil producer.)

- - - - - Financial Rand (South Africa - pro-gold producer and exporter.) Indexed: 1980 = 100

——— Deutsch Mark (West Germany - pro-gold central bank horder.) Indexed: 1980 = 100

Price for one ounce of gold.

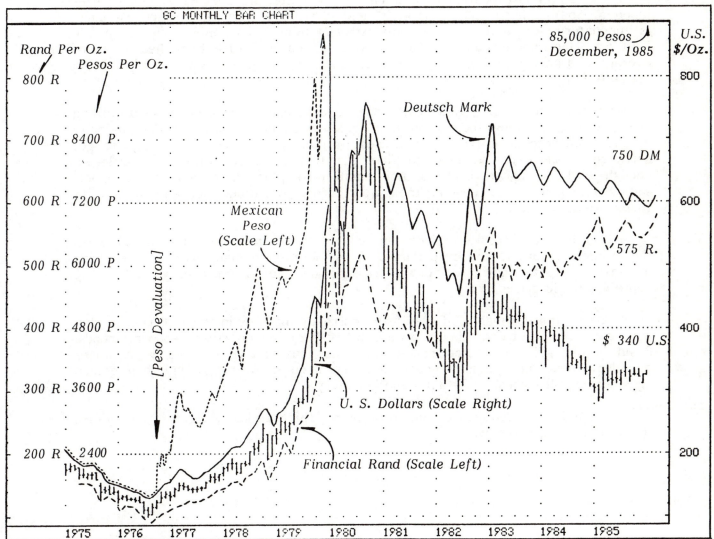

Commodity Quote-Graphics   TQ-20/20

Seasonal Gold Analysis

Gold is not naturally dominated by climate (i.e. the way crops are) nor by any gestation period (i.e. the way livestock is) but strangely enough has a pronounced seasonal price effect.

After the longer term secular trend has been removed, a distinct yearly high in or around February to a low around August is the main feature observed. After much research, we have traced it to a single, most probable source. The majority (65% - 80%) of newly mined world gold is marketed from South Africa in an almost continuous fashion. Raw materials are the economic life-blood of South Africa and so little is held in reserve. To get foreign exchange is mandatory for South Africa's mainstream mining economy. Being in the Southern Hemisphere however has created a seasonal effect of heavier-than-average marketing in our late summer; and lighter-than-average marketing in our late winter.

Contrary to rumors, this is not due to a strong, cold sirocco wind chilling the gold trees making them drop their gold seed pods. Since a high majority of the workforce is native, their interest is merely working long enough to get sufficient cash to return home to plant a new food crop. While not all leave, enough workers migrate back to their small farm plots during our winter (their summer) to plant, thus reducing their work force, gold production and availability to the world market.

This has an opposite effect during our late summer (their winter) when the workers return to the deep mines. This increase in manpower, the resulting increased output, and minor down pressure due to above average marketing depresses world prices.

Due to the dominance of credit and currency markets in the interrelationship with gold, secular trends should always be respected more than seasonal trends. Besides, the gold tree crop really isn't that susceptible to cold winds after all. However, South Africa's geese flock has been known not to lay their golden eggs during full moons. But that's another story.

A simple comparison of monthly price fluctuations year by year yields some interesting patterns.

Seasonal Gold Analysis

Gold's Seasonal Pattern – 10 Years, Plus Or Minus The Secular Trend.

Commodity Quote-Graphics   TQ-20/20

"The real price of everything . . . is the toil and trouble of acquiring it."
---Adam Smith

PART III

Correlation Anlaysis (to Gold)

Banking Reserves (U.S. Net Free)

Budget Deficit (U.S.)

Commodity Price Index

Consumer Price Index

Consumer Sentiment Index

Corporate Profits (U.S.)

Crude OIl

Dollar (U.S.)

Exchange Seat Prices

Gold Equities

Industrial Production

Interest Rates: Real Rate of return
                   Short Term
                   Long Term

Inventory to Sales Ratio

Money Inflation (World)

Money Supply (U.S. - M1)

Producer Prices

Reserve Assets: U.S.
                 Official
                 Real

Trade Deficit (U.S.)

"Hell is paved with good intentions,
but heaven goes in for something more dependable.
Solid Gold."
               ---Joyce Cary

Correlation Analysis

Gold as a standard of value.

While vehemently denied by socialistically trained monetary economists, such things as crude oil, paper currencies, interest rates, retail prices, other precious metals, and commodity prices in general, all have some relationship to the price of gold. These relationships may be direct or indirect; leading or lagging. However, in the long run, everything is dependent on gold, though it may be hard to believe.

History has shown that unless there is a store of value to money, no clothing, buildings, machinery, or even food would be produced. Contrary to myopic views of gold as nothing but another commodity, gold explains historic actions, political actions, wars, expansions and contractions of economic activity.

The 19th and 20th centuries have evolved into the age of paper inflation - destroying men, countries, and cultures without compassion.

Once the aforementioned concepts are accepted, a broader view and greater understanding can be had.

Historically, gold is THE store of value. It has been the basis for all money. Paper money, wire transfers, electronic computer blips, etc., are merely artificial representations of the issuing authority. Usually, a government issues paper currency to represent gold at a given value per ounce of a stated purity.

Paper money not redeemable in gold has ALWAYS collapsed in value, or reciprocally, inflated prices of goods and services as its quantity increased.

Generally speaking, in the long run, gold and paper currencies fluctuate together in price with gold being the reciprocal of the quantity of paper currency created.

The quantity of goods created at the producer level fluctuate with the price of paper currency which is interest rates. Both short and long term interest rates fluctuate in direct correlation to the price of gold. Longer periods of time better reflect this correlation, as short term is more erratic.

Overspending by any sovereign government (budget deficits) creates future price inflation and an eventual markup in the price of gold. This is best seen by inflation during war and how gold responds accordingly.

Sympathetic movement by parallel commodities such as platinum, silver, etc., reflect price movements of gold to a very high degree.

A series of correlations of gold to several interrelated items is presented in the following pages.

Net Free Banking Reserves (Scale Inverted)

Commodity Quote-Graphics TQ-20/20

Courtesy: Annual Statistical Digest, Federal Reserve System, 1974 through 1984.

U. S. Budget Deficit (Inverted,) Seasonally Adjusted Annual Rate

Commodity Quote-Graphics TQ-20/20

Courtesy: Federal Reserve Bulletins, 1974 through 1985, Federal Reserve System.

"Never make forecasts, especially about the future."
---Samuel Goldwyn

Commodity Price Indexes

The selection of a commodity price index that best shows the overall commodity situation relative to gold is described below. The most immediate observation is that gold, or perhaps all metals, leads the overall commodity universe in financial inflation. While there are parallel price movements, there is insufficient sympathetic movement to reach any positive conclusions.

The Commodity Research Bureau's Futures Price Index was selected to compare the overall commodity price structure to gold. The decision was based on a combination of factors that best balance data, variables, currency and availability.

First, it was necessary to eliminate indexes which are primarily denominated in foreign currency. Those indexes would require a great deal of adjustment to allow for currency differences. Otherwise, the index would be distorted.

Secondly, preference should be given to a weighted commodity index with current trade or futures activity favored. The revised Dow Jones Futures Index is heavily weighted towards three commodities that are not realistic in today's economy.

Third, where possible, the index should be futures based, not cash based. Situations arise where futures and cash prices do not converge and are highly distorted in their relationship. The index must reflect realistic price movement. For nearby gold futures, it must be a futures group index.

Fourth, it should have an extensive price history for tracking and preferably a base period similar to that used by the U.S. government, to be readily comparable.

Finally, it should be possible to divide the index into categorical subgroups so further analysis can be done.

The C.R.B. Futures Price Index has many details in construction and orientation that must be considered. While there are many distinct characteristics that some may feel make it inappropriate for comparison purposes, we feel the benefits outweigh the detriments. The following lists show the inherent biases.

Positive Factors

It is a daily computed index released after each day's trading.

It has a history of approximately 25 years compilation.

It has eleven subgroups available for study and monitoring of group price movements.

It is readily quoted on various newswires and, therefore, can be actively logged, plotted, and used to determine trends and changes in trends.

The base period of 1967 = 100 is a constant to numerous other data used by the U.S. Department of Commerce, Federal Reserve, and Labor Department.

Most of the commodities which comprise the index are produced in the U.S.; thus allowing more accurate price comparisons.

The majority of the commodities are quoted in U.S. dollars; therefore, more applicable when applied to other U.S. investment data for comparison.

Negative Factors

Of the 27 commodities in the C.R.B. Futures Price Index, 4 (approximately 15%) are Canadian based.

Ten of the 27 commodities (37%) are grains; therefore, grains dominate the overall price moves of the index.

Seventeen of the 27 commodities (63%) are crops; thus reducing the accuracy of the industrial commodity base by seasonal production factors.

There is no attempt at weighting the individual futures to any measurable scale of their trading or commercial dollar value.

It has a bullish bias in bear markets. The C.R.B. calculates its index by totaling futures for 12 months and rolling forward one future as the current future expires. This total is averaged; then adjusted to an index basis. Distant (in the far future) futures contracts have higher prices due to the cost of interest. When they are added to the index on a rollover calculation, the index is forced upward.

The opposite is true in a bull market. As the rollover futures is added and the current higher futures is dropped, the index is forced downward.

The eleven most publicized commodity indexes are:

1. Associated Press' <u>Commodity Index</u> - 34 commodities; weighted.

2. Bureau of Labor Statistics, U.S. Department of Labor's, <u>Tuesday Spot Wholesale Price Index</u> (Formerly the <u>2000 Commodity Wholesale Price Index</u>) - 22 commodities; not seasonally adjusted; 1967 = 100 base; monthly average BLS 1957/59 = 100. The BLS spot commodity indexes were begun in 1934.

3. Commodity Research Bureau's <u>Daily Futures Price Index</u> - 27 commodities; 1967 = 100 base; geometric average; unweighted; one year continuous averaging; expressed in terms of a percentage change in price relative to a base year. Also eleven sub-groups, and a spot price index comprising all 27 commodities. All indexes computed daily. Originally started in 1956 with a 1947/49 base; the same used for U.S. government indexes. Each decade when government departments change their base period, the C.R.B. does also.

4. Dow Jones' <u>Commodity Futures Index</u> - 12 commodities; 1924/26 = 100 base; calculated daily; weighted index; not an average. Calculated with two futures options for each commodity; approximately 150 days average or five months into the future. Begun in 1928 and revised in 1950 and again in 1975. Also Dow Jones Spot Commodity Index.

5. Dun & Bradstreet's <u>Daily Weighted Price Index</u> - 30 commodities; 1930/32 Average = 100 base.

6. Economist's [U.S.] <u>Dollar All Commodity Index</u> - 32 commodities; published weekly in the U.K. Commodities are weighted by three year moving averages of imports into industrialized countries; internationally traded industrial materials (18); and food commodities (14). Also available in Sterling and SDR's.

7. International Monetary Fund's <u>Spot Price Index</u> - 30 commodities; 1975 = 100 base; 37 wholesale price series; weighted by average export earnings; cash prices in U.S. dollars.

8. Journal of Commerce's <u>Daily Commodity Index</u>.

9. Moody's <u>Daily Index of Spot Commodity Prices</u> - 15 commodities; 1931 = 100 base; weighted by the ten prevailing economic activity. Revised in March 1973.

10. Painewebber, Inc.'s <u>Continuous Futures Index</u>. Developed in 1985 as a continuous price series, broad based futures index, relative to the 1975/84 range. Additional indicators on a group and individual commodity basis calculated daily.

11. Reuter's <u>Daily Index of the United Kingdom's Daily Commodity Prices</u> - 17 commodities; 1931 = 100 base; geometric average; internationally trade weighted; U.K. biased; spot or cash; computed daily.

With the advent of the computer age and all the data that can be monitored, numerous private indexes are being created daily. In 1966, when Mr. Schildgen was a clerk at the Chicago Board of Trade, he developed a weighted grain index to more accurately reflect what actually took place in the grains bull market that growing season.

Commodity Price Index/Gold Correlation

C. R. B. Commodity Futures Price Index - 27 commodities, subdivided into six groups.

Commodity Quote-Graphics   TQ-20/20

Commodity Research Bureau, 75 Montgomery Street, Jersey City, NJ 07302
Tel. (201) 451-7500

Commodity Price Index Bibliography

Commodity Index Report. Jersey City, NJ: Commodity Research Bureau, 1985.

The Dow Jones Commodities Handbook. Princeton, NJ: Dow Jones Books, 1978.

Federal Reserve Chart Book. Washington, DC: Federal Reserve System, 1985.

Futures Technical Advisor. New York: PAINEWEBBER, 1985.

International Financial Statistics. Washington, DC: International Monetary Fund, 1985.

Pring, Martin J. Pring Market Review. Washington Depot, CT: International Institute for Economic Research.

Consumer Price Index / Gold Correlation

Annualized % Change

Commodity Quote-Graphics TQ-20/20

Courtesy: Federal Reserve Chart Book, November 1985, Federal Reserve System.

U. S. Consumer Sentiment Index / Gold Correlation

Institute For Social Research, Ann Arbor, MI. 48106

Survey: 1200-plus households. Scale Inverted.   First Quarter 1966 = 100.

Commodity Quote-Graphics   TQ-20/20

Courtesy: Survey Research Center, University Of Michigan.

U.S. Corporate Profits / Gold Correlation

U. S. Corporate profits (Before Taxes) - Billions of Dollars

Commodity Quote-Graphics   TQ-20/20

Courtesy: U. S. Department Of Commerce

Crude Oil / Gold Correlation

Price of gold in terms of crude oil
(Barrels per troy ounce)

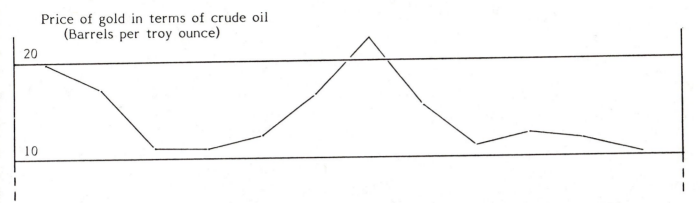

20

10

Arab Light Crude, Contract Price ——— Spot Price ⁓⁓ , Arab Heavy Crude, Contract Price — —

GC MONTHLY BAR CHART

$

— 35.00

— 30.00

— 25.00

Crude Oil Price ($/bbl.)

— 20.00

Crude Oil

— 15.00

Gold

— 5.00

800

600

400

200

1975 1976 1977 1978 1979 1980 1981 1982 1983 1984 1985

Commodity Quote-Graphics   TQ-20/20

Courtesy: Bank Credit Analyst, BCA Publications Ltd., 3463 Peel Street,
Montreal, Quebec, Canada H3A 1W7. Tel. (514) 842-8525.

U. S. Dollar - Foreign Currency / Gold Correlation

Trade Weighted U. S. Dollar (Inverted)   1973 = 100

Commodity Quote-Graphics TQ-20/20

Courtesy: Bank Credit Analyst, BCA Publications Ltd., 3463 Peel Street,
Montreal, Quebec, Canada H3A 1W7. Tel. (514) 842-8525.

Exchange Seat Prices/Gold Correlation

It is interesting to study the correlation between exchange seat prices and gold's price behavior during the last decade. There appears to be parallel movement between the two. Considering that purchasers or sellers of seats are acting in a business fashion and not speculating per se, this is a fascinating discovery.

Although the Commodity Exchange of New York (COMEX) is the traditional metal trading center, we used CBOT full seat prices, as this gave a broader representation against all activity during this period. Therefore, if you wish to apply this comparison to other markets, the CBOT full seat prices would be more applicable, as the CBOT covers the entire commodity spectrum — grains, metals, and financials.

Seat prices can be charted similar to any other active commodity. The overall activity and price patterns are similar to gold's but contain a little distortion at extreme price levels.

Chicago Board Of Trade - Full Memberships, Monthly Range of Prices.

Data from 9/83 to 12/84 is for month end seat prices only.

Commodity Quote-Graphics TQ-20/20

Courtesy; Chicago Board Of Trade.

Gold Equities / Gold Correlation

U. K. Financial Times Gold Equity Index (U. S. Dollar Adjusted) - Mostly South African mines

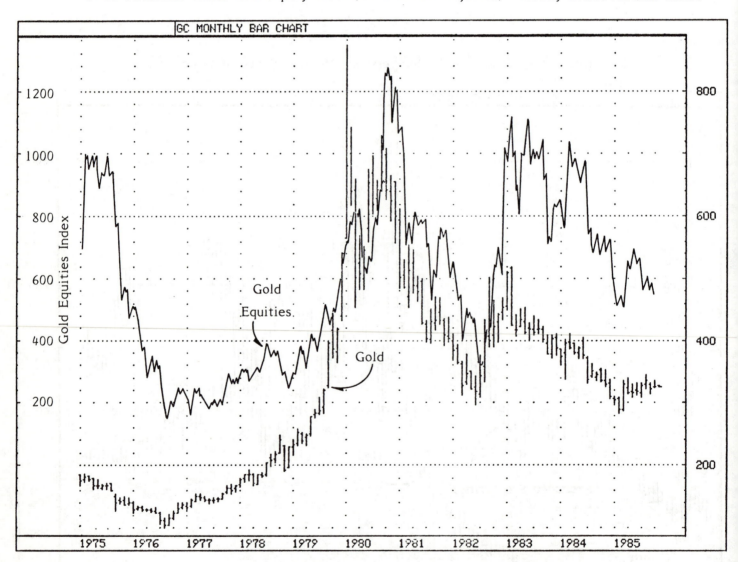

Commodity Quote-Graphics   TQ-20/20

Courtesy: Bank Credit Analyst, BCA Publications Ltd., 3463 Peel Street, Montreal, Quebec, Canada H3A 1W7. Tel. (514) 842-8525.

U. S. Industrial Production / Gold Correlation

U. S. Industrial Production; Index 1967 = 100

Commodity Quote-Graphics   TQ-20/20

Courtesy; U. S. Department Of Commerce

Real Interest Rate of Return

Six Month U. S. Treasury Bills Less The Consumer Price Index

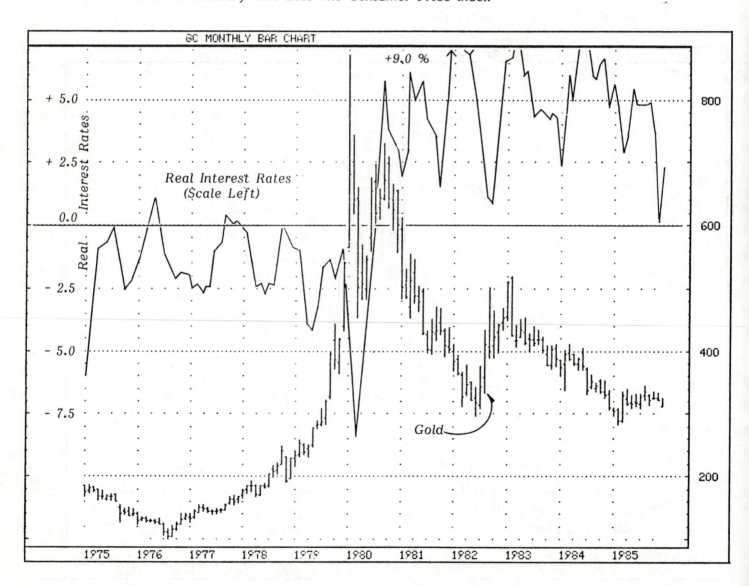

Commodity Quote-Graphics   TQ-20/20

Courtesy; Federal Reserve

Short Term Interest Rates / Gold Correlation

3 Month U. S. Treasury Bill Yields (Short Term) ————— Federal Funds Rate ⎍

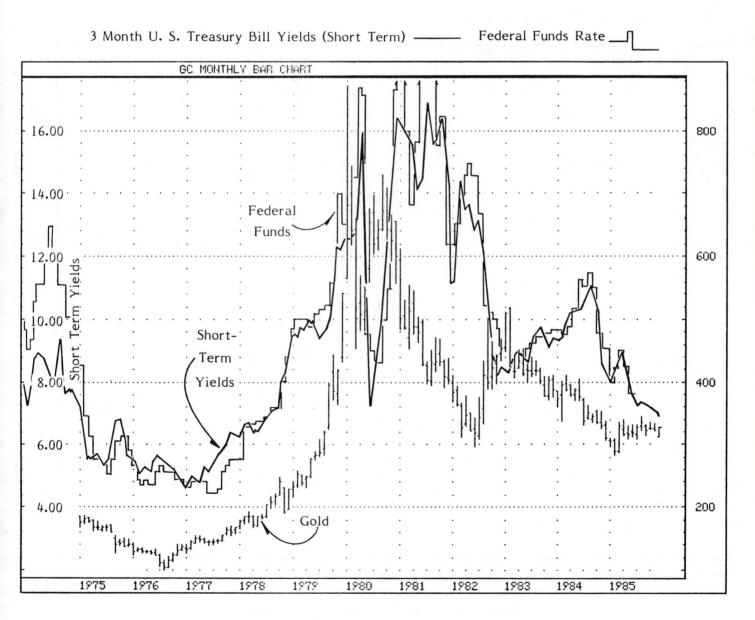

Commodity Quote-Graphics   TQ-20/20

Courtesy: Annual Statistical Digest, Federal Reserve System, 1974 through 1984.

Long Term Interest Rates / Gold Correlation

20 Year U. S. Treasury Bond Yields (Long Term) ———

Commodity Quote-Graphics   TQ-20/20

Courtesy: Annual Statistical Digest, 1974 through 1985, Federal Reserve System.

U. S. Inventory To Sales Ratio / Gold Correlation

GC MONTHLY BAR CHART

Inventory - Sales Ratio

Gold

Commodity Quote-Graphics   TQ-20/20

Courtesy; U. S. Department Of Commerce

World Money Inflation / Gold Correlation

Top Eleven Industrialized Nations Currency, Demand and Time Deposits, and Eurodollars ⎯⎯⎯

Commodity Quote-Graphics TQ-20/20
*Courtesy: Bank Credit Analyst, BCA Publications Ltd., 3463 Peel Street,
Montreal, Quebec, Canada H3A 1W7. Tel. (514) 842-8525.*

U. S. Money Supply (M1) / Gold Correlation

U. S. Money Supply (M1 - Annual % Rate of Change, Seasonally Adjusted) ————

Commodity Quote-Graphics   TQ-20/20
Courtesy: Annual Statistical Digest, 1974 through 1985, Federal Reserve System.

U. S. Producer Prices / Gold Correlation

Annualized % Rate of Change

Commodity Quote-Graphics   TQ-20/20

Courtesy: Bureau of Labor Statistics, U. S. Department of Labor.

U.S. Reserve Assets

Total reserve assets include total gold stock, foreign currencies beginning March 1961, reserve position in the International Monetary Fund, and special drawing rights beginning January 1970.

Total reserve assets for May 1972 include increase of $1,016 million resulting from change in par value of the U.S. dollar on May 8, 1972. Total gold stock increased $828 million, reserve position in the IMF, $33 million, and SDR's, $155 million.

Total reserve assets for October 1973 include increase of $1,436 million resulting from change in par value of the U.S. dollar on October 18, 1973. Total gold stock increased $1,165 million, reserve position in the IMF $54 million, and SDR's, $217 million.

Total gold stock is valued as follows: Through April 1972, $35.00 per fine troy ounce; May 1972 through September 1973, $38 per fine troy ounce; since October 1973, $42.22 per fine troy ounce.

Special drawing rights are valued through June 1974 as follows: January 1970 through April 1972, 1 SDR = $1.00; May 1972 through September 1973, 1 SDR = $1.08571; October 1973 through June 1974, 1 SDR = $1.20635.

Beginning July 1974, the U.S. reserve position in the IMF and holdings of SDR's are valued according to a technique adopted then by the IMF for valuing the SDR. The technique is based on a weighted average of exchange rates for currencies of selected member countries.

From March 1961 through October 1978, foreign currencies are valued at acquisition cost. Beginning November 1978, foreign currencies are valued at current market exchange rates.

Special drawing rights were increased by IMF allocations to the United States as follows: $867 million on January 1, 1970; $717 million on January 1, 1971; $710 million on January 1, 1972; $1,139 million equivalent on January 1, 1979; $1,152 million equivalent on January 1, 1980; and $1,093 million equivalent on January 1, 1981.

Current and back figures: U.S. International Transactions Section, Division of International Finance.

Courtesy: Federal Reserve System.

U. S. Reserve Assets / Gold Correlation

Foreign Currencies (Began March 1961) ——————   Reserve Position in the I. M. F. ·············

Commodity Quote-Graphics   TQ-20/20

Courtesy: 1984 Historical Chart Book, Federal Reserve System

Official U. S. Reserves / Gold Correlation

Total Reserve Assets — — — — —

Total Gold Stock (Official Price, October 1973 - $ 42.22/Oz.) ————

Commodity Quote-Graphics   TQ-20/20
Courtesy: 1985 Historical Chart Book, Federal Reserve System.

Real U. S. Dollar Reserves / Gold Correlation

Real U. S. Dollar Total Reserves
Foreign Currency, I. M. F. Reserve Position, & Special Drawing Rights ....
Total U. S. Gold Stock (Free Market Price X Official Gold Stock) ————

Commodity Quote-Graphics   TQ-20/20

Courtesy: 1985 Historical Chart Book, Federal Reserve System.

U. S. Trade Deficit / Gold Correlation

U. S. Trade Deficit (Inverted,) Seasonally Adjusted Annual Rate

Commodity Quote-Graphics TQ-20/20

Courtesy: Federal Reserve Bulletin, 1974 through 1985, Federal Reserve System.

"The Almighty Dollar, that great object of universal devotion."
---Washington Irving

PART IV

Technical Approaches
Accumulation/Distribution Analysis
ADX - Smoothed Average of Directional Movement Index
Astrological Analysis
     Lunar Cycles
     Eclipses
Bar Chart
Centered Moving Average Analysis
Commodity Channel Index (CCI) Analysis
Complementary Angle Analysis
Contrary Opinion Analysis
Cycle Analysis
     Harmonics
     Periodicity
Elliott Wave Analysis
Fan Line Analysis
Fibonacci Progression Analysis
Fifty Percent Retracement Rule
Formation and High-Low Analysis
Fourty-Five Degree Angle Analysis
Gann, W. D. Angle Analysis
Harahus Pentagon Analysis
January Annual Syndrome Analysis
Moving Average Analysis
     Comparison
     Glossary
Option Analysis
     Glossary
Oscillator Analysis
Parabolic Analysis
Parallel Channel Line Analysis
Percentage Retracement Analysis
Point and Figure Analysis
Price Box Congestion Analysis
Psychological Crowd Profile Analysis
Relative Strength Index (RSI)
Speed Resistance Line Analysis
Spread Analysis
     Glossary
Stochastic Analysis
Support and Resistance Analysis
Swing Chart Analysis
Three and Four Dimensional Chart Analysis
Trendline Chart Analysis
Volume and Open Interest Analysis

*"You never see the stock called Happiness
quoted on the stock exchange."*
    ---Henry Van Dyke

Technical Approaches

A technical approach is the direct observation of price action, volume, open interest, interrelationships, indexing or cross correlation of markets in order to make market decisions. Simply gathering data and mechanically applying it is insufficient by itself. The data must undergo subjective human evaluation resulting in an interpretive decision, usually guided by standardized criteria. Methods used in the analysis and manipulation of market data are called technical analyses.

The main advantage of using a technical analysis for making positional decisions is that historical market prices are inflexible. Mathematical (technical) methods of applying an analysis cannot be subjectively manipulated. Most non-technical approaches rely on outside opinion which can be inconsistent. Using a technical approach, outside opinions are not intrinsic and need not be relied upon.

For technical approach purposes, the market is defined as the sum total of everyone's investment in it. No one's opinion by itself influences market prices unless they "put their money where their mouth is". A long and a short's opinions have strength only in proportion to the amount of money they have committed to their respective positions.

Traders and investors involved in a market create a continuum, commonly called a trend. This trend carries into the future until the net balance of shorts or longs changes, thereby reversing it. Since the total effort of using a technical analysis is to get a reliable price projection, it is reasonable to assume that using market data gives a better indication than extraneous data.

Only Two Technical Approaches

There are actually two types of technical approaches for investing — trending or trading. Every technical approach devised either assumes that market prices are trending up or down (trending) or fluctuating around a median level or medial (trading or whipsawing). In a trending market, investors buy when breakout signals suggest higher prices. They also sell when breakout signals suggest lower prices. They buy high to sell higher and go short to cover their positions much lower. Trading market approaches sell rallies anticipating prices returning to a median range, and buy low prices to catch rallies back to the medial.

Markets tend to be either in a trading or a trending pattern as supply and demand constantly shifts. Markets tend to move sideways approximately 60% to 80% of the time. Most money is made, however, when prices trend up or down because of the magnitude of price changes. An individual's attitude usually leans toward either the trending or trading approach. Dramatic price changes or relative price consistency will determine which attitude will be predominate for profits at that time. Experienced investors and traders recognize that the overall market also experiences phases from strongly trending to strongly whipsawing and back again.

Trading Approaches

Short term active traders lean heavily toward whipsaw or medial approaches. They prefer greater activity, shorter term trading cycles with commensurately smaller and quicker profits and losses. They constantly refine their systematic approach by analyzing trade results, trying to improve profit to loss ratios, reduce costs, and maximize profits, as any business manager would do in running a company.

We believe the most used of all trading approaches is the oscillator. It has been proven extensively that prices fluctuate around a median price level most of the time. Using cycle analysis to show fluctuation, the apparent cycles appear with varying degrees of reliability. Through detailed analysis, market analysts measure, define and use these studies in varying ways in their trading plans. When a commodity's price is going sideways, assuming it has a 30 day cycle, the difference between the actual price and a 30 day moving average can be plotted against a flat line representing the average. When prices get into overbought or oversold areas, a trader looks for signs of prices returning to the median area. (See Oscillator Analysis.)

Each commodity price structure has its own inherent dominant cycle, characteristics, volatility and peculiar traits. Silver and gold occasionally have cycle lengths of roughly 30 and 45 trading days respectively. In contrast, U.S. Treasury Bills seem to have a much shorter cycle of 15 to 20 trading days.

With the two technical approaches having exactly opposite orientations, a person can become disenchanted very quickly. Some technical traders will be buying exactly where other technicians will be selling. Whether a person is inclined toward aggressive trading or conservative positioning depends on their patience, experience, the amount of risk capital, as well as other influencing factors.

Trending Approaches

Over the years, we observed that all markets, viewed as a universe of commodities, generally fall into one of three levels of price trending activity. Depending on the individual's avariciousness, trending approaches used will be oriented toward short, intermediate, or long term time frames.

A few experienced technicians have observed that the commodity futures universe can be categorized by the percentage of actively trending subjects annually. If they could know with some degree of certainty the percentage of commodities which were going to be dynamic the next year, they could out-perform others in their results by shifting to the time system that would better their results.

System Time Frame

	Short Term	Intermediate Term	Long Term
Dynamic Price Changes 50% or More 1972 Russian Grain Deal 1979 High Inflation Rapidly Changing Interest Rates		*1972* *1980* *1981*	*1973* *1979*
Average Number of Strong Moves Generally 20-40% 1974 All Commodities		*1974* *1975* *1976* *1978* *1982*	
Very Quiet Lackluster Price Period Generally Under 10-15% of All Commodities Trend 1969-70, 1 to 2 Bull Markets Only	*1968* *1969* *1970* *1971*	*1977* *1983* *1984* *1985*	

Influential Factors

The subconscious effect of a price chart will influence a person's judgment of current price position and anticipated future move. After compiling hundreds of research reports, it was discovered that readers respond to a predominantly placed price graph by subconsciously focusing on the center of the chart and dividing the chart into nine areas of activity. Subconsciously, the person relates the price as it is actually shown toward the center of the chart. If the price is close to the far right, the subconscious mind says the move is almost over. If to the far left; it has just begun. If close to the top of the chart, (in a bullish price trend) the price has gone up too far. If near the bottom; it has just begun. This subconscious reaction actually induces prejudgment on the part of the viewer.

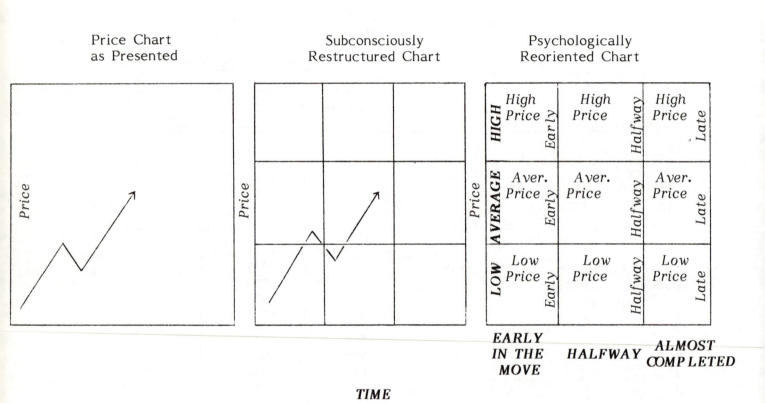

Price Chart as Presented · Subconsciously Restructured Chart · Psychologically Reoriented Chart

TIME

Experienced marketing specialists utilize this psychologically influencing factor of price placement within a chart to increase enthusiasm and acceptance of an investment promotion. An incorrectly biased chart or "psychologically bearish" price may induce a negative response, when the intended theme was bullish. In effect, the sales attempt becomes self-defeating.

Below are examples of charts with the psychological reactions noted.

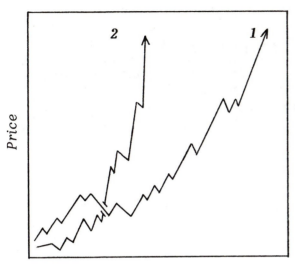

Time

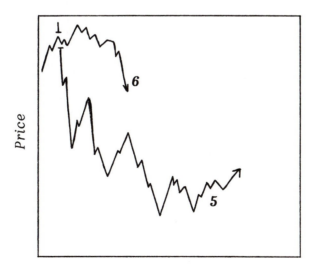

Time

1.   It's too late and too expensive to get in.

2.   Wait for the reaction because it is half over, but still a very bullish move.

3.   It's all over.

4.   Ideal bullish situation; buy now while it's still early and priced low.

Time

5.   Ideal time for investors to begin buying; can't lose much compared to how low its been and have the world above to gain as prices go back to near old highs.

6.   Ideal positioning for recommending a bear strategy position move. However, the majority of people are optimistic in nature and rarely respond to any recommended bearish strategy.

In the following pages, numerous orthodox and unorthodox technical analyses are presented. As long as the requirements of price oriented mechanical tools and directly observed data were met, we tried to present it. We attempted to be objective and simply present various analyses in how they apply to our long term gold chart. Some approaches that use strong methodology and show a high reliability in practical application are emphasized. Some approaches that are too subjective, non-analytical, and unreliable when applied are only briefly mentioned. Approaches originally devised for very short term trading purposes, for example, were difficult to apply to long term analysis.

"When it is a question of money, everybody is of the same religion."
---Voltaire

Accumulation & Distribution Analysis

This analysis is best seen by analyzing general categories of price volatility and participants at different levels of activity. Old time traders call this a pattern of behavior rather than an exacting analytical study of price patterns. Simply put, there are three levels of activity that explain where you are at in any cycle. This requires the participant to have experienced at least one full cycle, preferably from low to high, and back to low again. The more cycles experienced, the greater number of different commodities or stocks experienced, the better the judgment as to where you are in the cycle. To stay in keeping with our theme, we will refer to the gold commodity futures market due to its high liquidity.

There are just four phases to this approach:

1. <u>Accumulation</u>: Bottoming pattern from a prior high level occurs as small daily price ranges reflect a lack of interest on the part of the general public. No publicity or even negative opinions prevail in the financial press, as experts predict gold's death on the basis of strong fundamentals. Professionals, banks, individual traders, etc., (strong hands) who have been through this before, start accumulating. Their experiences over many cycles has given them patience, judgment, and cast iron stomachs.

2. <u>Markup</u>: Gradually rising prices signal "green" to semiprofessionals (part-time investors) to enter into the market to accumulate their share of the pie. Some publicity begins to occur, but only in trade journals; not the general media. Greed begins to show in the language of commission house publications and traders, as they reinforce their own positions.

3. <u>Distribution</u>: Topping occurs as the primary short holders finally cover their gold positions. A new wave of enlightened bullish neophytes swarm into the market, as talk of easy profits proliferate. Strong hands now leave their positions, usually on signs that there is too much of the general public in the market, there is too much publicity, and there is no economic basis for gold being where it is. Publicity becomes excessive by the general media. Financial guru books that took a year to write and six months to publish are being bought to reinforce what is happening. Weak hands now dominate market action in acquiring long positions at price levels three times higher than what had been years before. Investors now have confidence and reasons to explain their actions.

4. <u>Markdown</u>: Gradually dropping prices occur with prices actually falling sharply, sometimes due to a reason — other times not. All reasons for why gold's price is where it is are now known and accepted. Financial stories of overtrading by some and huge fortunes being compiled by others come to light. Recent buyers all seem to have some degree of loss, but are confident they will make their fortune with a little more patience.

<u>Accumulation</u>: Wounds are being licked. Disgruntled buyers (longs) who bought at higher levels are forced to leave their positions as their threshold of economic pain has been breached. The process of eliminating most of the old participants creates the void for the new players the next time around. This is, of course, the cycle completed and the beginning of a new cyclical pattern.

See Psychological Crowd Profile for such emotions as fear, hope, greed, and panic to understand the human psyche in different market situations. The Accumulation/Distribution analysis is evaluative, as it looks at the response of mass emotion and crowd thinking.

Accumulation & Distribution Analysis

GC MONTHLY BAR CHART

Commodity Quote-Graphics   TQ-20/20

ADX

Smoothed Average of Directional Movement
Index (DX)

The ADX is a smoothed average of the directional movement index. Once the
directional movement calculations have been done, the ADX can be calculated
by dividing the difference between +DI and -DI by the sum of +DI and -DI.
Multiplied by 100, the resulting value is shown as a positive figure.

$$DX = 100 \; \frac{(+DI) - (-DI)}{(+DI) + (-DI)}$$

continued...

Commodity Quote-Graphics   TQ-20/20

ADX

Smoothed Average of Directional Movement
Index (DX)

The example shown is a 14 bar ADX, plotted against the monthly gold chart, from early 1977 through September 1985.

Note that most of 1985's plot range is similar to 1983's on balance. Gold's real price ranged in the low 400 dollar area during 1983. In 1985, gold's price ranged mostly in the low 300 dollar area. The ADX showed neutral on the scale or even a possible turnaround. This would seem to imply a turning to the upside of the major downtrend that has dominated gold since 1980.

EXPANDED SCALE

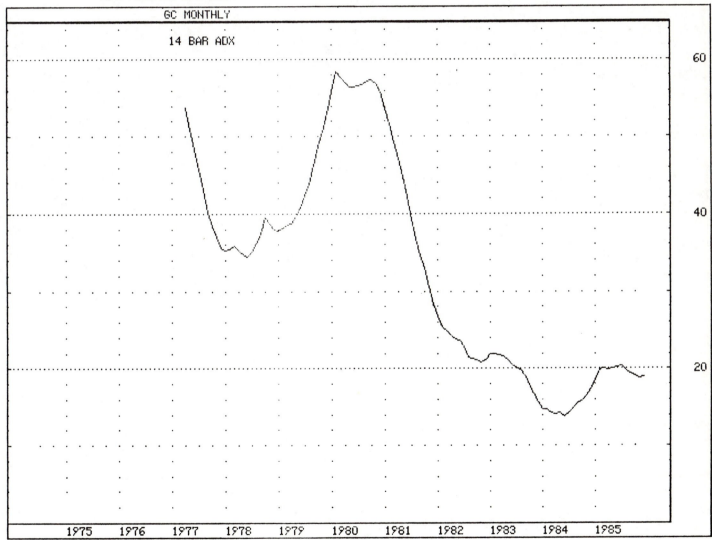

Commodity Quote-Graphics TQ-20/20

"Millionaires don't use astrology;
billionaires do."
                        ---J. Pierpont Morgan

Astrological Analysis

Astrology is the study of positions and aspects of heavenly bodies with a view to predicting their influence on the course of human affairs. Applied to gold, this means astrology is the study of the heavenly bodies with a view to predicting their influence on the price of gold.

Most important is the ability and experience of the astrologer in interpreting the natal astrological aspects and applying progressions and transits to the current and future.

Planets traversing the twelve zodiacal houses tend to influence the area which rule those houses and/or affect other planets in certain constant patterns. The interpretation of these geocosmic relationships is an art (subjective) and a science (objective). Analyses include progressions, directions, transits and degrees of orbs.

Perhaps the best study of planetary movements, transitions and interrelationships is R. A. Merriman's The Gold Book: Geocosmic Correlations to Gold Price Cycles. Essentially he summarizes his findings as: 1) several consistent relationships exist between gold price cycles and the retrograde (apparent reverse) and the direct periods of each of the planets; 2) certain major and minor geocosmic aspects (angles between two planets) occur and have exhibited a 90% reliability within four trading days. The latter is perhaps the most important finding of his work. Geocosmic aspects coinciding with major cycle reversals which have approximately 45% or greater association, are termed "level one" catagory. They are as follows:

		Occurrences	Percentage
1.	Saturn/Neptune	6 of 6	100%
2.	Neptune Retrograde	6 of 7	85%
3.	Jupiter/Saturn	5 of 6	83%
4.	Mars Stationary	6 of 8	75%
5.	Jupiter/Neptune	2 of 3	67%
6.	Mercury Conjunct or Waxing Trine to Mars	11 of 17	65%
7.	Venus/Mars	18 of 28	64%
8.	Venus Stationary	6 of 10	60%
9.	Mars/Jupiter	7 of 12	58%
10.	Venus/Uranus	20 of 36	56%
11.	Saturn Stationary	7 of 13	54%
12.	Sun/Uranus	16 of 36	44%

Other levels of associations are too numerous to mention here. With a frequency of 90%, a combination of three or more major planetary cycles will tend to be present within six trading days of a gold price cycle culmination. There are a total of 35 aspects found to be significant.

The following charts show numerous astronomical calculations for the positions of planets. These are then interpreted astrologically.

The two computer drawn astrological charts of gold; natal (contract initiated at 10:00 a.m. E.S.T., December 31, 1974) and gold's graphic ephemeris for 1986 are courtesy of Astro Computing Services.

Natal Chart

Plotted as of the initial moment of trading of the gold futures contract at the Commodity Exchange of New York City. Plotted on a Placidus house system (horizon adjusted for the ellipticity of the earth) and tropical zodiac (determined where the earth's ecliptic and equator cross at 0° Aries - the vernal equinox; and 0° Libra - the autumnal equinox).

Planetary positions are given in signs and measurements, in the upper left corner of the page. Ruler (R), detriment (D), exaltation (E), or fall (F) are traditional categories of relationship between the planet and the sign it occupies.

In the middle left side of the page, triplicity (element) and quadruplicity (quality) summaries are given in fire, earth, air, and water signs as well as the cardinal, fixed, and mutable qualities of the signs.

In the lower left corner, the aspectarian compiles all major and many minor elliptical aspects, parallels, and contraparallels in declination between the planets, ascendent, mid-heaven (MC) and true node of the moon. Nearest midpoints, halfway between any two factors, are considered sensitive points and are also shown.

Graphic Ephemeris

Developed by the German school of Rheinhold Ebertin and his son, Baldur. The graphic ephemeris shows transiting contacts, which are multiples of 45° aspects, such as conjunctions, squares, and oppositions.

The elapse (time progression) is seen on the horizontal axis; and the degrees of the signs on the vertical axis in 45° aspects. Natal planetary positions are on the outer vertical scale with horizontal lines.

The major (outer) planets are relatively flat as they progress (move down) or retrograde (move back up) in their apparent orbit as seen from earth. Fast moving (minor) planets are shown as nearly vertical lines. The moon is not shown in transiting but only on the far left natal axis. Where any planet's transit line intersects any of the horizontal natal lines, there is an angular aspect occurring.

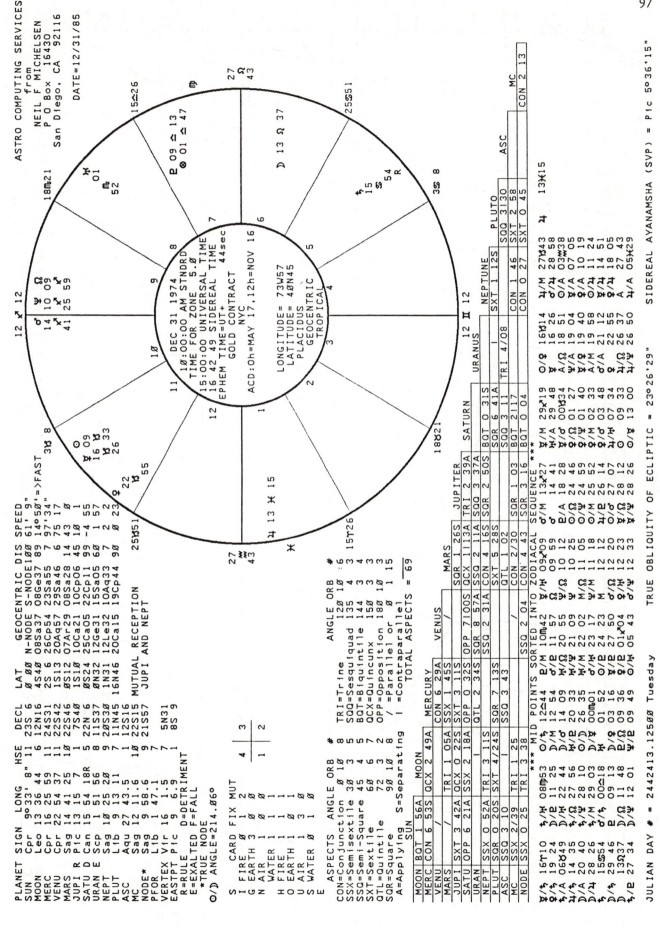

GRAPHICS FOR: GOLD CONTRACT NYC BIRTH DATE: DEC 31 1974 TIME: 10h 0m 0 ZONE 5.0 STANDARD TIME

98

— NATAL   — — TRANSITS, TIME ZONE   6   TROPICAL

Astrological Analysis

Transits and progressions occur whenever a planet forms an aspect to another planet, the sun, the moon, or any of the house cusps. These transits indicate trend changes and new issues.

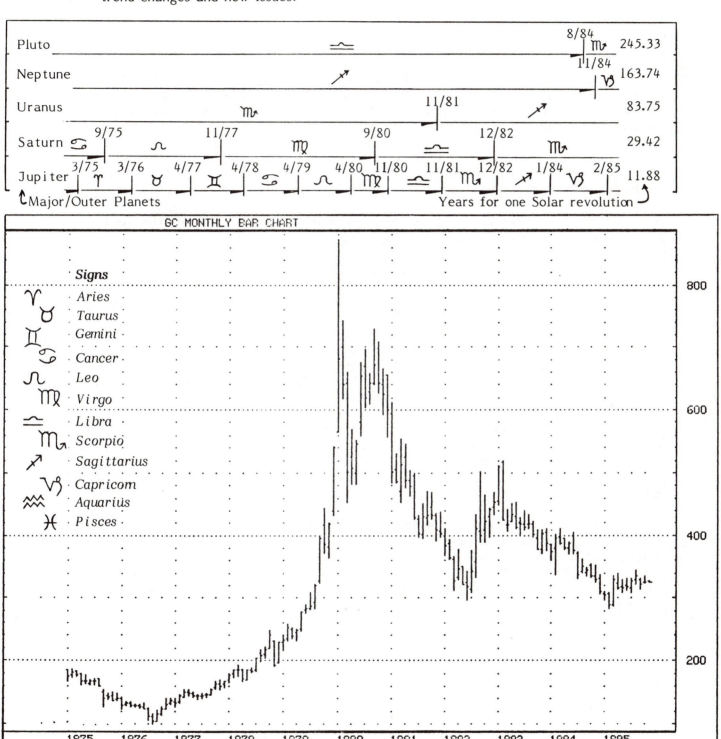

Commodity Quote-Graphics   TQ-20/20

Because of their much smaller orbits, Mercury, Venus, the Earth, and Mars progress much faster and have more frequent aspects than the outer planets.

Lunar Cycles

Researchers have tried to find a correlation between lunar phases (preferably the full moon) and the stock market. Ian McAvity confirmed lunar cycles having a full moon/high, new moon/low effect on the stock market. Research was based on over 60 lunar cycles (1977 through 1981).

While a simple six month observation cannot be statistically significant, it does give "food for thought". An empirical comparison of gold price highs and lows to phases of the moon did not show anything conclusive.

Thirteen representative dates of six lunar cycles in 1985 plotted onto a daily chart for observation show the following:

Highs (New Moon)	Lows (Full Moon)
6/18/85 High	7/2/85 Low
7/17/85 High	7/31/85 No
8/16/85 High	8/30/85 No - Uptrend violation to the downside.
9/14/85 No	9/28/85 Possibly
10/13/85 No	10/28/85 No
11/12/85 No	11/27/85 No - Uptrend violation to downside
12/11/85 No - Actually a significant low.	

There is simply insufficient consistency in a full moon/new moon - high/low cycle association to be considered reliable. The market in December 1985 is a lackluster, sideways trading affair. There is a definite lack of the public or mass of investors who may change these findings when they re-enter the gold market.

There are professional speculators in weather related commodities who use lunar cycles to determine the effect of artic cold fronts crossing the continental U.S.' width into the Florida citrus area. Supposedly, during only one part of the lunar cycle will the cold be stationary long enough to damage the citrus crop. We have not done any analysis on this premise as yet and cannot comment.

Lunar Cycles

New Moon——●   Full Moon——O   Six Months Daily Chart

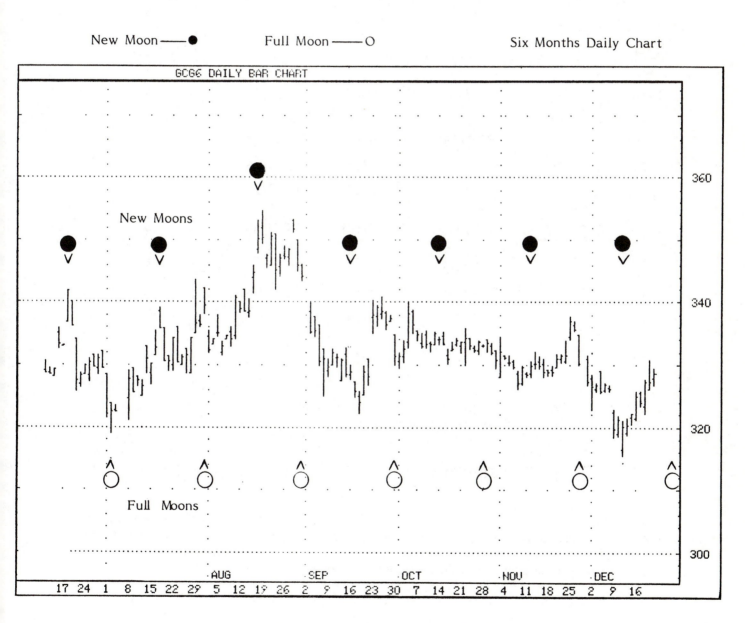

Commodity Quote-Graphics   TQ-20/20

Solar and Lunar Eclipses

A common fallacy in investment houses is eclipses have significance in gold price turning points. Since solar and lunar eclipses occur infrequently, we decided to briefly study both over the past decade.

Solar eclipses occur when the moon moves directly between the sun and the Earth. Either full or partial lunar eclipses occur when the moon moves into Earth's shadow.

Intermediate turning points for gold's price falling within one week of an eclipse date are shown below. The most significant highs and lows seem to have no relationship to eclipses except for one solar eclipse in 1982.

Year		Eclipses			A	B
1975	O 5/11	C 5/24	O 11/03	C 11/18	0	4
1976	O 4/29	C 5/13	O 10/23	C 11/06	0	4
1977	C 4/03	O 4/18	C 9/27	O 10/12	0	4
1978	C 3/24	[O 4/07]	C 9/16	O 10/02	1	4
1979	O 2/26	C 3/13	O 8/22	C 9/06	0	4
1980	O 2/16 C 8/25	C 3/01	C 7/27	O 8/10	0	5
1981	[C 1/20]	O 2/04	[C 7/16]	[O 7/30]	3	4
1982	C 1/09 O 12/15	[O 6/21] C 12/30	C 7/06	O 7/20	1	6
1983	[O 6/11]	[C 6/25]	O 12/04	C 12/19	2	4
1984	C 5/15 O 11/22	O 5/30	C 6/13	C 11/08	0	5
1985	C 5/04	O 5/19	C 10/28	O 11/12	0	4
				Total:	7	48 (14%)

Legend: A = Number of eclipses within one week of a turning point.
          B = Total number of yearly eclipses.
          O = Sun
          C = Moon
          [＿＿＿] = Turning point occurred within one week of this eclipse.

Significant highs were not reversed during an eclipse, and only a few significant lows turned to the upside near an eclipse. Statistically speaking, we found it completely unreliable for any long term analysis as there are insufficient meaningful turning points within one week of an eclipse.

Astrological Analysis Bibliography

Freeman, Martin. Forecasting by Astrology. Wellingborough, Northamptonshire, England: The Aquarian Press, 1982.

George, Llewellyn. A to Z Horoscope Maker and Delineator. St. Paul, Minnesota: Llewellyn Publications, 1972.

Hand, Robert. Planets in Transit: Life Cycles for Living. Rockport, Massachusetts: Para Research, Inc., 1976.

McAvity, Ian. Full Moon & The Market. Toronto, Canada: Deliberations Research, Inc., 1982.

Merriman, Raymond A. The Gold Book/Geocosmic Correlations to Gold Price Cycles. Birmingham, Michigan: Seek-It Publications, 1982.

Michelsen, Neil F. Astro Computing Services 1985/86. San Diego, California: ACS Publications, 1985.

Michelsen, Neil F. The American Ephemeris For The 20th Century: 1900 to 2000 at Midnight. San Diego, California: Astro Computing Services, 1980.

Pottenger, Maritha. Astrolocality Maps. San Diego, California: ACS Publications, 1983.

Stern, Jess. A Time For Astrology. New York: Coward, McCann & Geoghegan, Inc., 1971.

Thomas, Robert B. Old Farmers Almanac. Dublin, New Hampshire: Yankee Publishing, 1985.

Townley, John. Astrological Cycles and Life Crises Periods. New York: Samuel Weisner, Inc., 1977.

Bar Chart Analysis

A bar chart is usually thought of as a high, low, and close plot of prices with a standardized time frame such as a day, week, or month. With computer capabilities, many traders monitor hourly, half-hour, fifteen minutes, ten minutes, five minutes, and even one minute bar charts. The low cost of commissions for large volume traders, floor traders and institutional traders make these shorter term charts more appropriate. Smaller point moves are more meaningful to these professionals because they trade greater quantity.

Some seasoned traders prefer charts showing only closing prices. They believe the closing price is the only significant part of a bar chart's history. The reason the last or closing price is meaningful is that much of the trading activity within the bar plot is usually negated by the final or close. For long term trend determination, inter-period trades are mostly offset within that time period. The best example of this is floor traders aggressively trading large volumes of contracts daily. By the end of the day, their intention is to be flat — neither long nor short. As a result, plotting only daily closing prices, unless they range over significant support or resistance levels, will show a different and clearer trend pattern.

The following bar chart shows this best as the "closes" of each month (the last day of the last week of each month) are connected. Significant trends, fan trendlines, and parallel trendlines are indicated. Violations of trendlines are indicated by "O's".

Monthly Closes (Lasts) – Connected

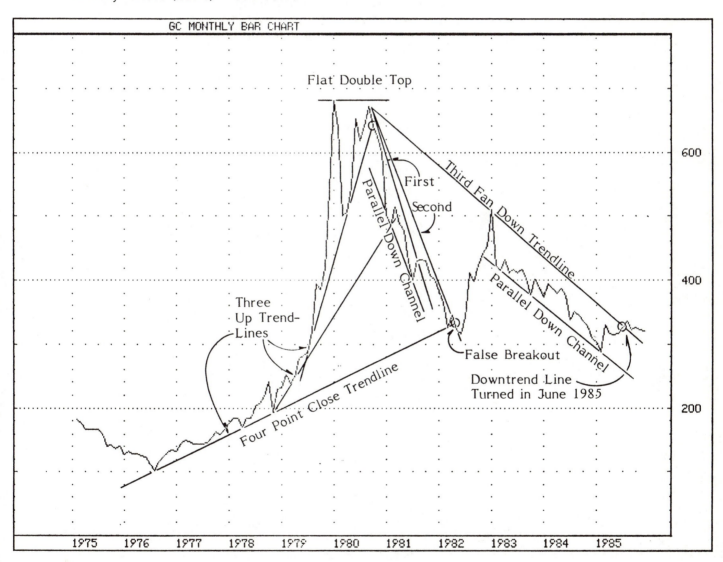

Commodity Quote-Graphics   TQ-20/20

*"The man who has a million dollars
is as well off as if he were rich."*
---John Jacob Astor III

Centered Moving Average Analysis

A centered moving average is a derivative of an ordinary moving average. It is an advanced form of price analysis which benefits the user in two ways. First, it defines the major trend it is designed to follow. Second, it gives a mechanically graphic measurement for both overbought and oversold parameters within the longer term trend scenario.

After being computed, moving averages are usually plotted at the time of most recent price. In our example, we took a 13 bar (month) moving average and plotted it at the center of the time period — 7 months. This is called the lagged plotting of data. If our period of moving average was 10 bars, the centering would have placed it at 5-1/2 bars.

The result is a moving average plotted in the middle of prices as they occur. Prices flucutate both up and down but tend to stay within a certain percentage band located around their trending average. This creates a band or channel effect that can be graphically demonstrated and even used for positioning purposes. Even when prices exceed this band, they still return close to the moving average center area.

When seen on a long term chart, such as our 10 year gold plot, prices fluctuate, but always with a bias toward the dominant trend. When prices extend beyond the normal extremes, they don't stay there very long. (See Chart A.) When the long term price trend reverses, say from up to down, the new trend maintains prices at a consistent rate of downtrend within the band. Prices still stay within the band constructed around the centered moving average.

Analysts who use centered moving averages know that when prices reach the extreme high or low of the price band, the probability is greatest for a reaction back toward the center. If the trend is down, they know where not to add on to their shorts. They also know where to exit their profitable positions and to wait for a reaction. Therefore, the band can be used as a short term trading tool within a longer term trending pattern. Its use is variable, either long or short term.

With the aid of the computer after centering the 13 bar average we experimented to find the best percentage band above and below the centered average. After many trials, a 16% band above and below the center average proved best, as shown in Chart A.

A variation of the centered moving average with upper and lower bands only is a hand drawn price envelope (see Chart B). It is created by visually drawing lines connecting the highs to each other in a smoothed fashion. Then the lows are connected in the same manner. This creates an envelope around any given price data. As this is hand drawn; exact methods, rulers, nor mathematical calculations are used. It is amazing how close the overall envelope is when compared to a computer drawn percentage band.

Since no computer is needed to calculate moving average data, nor backspace it to the appropriate bar plot to lag the data, nor construct different percentage calculations to see which band best fits the prices, the main advantages of envelope analysis are its convenience, simplicity, and quickness for devising a useful analysis.

Many technicians do not use hand drawn envelope analysis, as they prefer exact points telling them where to go long or short.

Centered Moving Average Analysis

Computer Drawn
Chart A

Moving Averages: 13 Bar, Lagged Plot By 7 Bars (Half), Plus Or Minus 16%.

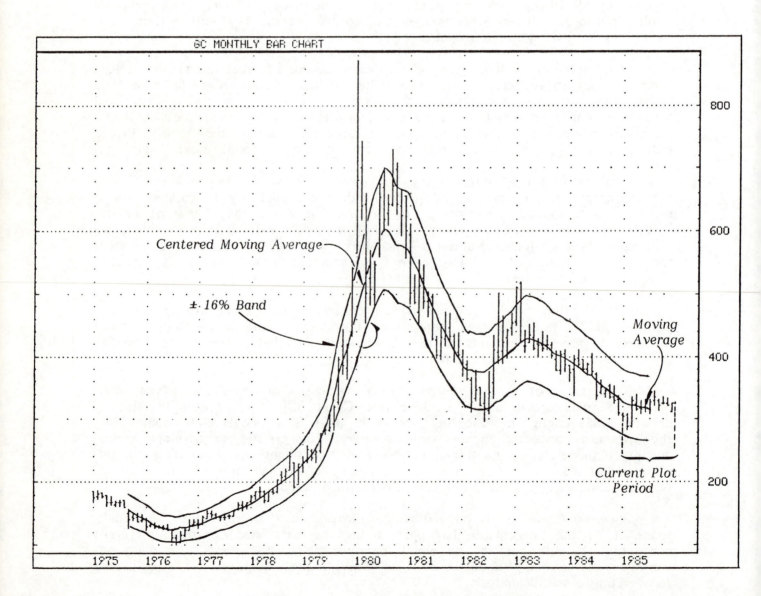

Commodity Quote-Graphics   TQ-20/20

Centered Moving Average Analysis

Envelope Analysis
Chart B

Price Envelope Analysis: Approximately 95% Of All The Price Movement Fits Within The Eye Fitted, Hand Drawn Band.

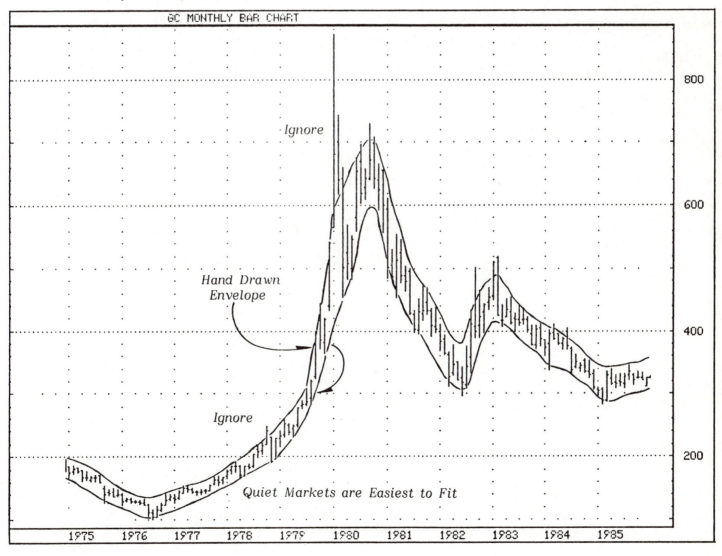

Commodity Quote-Graphics   TQ-20/20

"I cannot afford to waste my time making money."
---Jean Louis Agassiz

CCI

Commodity Channel Index Analysis

The commodity channel index is used primarily for predicting cyclical trends. Therefore, its use is that of noting divergence to price fluctuations and trends.

To calculate the channel index, first calculate a simple moving average with the time frame desired. For our example, we selected a 12 bar moving average. We then calculated the mean deviation. This is an average of the absolute value of differences between the current value used in the average, and each price used to calculate that average.

$$CCI = \frac{(Current\ Price - Current\ Average) \div Mean\ Deviation}{.015}$$

We have shown the CCI against gold's long term price for direct comparison (Chart A) and by itself for closer examination (Chart B).

For the example, we selected a 12 month bar period which is consistent with other studies. This eliminates seasonal effects and all annual influences on gold prices.

Prices stayed within the commodity channel index at plus 90 to plus 110 from late 1976 (the first index plot) through late 1978. In October, when prices began to run bullishly, President Carter's October 31st speech to defend the U.S. dollar collapsed gold prices for 4 weeks. The bar channel index dropped from a reading of plus 140 to 0. Prices immediately rose, with the channel index re-establishing itself in the prior plus 40 to plus 110 range. After June 1979, when gold prices began to escalate at a geometrically compounded rate, the channel index shot up to eventually reach plus 230 in January 1980. When prices collapsed during the winter of 1980, so did the index, but only to the low range of its previous area — plus 40 to plus 80.

September 1980 saw the real top of gold prices occur and then erode into a bear market. The channel index fell through zero (December 1980) and then worked its way down to the minus 40 to minus 110 area, where it stayed for the next 15 months. Please note that this is the same range for the index as the bullish period was, only in the opposite negative territory.

Only after June 1982, with gold's phenomenal rally to over $500 an ounce in January 1983, was there any positive sign from the channel index. The index climbed to plus 130, but then collapsed in sympathy to gold's vicious February break to resume its bear trend. The index moved back down to the minus 30 to minus 135 range for the next 18 months as gold prices continued their steady decline.

March of 1985 saw gold prices rally to violate immediate downtrend lines after hitting $287 in February, or $15 lower than June 1982 levels. The index rallied to just above the zero level for the next few months; not enough to say the trend has turned but the trend apparently is no longer distinctly bearish.

Gaining familiarity with this approach necessitates applying different bar periods to many various commodity charts. We feel it is an excellent tool when read correctly, when an adequate bar period for computation has been chosen, and when it is used against a dynamically trending commodity instead of a trendless one.

CCI

Commodity Channel Index

Chart A

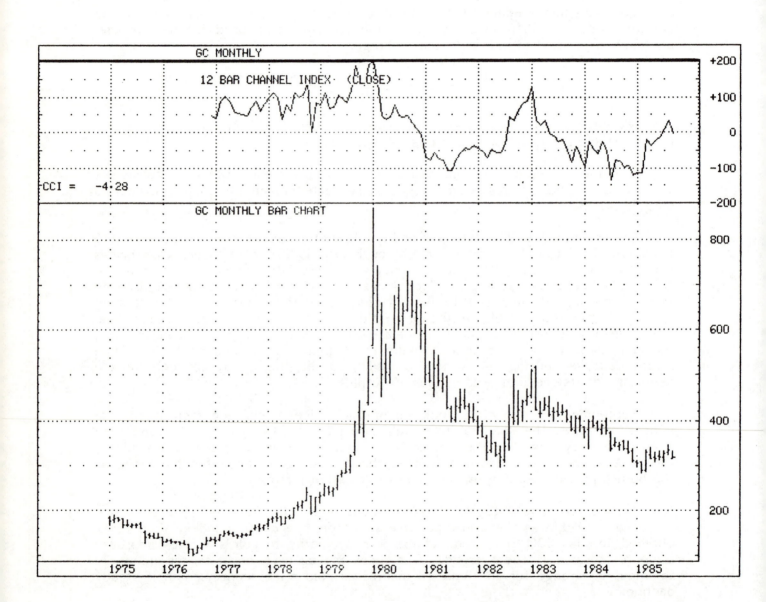

Commodity Quote-Graphics   TQ-20/20

CCI

Commodity Channel Index

Chart B

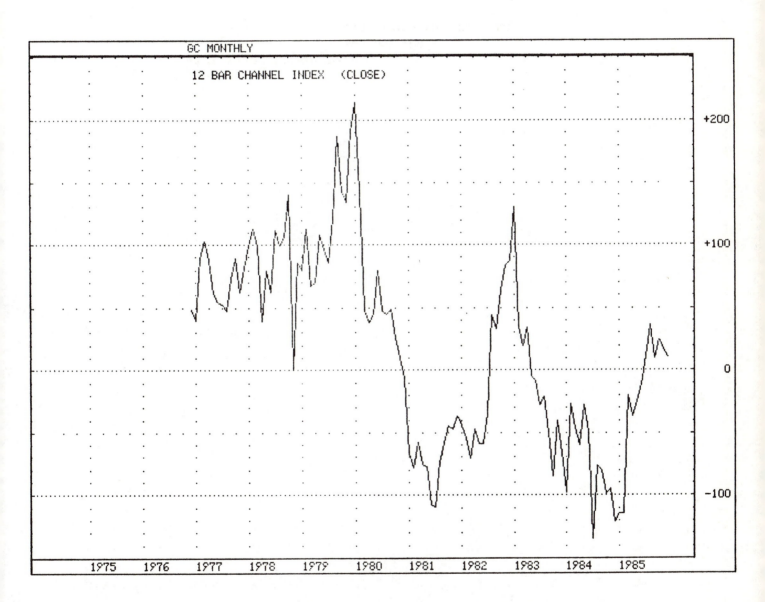

Commodity Quote-Graphics   TQ-20/20

"There are only two emotions in Wall Street:
fear and greed."
---William M. LeFevre, Jr.

Complementary Angle Analysis

One approach rarely used by commodity technicians is complementary angle chart analysis, sometimes called 90° complementary angle analysis. Perhaps the reason it is rarely used in commodity charts is that it doesn't appear to be relevant for short or long term charts. (See Chart C.) When applied to gold's long term bar chart, it did not appear to be useful. However, as we are trying to be objective, it does appear to work for long term stock analysis. Therefore, we decided to deviate from our normal presentation and show examples of complementary angle analysis as applied to stocks.

Best explained by the investment advisor Richard Ney in his two famous books, The Wall Street Jungle and The Wall Street Gang, this approach is useful in decade-long stock trend analysis. Complementary angle examples in The Wall Street Gang show clearly developed analyses on such blue chip stocks as General Motors, Grumman, Sears, and United Airlines over 30 and 40 years. Charts used for this form of analysis by Mr. Ney and shown here for your benefit are courtesy of Security Research Company [208 Newbury St., Boston, MA 02116].

We would like to point out that the price scale used is semi-logarithmic (ratio) scale to the base two. A move up from 10 to 20 has the same percentage increase (100%) as does 20 to 40, or 40 to 80. A move down from 100 to 50, or 50 to 25 is a 50% drop or 1/2 ratio; again equally measured on a semi-logarithmic scale chart. Currently there is no source to our knowledge that offers such plotting of commodity prices, long or short term, on semi-log scale. Trading on as little as 1% to 5% margin, makes most market participants interested in shorter term price fluctuations. This effectively nullifies almost all demand for semi-log scale long term charts.

We decided to show two distinct applications of this approach on two stock charts, Bristol-Myers Co. and Associated Dry Goods Corp. We picked these two because they both showed well defined complete downmoves and the resultant complementary angle trends.

Complementary angle analysis concentrates on three angles to be used for both advancing and declining phases. When a stock such as Bristol-Myers has a significant price decline, the "principal" angle (AB) is created from a line drawn from the stock's major low (A) to its prior high price (B). This move has within its price action the long term future price trends. The price scale of the SRC charts is always on the right side, and actual prices of stock are adjusted for stock splits and dividends.

While principal angles are formed from a major low of a stock decline, each major low's principal angle has a function that distinguishes itself from other principal angles. The steeper the angle, the shorter term is its influence.

A "secondary" angle (AC) is created by drawing a line from the major price low (A) to the preceeding low (C). The difference of the two angles is termed the "acute" angle ($\angle$ AB - $\angle$ AC).

Distinct from the principal angle is its "complementary" angle, or its difference from 90°. In the Bristol-Myers' example, the principal angle is 39°. The complementary angle therefore is 90° - 39° = 51°. Note the plot from "A" upwards for some 15 years duration. Simply put, this trend is drawn off the exact low at exactly 90° to the angle of the principal downtrend. Parallel trend-lines to this new, upwardly drawn complementary angle are constructed off significant highs and lows, defining limits and channels that hold for decades.

To refresh your knowledge, a straight line drawn on semi-log scale is actually a curved plot when drawn on an arithmetically scaled chart. This shows a compounded rate of price movement. Why major price collapses tend to create the next upmove for 15, 20, 30 years or longer is a real mystery.

According to Mr. Ney, while the complement of a stock's secondary angle sometimes occurs for future trend channels, the complement of the principal angle seems predominate.

When all the angles' complements are put onto the chart, they tend to intersect at various points in the future. These points of intersection indicate price objectives. Attainment of a price objective is frequently a price trend change.

What is most relevant about Mr. Ney's approach is that these relationships seem to pervade the life cycle of these economic assets. The major collapse appears to create its future upward movement. The rate of climb is a by-product of the prior rate of collapse. Therefore, price history is a continuum with major moves in the past both influencing and defining what the future may hold.

With the advent of computers and their millions of calculations per second capacity, accurate plotting of commodity prices onto semi-log scale charts is imminent. Creative minds will apply what Richard Ney has developed and published in this area. In fact, what Mr. Ney has developed and not yet made public may be more revealing in depth.

We recommend that you contact Mr. Ney at his current address to obtain the most recent methodology and advice in this area. His newsletter, "The Ney Report", is published at: P. O. Box 90215, Pasadena, California 91109.

Chart A

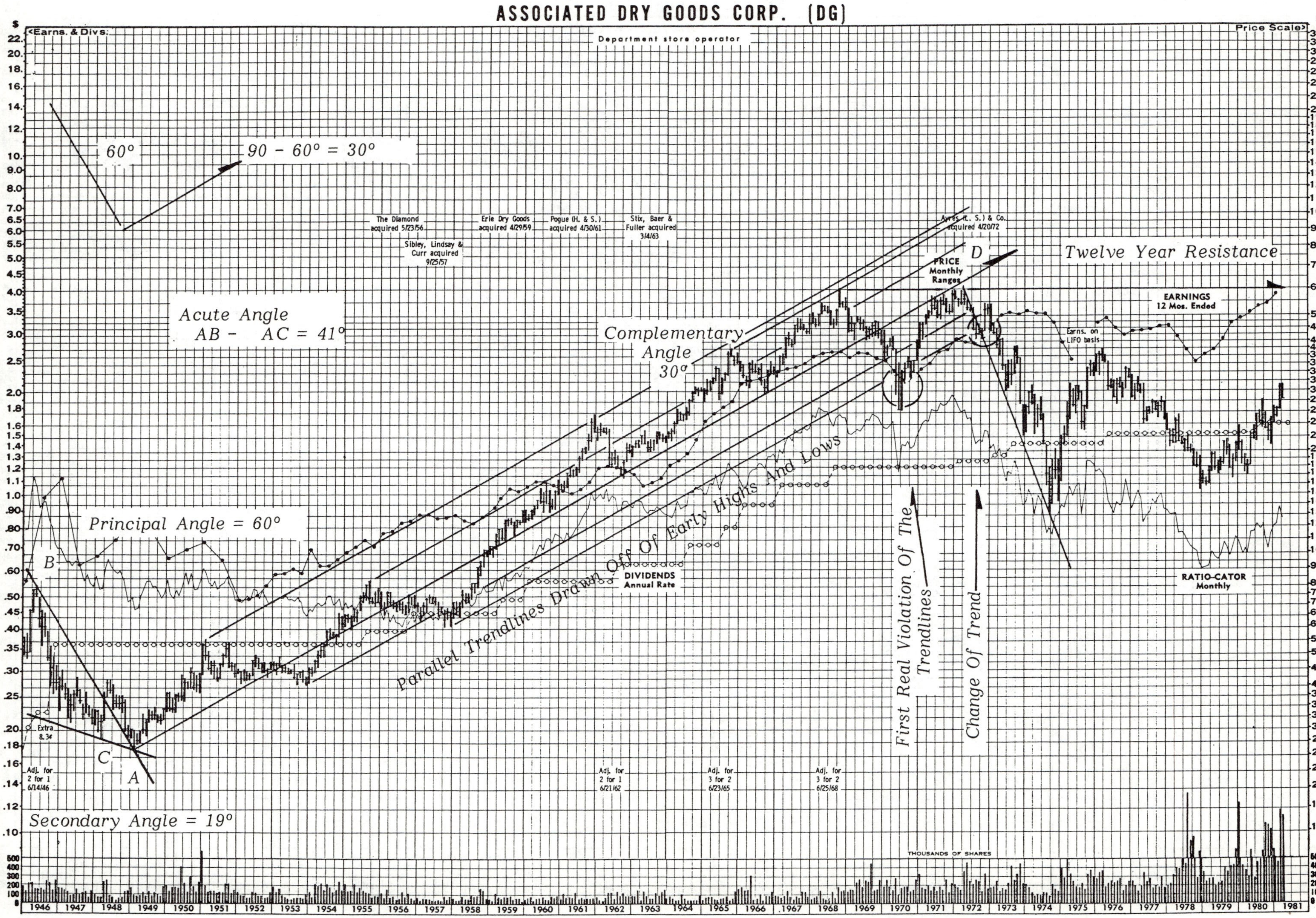
ASSOCIATED DRY GOODS CORP. (DG)
Department store operator
<Earns. & Divs.
Price Scale>
60°
90 - 60° = 30°
Acute Angle
AB - AC = 41°
Principal Angle = 60°
Secondary Angle = 19°
Complementary Angle 30°
Parallel Trendlines Drawn Off Of Early Highs And Lows
First Real Violation Of The Trendlines
Change Of Trend
Twelve Year Resistance
A
B
C
D
The Diamond acquired 5/23/56
Sibley, Lindsay & Curr acquired 9/25/57
Erie Dry Goods acquired 4/29/59
Pogue (H. & S.) acquired 4/30/61
Stix, Baer & Fuller acquired 3/4/63
Ayres (L. S.) & Co. acquired 4/20/72
PRICE Monthly Ranges
EARNINGS 12 Mos. Ended
Earns. on LIFO basis
DIVIDENDS Annual Rate
RATIO-CATOR Monthly
Adj. for 2 for 1 6/14/46
Adj. for 2 for 1 6/21/62
Adj. for 3 for 2 6/23/65
Adj. for 3 for 2 6/25/68
Extra &.34
THOUSANDS OF SHARES
1946
1947
1948
1949
1950
1951
1952
1953
1954
1955
1956
1957
1958
1959
1960
1961
1962
1963
1964
1965
1966
1967
1968
1969
1970
1971
1972
1973
1974
1975
1976
1977
1978
1979
1980
1981

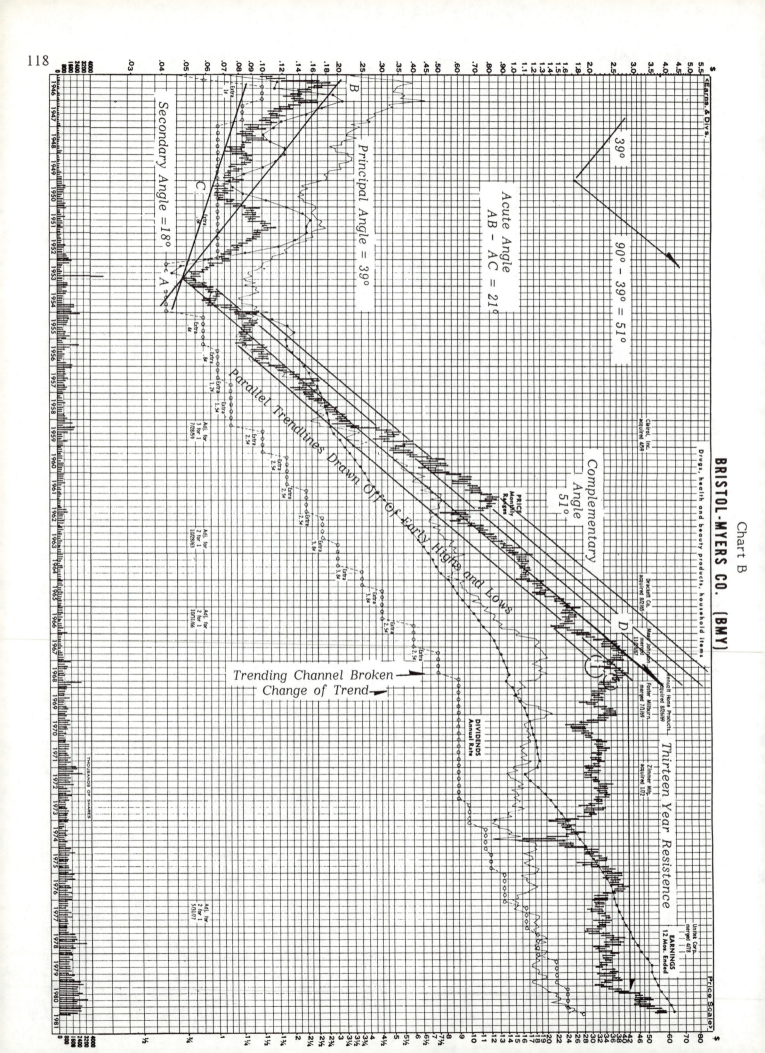

Chart B

BRISTOL-MYERS CO. (BMY)

Drugs, health and beauty products, household items

118

Complementary Angle Analysis
Chart C

Used primarily by short term traders, the 90° complementary angle approach is simplicity itself. Its main tenant is the angle of bearishness is complementary to the angle of bullishness totaling 90°. This is a right triangle and is shown below in graph form. The main or initial angle 'A' has a 34° slant to the horizontal. The difference between this angle and a right angle is angle 'C' or 56°, the two angles totaling 90° shown as angle 'C'. Its application on our long term chart leaves something to be desired.

Commodity Quote-Graphics   TQ-20/20

Chart D

In applying complementary angle analysis to gold on a semi-log scale, we found it did not work as it did for stock prices. The angle AB of 43° in 1975-76 created angle AC which was 47° to the horizontal, and the complement to AB. The next decline from 1980 to 1982 created the principal A'B' of angle 42°. Its complement A'C' of 48° was somewhat followed by prices until early 1983. The market then seemed to completely walk away from its bullish trend with a pattern of constant, shallow trending erosion. Prices did not follow the original angle AC in any parallel channel trendlines drawn off of developing highs and lows. The application of this analysis to gold is negative and appears only to work for long term stock prices. But we can't think of anyone who holds onto their stocks for 35 to 40 years anymore.

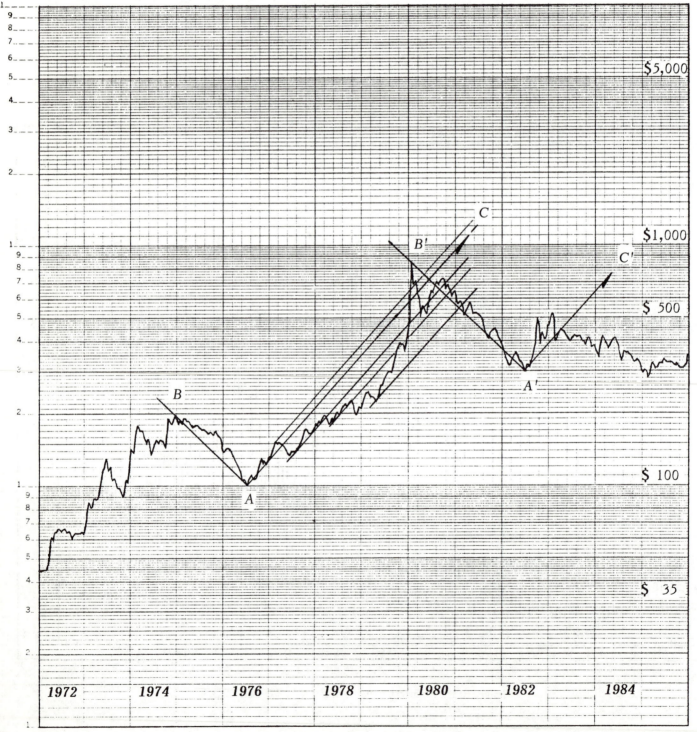

Complementary Angle Analysis Bibliography

Ney, Richard. The Wall Street Gang. New York: Praeger Publishers, 1974.

Ney, Richard. The Wall Street Jungle. New York: Grove Press, 1970.

The SRC Green Book of 3 - Trend 35-Year Charts 1946-1981. First Edition. Boston, MA: Securities Research Company, 1981.

"If you want to succeed you should strike out on new paths rather than travel the worn paths of accepted success."
---John D. Rockefeller

Contrary Opinion Analysis

This approach to understanding markets could have been placed in the Psychological Crowd Analysis. However, since contrary opinion is the ability of one person to oppose the crowd mentality, we felt it appropriate to separate it from analyzing crowd behavior and logic — or illogic as the case may be. Contrary opinion is action in direct opposition to the crowd's behavior pattern.

In the majority of markets the larger number of people consistently lose their money to the smaller number of people. This is a regular process of distribution in every form of investment, speculation, and trading. This is also true in the commodities markets, but happens in a much shorter time period due to smaller margin requirements. As a result, people eventually wind up following full time professionals for making trading decisions. Professionals could be brokerage firm newsletters, or special reports, independent trading advisors, and even retail account brokers. The various writers of trading information and opinion set the pattern for the public's bullish or bearish attitude. Advisors, wanting a favorable acceptance of their recommendations, reinforce or recommend their opinion when the market has already partially moved in the direction they lean toward. Guess where most recipients of this advice buy — near the high. Guess where most recipients of this advice sell — near the low.

By monitoring a statistically significant number of advisory services and brokerage house opinions, some observations can be made. A West Coast chart and advisory service, Sibbet-Hadady Publications, Inc. [Financial Building, Suite 200, 380 E. Green St., Pasadena, California 91101] takes a weekly poll of bullish opinion. It is then listed on a scale of 0% to 100% for each commodity and plotted against a price scale. A balanced market tends to have contrary opinion levels around 50% to 60% bullish. Overbought and oversold border areas of the bullish consensus occur around 70% and 30% respectively, where price changes in trend are likely to start. As the consensus approaches 10% to 0%, the probability of the trend reversing to up increases drastically. As the consensus reaches 90% to 95% or even 100% bullish, the probability of the trend to turn down is strong. We just could not find any graphic manner in which to present this technical tool on our long term chart. Instead, we decided to show ten of the most famous quotations of the last decade and when they were made on our long term gold chart.

Contrary Opinion Analysis

— Famous Quotes on Gold and Money
and When They Occurred —

1. $35   Late 1960's: "When gold is not going to be supported by the federal government at $35 anymore, it will crash to $6 an ounce."
—Rep. Henry S. Reuss (D-Wisc.) Chairman of the House Banking Committee.

2. $190   Dec. 1974: "Gold will go to $600 and the stock market will crash."
— Leading gold-bug newsletter from Switzerland.

3. $110   June 1976: One of America's top N.Y. money banks stated in its newsletter that gold "... will probably collapse down to around $65 an ounce."

4. $150   Mid 1977: "With the initial auction by the I.M.F. [International Monetary Fund] gold has nowhere to go but down."
—Secretary of the Treasury.

5. $240   March 1979: "Gold and the Dow [Dow Jones Industrial Stock Index] will trade at the same price."
— Gold-bug newsletter.

6. $800   Dec. 1979/Jan 1980: "Gold is going to $1,000."
"Gold is going to $3,000."
"Gold is going to $4,000."
— Three different gold-bug newsletters.

7. $300   June 1982: One famous gold oriented technical newsletter proclaiming to be the "original gold-bug" gave his "much vaunted all out one and only gold and silver sell signal" to get out of investment holdings of gold. This was often referred to as his MVAOOAOGASSS. This was the major bottom!

8. $475   Dec. 1982: "We predict $3,600 gold by late 1985 - early 1986 at the latest."
— Leading gold oriented technical advisory from Costa Rica.

9. $320   Dec. 1984: Business Week's lead article with predominant cover was "The Death of Mining". This mainly referred to gold and other mining stocks.

10. $285   Feb. 1985: The U.S. dollar was constantly called "superdollar" in its 4 year climb against other industrialized currencies. The "superdollar" title was also given to contrast it to the now lowly gold market, applied retrospectively. This term was used extensively by the "establishment" money trade (bonds, stocks and currencies). Ironically, this was the high for the U.S. dollar after which it proceeded to collapse.

•

Contrary Opinion Analysis

Famous Quotes On Gold, Money And The Stock Market

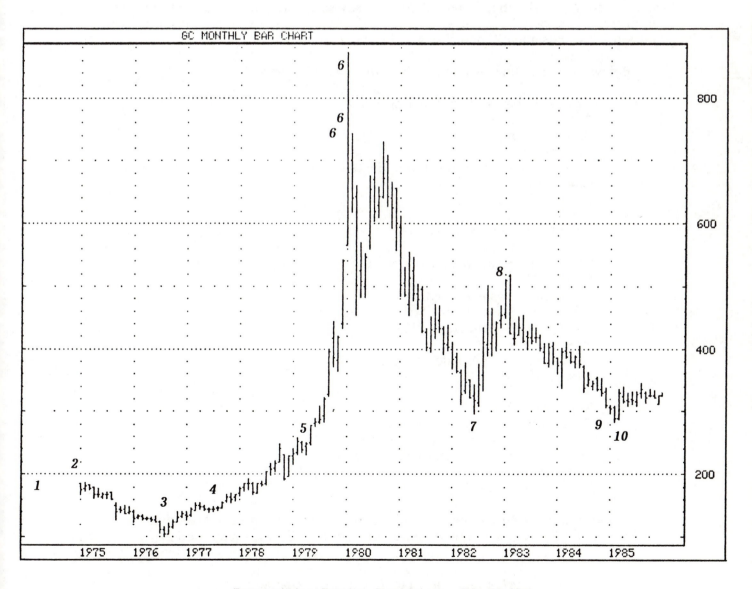

Commodity Quote-Graphics   TQ-20/20

The "Establishment" in Financial Parlance, Business Publications and News Media

Traders and investors who want to maintain their individuality and independence in judgment avoid reading the "establishment" publications and viewing "establishment" media. The reason is the facts presented are subjected to degrees of editorialization, which is usually untimely.

For example, a market which is not really trending (gold in 1985) is not publicized. It is not news. The more a market trends, the more it is written or talked about and the more it is editorialized. Therefore, most stories are done after an extended market trend, such as at the top of a bull market (gold in 1980 or stocks in 1986) or the bottom of a bear market (crude oil in 1986).

Therefore, an investor who has a practical grasp of this situation, will apprise himself of what the "establishment" media is editorializing. If a market is being over-editorialized, his position in that market will be opposite the current trend since he feels the trend is due to reverse. Even specialized investment newsletters can be classified as "establishment". Any extreme, absolute statements by "establishment" media should be cause for caution.

Below is a sampling of current "establishment" media.

ABC - American Broadcasting Co. (T)
Associated Press (NS)
Barron's (N)
Business Week (M)
CBS - Columbia Broadcasting System (T)
Chicago Commerce (M)
Chicago Tribune (N)
CNS - Commodity News Service (NS)
Crain's Chicago Business (M)
The Dine's Letter (NL)
FNN - Financial News Network (T)
Forbes (M)
The Gold Newsletter (NL)
The International Harry Schultz Newsletter (NL)
International Moneyline (NL)
Investors Daily (N)
NBC - National Broadcasting Co. (T)
New York Times (N)
Newsweek (M)
Reuters (NS)
Time (M)
U.S. News & World Report (M)
UPI - United Press International (NS)
Wall Street Journal (N)
Wall Street Week (T)

(NL) Gold Oriented Specialty Newsletter   (M) Business Magazine
  (N) Newspaper   (NS) News Service   (T) Television Media

"All I know is what I read in the papers."
— Will Rogers

Contrary Opinion Bibliography

Angell, G. "Thinking Contrarily" [Interview of R. Earl Hadady] Commodities Magazine, Nov. 1976, pp. 22-23, 36-37.

Band, Richard E. Contrary Investing. Arlington, Va: Alexandria House Books, 1985.

Hadady, R. Earl. Contrary Opinion. 1983.

LeBon, Gustave. The Crowd. 1895.

Mackay, Charles. Extraordinary Popular Delusions and The Madness of Crowds. 1841.

"The Bullish Consensus." Market Vane, [Advisory Service] 61 S. Lake Ave., Pasadena, Ca. 91101.

Neill, Humphrey B. The Art of Contrary Opinion Thinking. 1954.

"Contrary Investing: How the Smart Money Buys Low and Sells High." World Market Perspective, Sept. 1985.

Cycle Analysis

On the monthly plot used throughout this study, the most obvious cycles are the 19 week, the seasonal or 48 to 52 week, and the powerful 5 1/2 year cycle. For comparitive purposes we have added Samuel Benner's business cycle projections at the extreme low to show what was forecast for this period back in 1875.

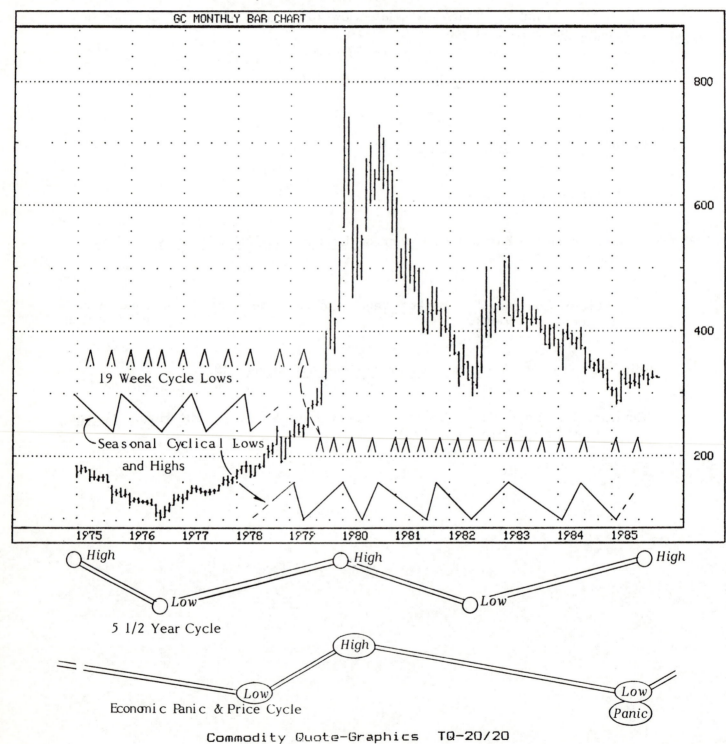

Commodity Quote-Graphics   TQ-20/20

Cycle Harmonics

To better understand the nature of cyclic behavior and their causes, professionals use many forms of mathematics to research time series, wave-form, timing and strength.   Cycle harmonics shows the associations and relationships between cylces of different lengths.   The listing below shows a few of the more well known interrelationships.   A music student understands harmonics better due to everyday familiarization and use of musical scales.   Harmonics are merely cycles within longer cycles.

Most Common Cycle Lengths

2x Harmonics   3x Harmonics

4.0	Years
5.89 – 6.01	Years
7.96 – 8.02	Years
8.95 – 9.94	Years
11.19 – 12.84	Years
16.7 – 18.2	Years
22.0	Years
54.0	Years
164.0	Years

While there are interrelationships with other ratios, the above ratios show the harmonious intertwining of their time periods and presumably, their source and nature.

Foundation for the Study of Cycles, Inc., 124 S. Highland Ave., Pittsburgh, Pennsylvania 15206.

All Gold Associated Cycles

Direct and indirect, listed in order of periodicity from longest to shortest.

Source	Period	Range (If Any)	Definition
Herbst	520 Yrs.		Gold "Purchasing Power"
Jastrom	112 Yrs.	106 - 118 Yrs.	English War Cycle
Williams	56 Yrs.		Panic Highs/Economic Activity
Kondratieff	54 Yrs.	52 - 56 Yrs.	Wholesale Prices/Inflation/Economic Activity/Wheat Prices/Stock Market Prices/Interest Rates/Sunspot Numbers Also known as the "K-Wave".
Herbst	53.83 Yrs.		Gold "Purchasing Power"
Herbst	42 Yrs.		Gold "Purchasing Power"
Foundation & Williams	22.11 Yrs.	9 - 34 Yrs.	Since 1781 - Panics/Wars/Gold Tops/Sunspot Highs
Benner	18 Yrs.	16 - 20 Yrs.	Economic Panics/Wars
Foundation	11 Yrs.		Sunspot Cycles/Wholesale Commodity Prices
C.R.B., Foundation & Bressert	9-1/2 Yrs.		Wholesale Commodity Prices/9.26 Yr. Silver Cycle
Benner	9 Yrs.	7 - 11 Yrs.	Hard Times/Low Prices
Benner	9 Yrs.	8 - 10 Yrs.	Good Times/High Prices
Foundation	5.58 Yrs.		Since 1850 - Silver/Commodities/Interest Rates
Williams	5.42 Yrs.	5.1 - 5.75 Yrs.	Since 1969 - Gold Cycle/Wholesale Commodities
Merriman	118 Wks.		68 week dominant with 50 week inferior cycle.
Bressert	48/52 Wks.		Seasonal Gold
C.R.B. Index	11 Mo.		Wholesale Commodity Prices

Bernstein	23 Wks.		Gold
Bressert	19 Wks.	16 - 23 Wks.	Gold "Primary" Cycle
--	13 Wks.	11 - 14 Wks.	Gold
Bressert	9.5 Wks.		1/2 of 19 Week Cycle/Harmonic Cycles
Bressert	5/7 Wks.		1/3 of 19 Week Cycle/Harmonic Cycles
--	56 Day		Double 28 Day Cycle/Most Commodities
Lunar	28 Day		Gold/Most Commodities
Bressert	21 Day		Gold
Lunar	14 Day		1/2 of 28 Day Cycle/Harmonic Cycles
--	4/7 Day		Floor Trade/Public Cycle

Cycle Periodicity

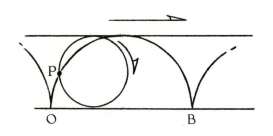

Perhaps the most interesting of all facts regarding cycles is that measurements of raw data, after detrending, usually show a peak-to-peak or trough-to-trough bias. Rarely does cycle data clearly show defined peaks and troughs concurrency. Rather, such as in long term price data, highs seem to be the predominant points for establishing the existence of long term cycles. The observable lows are spurious and in general more erratic. In shorter term data, the lows seem to be more clearly defined with less consistent highs.

The above drawing shows a point (P) on a rotating circle. When the circle makes over one full revolution begining at a point (O), two distinct troughs are seen (O and B). There are no distinct highs or peaks. The mathematical term for this is a cycloid.

On a measured scale, it appears the rotating or cyclic force has a single point affecting other things. This implies a single point of energy or force having a circular motion periodically influencing masses of people to behave in a cycloid manner. The natural conclusion leans toward astronomical occurrences. The numerous circular orbits and interrelation to other bodies gives many possible sources of influence. We suggest the reader see the section on astrological analysis.

Cycles of unrelated natures seem to repeatedly trough or peak together. The best study of cycles to date was done by the late Edward R. Dewey, covering 309 cycles. To hold the study to workable levels, he limited it to all then observed cycles of four years or longer. To be included in the study, each cycle had to have at least three examples. All 309 cases grouped themselves into what he called "master cycles". Nineteen master cycles are as follows:

```
16 examples of   4.0   year periods
10 examples of   5.9   year periods ( 5.89 to  5.92)
37 examples of   6.0   year periods ( 5.98 to  6.01)
37 examples of   8.0   year periods ( 7.96 to  8.02)
31 examples of   9.0   year periods ( 8.95 to  9.14)
28 examples of   9.2   year periods ( 9.17 to  9.34)
 7 examples of   9.5   year periods ( 9.41 to  9.54)
24 examples of   9.6   year periods ( 9.58 to  9.7 )
16 examples of   9.9   year periods ( 9.75 to  9.94)
 6 examples of  11.2   year periods (11.19 to 11.3 )
 3 examples of  12.0   year periods (12.0  to 12.05)
11 examples of  12.6   year periods (12.4  to 12.84)
 5 examples of  16 2/3 year periods
 6 examples of  17 1/3 year periods
 9 examples of  17.7   year periods
14 examples of  18.2   year periods
10 examples of  22     year periods
35 examples of  54     year periods
 4 examples of 164     year periods
```

We grouped these master cycles even further to allow for possible inadequacies (not enough measured cycles, poor data, wobble, unknown extraneous forces, and so on). (See Cycle Harmonics.) These are "Grand Master" cycles; 4, 6, 8, 9, 12, 17, 22, 54, and 164 years; that are dominant in all things, but especially economic price data.

An Example of Cycle Synchrony
The 5.9 Year Cycle

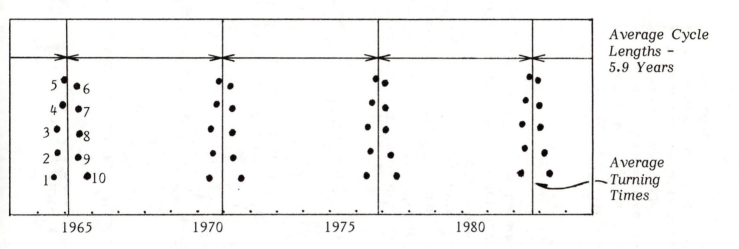

Cycles: 1) Business Failures, Inverted   6) Grouse Abundance
         2) Railroad Stock Prices   7) Pig Iron Prices
         3) Combined Stock Prices   8) Sunspot Numbers
         4) Coal Stock Prices   9) Cotton Prices
         5) Copper Share Prices   10) Copper Prices

Edward R. Dewey, "Cycle Synchronies," Cycles Magazine, August 1970. [Above table has been updated from original. Ed.]

Coincidentally, all but three of the master periods are multiples of the orbital period of earth or fractions of the five outer planets' orbits. The elliptical orbits and variations in speed of the planets can be better examined to show variations around the cyclical norm when orbits are divided by 2, 3, 4, etc., up to 12 segments. For example, Saturn's orbit of 29.5 years, when segmented by 5, shows real cyclic ranges from 5.39 to 6.53 years, due to its elliptical form. The average length of 5.9 years when multiplied by 5, gives the siderial period of 29.5 years to complete one orbit.

Farmer Benner's Business Forecast

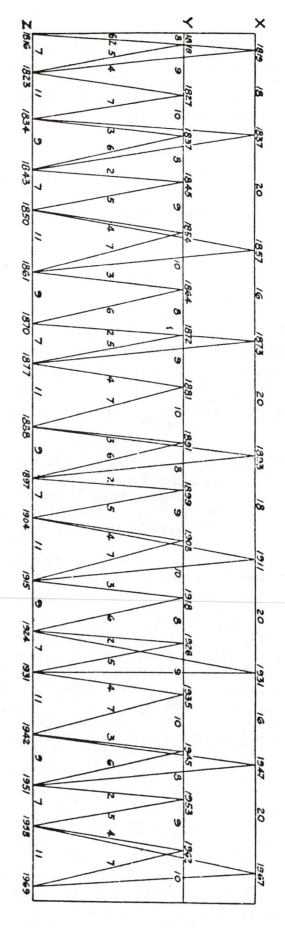

THIS chart, showing the trends of business in the United States from 1816 to 1967, was published by Farmer Benner in Cincinnati in *1871*. Students of economics say it has hit the nail on the head up to the present time. The chart shows that the *1931* depression officially ended with the year, and that for four years, *beginning in 1932, business will be on the up-grade.*

Key to Chart

X—Years in which panics have occurred and will occur again. Their regular cycles are 16, 20, 18, 20 years.

Y—Years of good times, high prices and the time to sell stocks and values of all kinds. Their cycles are 8, 9 and 10 years.

Z—Years of hard times, low prices and a good time to buy stocks, corner lots, etc., and hold until the boom, then unload. Their cycles are 9, 7 and 11 years.

The late John H. Patterson of The National Cash Register Company, kept this chart ever before him and it had a great deal to do in the planning of his operations during past periods of depression.

The man who made this chart died in 1884, and this chart was first published in Cincinnati Ohio, in 1871—75 years ago. If you will study it carefully, you will note the accuracy with which this chart has hit the business cycles.

135

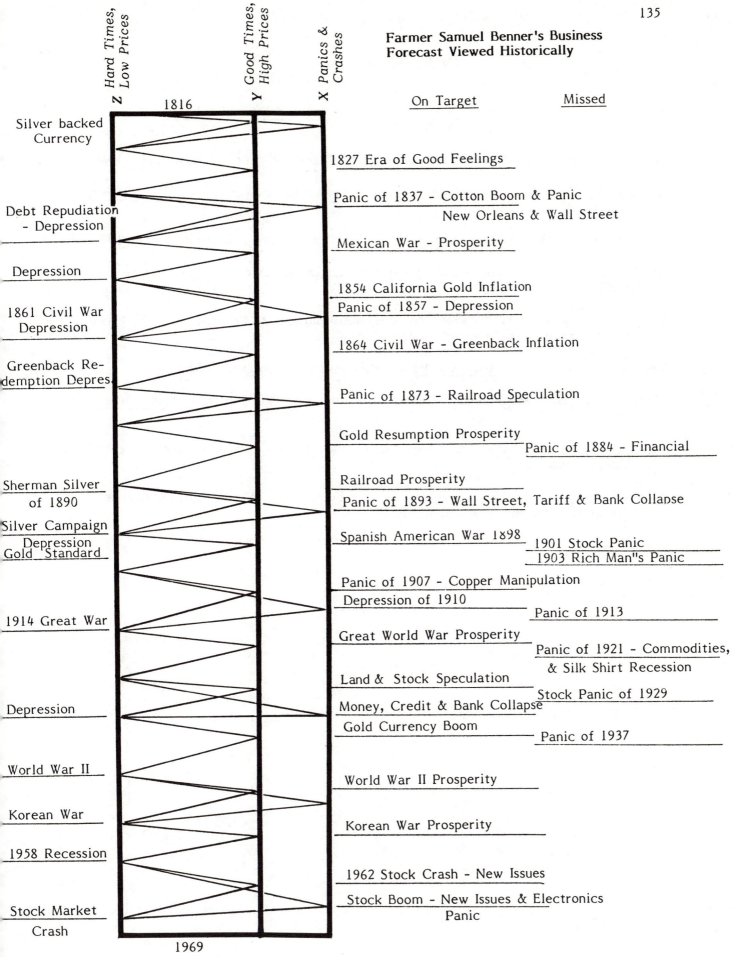

Farmer Samuel Benner's Business
Forecast Viewed Historically

On Target   Missed

Z Hard Times, Low Prices   **Y** Good Times, High Prices   **X** Panics & Crashes

1816

Silver backed Currency

1827 Era of Good Feelings

Debt Repudiation - Depression

Panic of 1837 - Cotton Boom & Panic
New Orleans & Wall Street

Mexican War - Prosperity

Depression

1854 California Gold Inflation

1861 Civil War Depression

Panic of 1857 - Depression

1864 Civil War - Greenback Inflation

Greenback Redemption Depres.

Panic of 1873 - Railroad Speculation

Gold Resumption Prosperity

Panic of 1884 - Financial

Sherman Silver of 1890

Railroad Prosperity

Panic of 1893 - Wall Street, Tariff & Bank Collapse

Silver Campaign Depression
Gold Standard

Spanish American War 1898

1901 Stock Panic

1903 Rich Man"s Panic

Panic of 1907 - Copper Manipulation

Depression of 1910

Panic of 1913

1914 Great War

Great World War Prosperity

Panic of 1921 - Commodities, & Silk Shirt Recession

Land & Stock Speculation

Stock Panic of 1929

Depression

Money, Credit & Bank Collapse

Gold Currency Boom

Panic of 1937

World War II

World War II Prosperity

Korean War

Korean War Prosperity

1958 Recession

1962 Stock Crash - New Issues

Stock Boom - New Issues & Electronics Panic

Stock Market Crash

1969

Cycles Bibliography

Benner, Samuel. Benner's Prophecies of Future Ups and Downs in Prices. Cincinnati, Ohio: Chase & Hall, 1875.

Bressert, Walter J. "Special Report - Gold" Hal Market Cycles, June 1984.

Herbst, Anthony F. "A 54-Cycle in the Purchasing Power of Gold" Cycles, March 1981.

Jastram, Roy. The Golden Constant. New York: John Wiley & Sons, 1977.

Kondratieff, N. D. "The Long Waves in Economic Life" Cycles, December 1973.

Merriman, Raymond A. "Cycles Indicate Bull Market in Precious Metals Could Be Underway" The Merriman Market Analyst.

Merriman, Raymond A. The Gold Book. Birmington, Michigan, 1982.

Owen, A. M. D. "Megatrends: Markets to the Year 2000" Newsletter Digest, 1983.

Williams, David. "Cycles in Silver, Gold and Economics" Lecture presented March 1982.

Wilson, Louise L. Catalog of Cycles, Part I - Economics. Pittsburgh, Pennsylvania: Foundation for the Study of Cycles, 1964.

Elliott Wave Analysis

This analysis is a subjective interpretation of identifying wave patterns of prices. Developed and published by Ralph N. Elliott in the 1930's, his "wave principle" theory was based on analyses of the Axe-Houghton stock index in the United States. Because of its subjective process, this analysis requires an exceptionally imaginative mind that can visualize price patterns and continually re-interpret them. The correct interpretation gives an idea of position within the overall picture. The problem is in knowing when your interpretation is correct.

According to Elliott, price fluctuation ebbs and flows in patterns similar to that found in nature, both in amplitude as well as repetitiveness. Prices seem to move forward in trend in five waves; three forward with two intermediate reactions. Prices then move against the trend in three waves; two counter with one reaction. As illustrated below, this pattern is five waves trending, with three waves countertrending, totaling eight waves to complete a cycle. Elliott labeled this 1-2-3-4-5 and A-B-C for pattern determination.

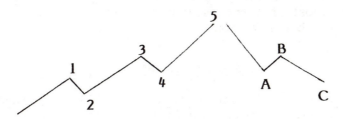

On further examination, it was found that upmoves within the upwave contained five subwaves similar to the more readily observable five wave pattern. The same thing was observed on an even shorter time scale. This cycle within a cycle configuration also expands into larger and larger phases. When examined in detail, the same is true of downwaves having patterns similar to the full cycle. At this level of analysis, there are 34 waves for a full cycle. The following drawing can be expanded to show that these waves are part of greater waves and vice-versa.

Elliott identified nine magnitudes of waves in stock prices covering the prior seventy years. Some analysts have carried this wave principle back for retail price levels over hundreds and even thousands of years. While there are exceptions, variations, and complexities within Elliott's theory, which complicate the judgment involved, the overall principles have often been reliable.

Contemporary wave principle followers offer "secondary" or alternate counts as to how they interpret the wave patterns when patterns are not clear.

This theory has been applied not only to stock indexes and individual stocks, but also to commodities, real estate, collectibles, currencies, bonds, etc. It has even been applied to raw data in the scientific measurement of different natural phenomena.

While Elliott developed his wave principle from stock index analysis, we have extrapolated both the degrees of movement scale, as well as two attempts of wave pattern identification. The latter is the result of showing the 10 year gold chart to a number of market technicians familar with the Elliott Wave Principle. All we achieved was a collection of differing opinions. We have summarized the two most frequent estimates of wave counts and labeled them simple and complex for obvious reasons.

Gold Wave Cycles

Degree of Movement (Elliott's Terminology)	Length of Time* (Our Estimate)	Most Recent (Our Estimate)
Grand Super Cycle	50 - 70 Years	1928 - 1980 (?)
Super Cycle	12 - 30 Years	1967 - 1980 (?)
Cycle	2 - 10 Years	1980 - 1985
Primary	3 Months - 2 Years	1985 - (?)
Intermediate	4 Weeks - 18 Months	
Minor	5 Days - 6 Months	
Minute	Days - 8 Weeks	
Minuette	Hours - Days	
Sub-minuette	Minutes - Hours	

*Not absolutely reliable but encompasses 90% of movements for the phase listed on the left. Note how lengths of time overlap other phases of both greater and lesser duration.

Elliot Wave Analysis - Simplistic View

Chart A

Cycle Count 1, 2, 3 A, B, C
Simplified Wave Patterns

Note: Bearish counts are underlined.

Commodity Quote-Graphics TQ-20/20

Elliot Wave Analysis - Complex View

Chart B

Cycle Count (1), (2), 3 A, B, C
Primary Count 1, 2, 3 A, B, C
Simplified Wave Patterns

Note: Bearish counts are underlined.

Elliott Wave Analysis Bibliography

Bolton, Hamilton. The Elliott Wave Principle of Stock Market Behavior. Montreal, Canada: ONRA, Ltd., 1960.

Elliott, R.N. "The Wave Principle" Montreal, Canada: ONRA, Ltd., 1969. [Originally published 1939 by Financial World.]

Frost, Alfred J. and Robert R. Prechtor, Jr. Elliott Wave Principle - Key to Stock Market Profits. New York: Haddon Craftsmen, Inc., 1978.

Fan Line Analysis

-Rule of Three

Considered part of formation analysis, experienced traders use fan line analysis to determine major bottoms. Using major bull market blow-off highs, (such as 1980 for gold) trendlines are drawn off the significant or highest high. These are called fan trendlines because of their pattern. Experience has shown that major lows are usually established after two and most definitely after three fan lines are drawn. The lows usually develop into what is called a rounding bottom or an extended multiple low pattern. Since the business and interest rate cycles run 4 to 6 years, it requires at least 8 to 12 years of experience to gain familiarity with the application of this analysis.

The third fan line drawn off of a major high usually signifies the end to a bear market over 80 percent of the time. It is merely a matter of judgment as to which fan lines are valid. The chart below shows the three fan lines known to date for gold. The first down fan line was violated by prices turning back up in just four months. This fan line may or may not be considered valid for count toward the rule of three. The circles listed 1 through 5 show where the downtrends were violated, with 3, 4, and 5 failing to show any rallying strength in price.

Fibonacci Progression Analysis

Of all the technical approaches presented, this is the most pedigreed by usage — in nature itself. The correct mathematical name is the golden ratio — the ratio of natural progression of prime numbers both in an increasing and decreasing series.

Fibonacci progression was used extensively in market analysis by R. N. Elliott in his wave theory (see Elliott Wave Analysis). Published in 1202 A.D. as the Liber Abaci and later in 1220 A.D. in Practica Geometria, the Italian Leonardo of Pisa (Leonardus Pisanus (Latin) or simply Fibonacci) showed this mathematical progression using an involute process. (1 + 1 = 2; 2 + 1 = 3; 2 + 3 = 5; 3 + 5 = 8; 5 + 8 = 13; etc.) Using any number in the series as a multiplier or divisor, a ratio evolves of 1.618 or 0.618 respectively. Using alternate numbers in the sequence, the ratio becomes 2.618 or its inverse 0.382. This ratio is observable in numerous natural phenomena; the branching of trees, sea shells' spirals (i.e. the nautilus) sunflower seed growth, the human inner ear, etc.

This ratio's appearance is pleasing to the human eye, probably due to its constant occurance throughout nature. Michaelangelo's Cistine Chapel mural, da Vinci's The Last Supper, the Great Pyramid on the Giza plain, and classical Greek temples (i.e. the Parthenon) all have this mathematical constant in their design. It occurs throughout music, art, literature, architecture, furniture and decoration. The mind will accept this relationship as long as it is graphically depicted in ratio form or logarithmic plot such as the nautilus shell. For this reason, it has been named the golden rectangle, golden ratio, and golden mean.

The application of Fibonacci to make interpretation is in time periods and price movements. Chartists apply Fibonacci to daily, weekly, monthly, and annual prices for time interpretation. Price movement, percentage retracement, percentage expansion, and series analysis are constantly being done by application of the golden ratio.

We cannot explain why the golden ratio does not constantly occur in every commodity, stock, and other man-made markets. We can only theorize that as these markets are man-made, man has something to do with the deviation from the golden ratio. Fibonacci progression reliability is a matter of percentage, judgment, and personal belief.

We have plotted counts onto a monthly chart for you to use (see Chart A). Price movement is also fascinating when the Fibonacci progression is applied to price ranges and multiples of the artificial base price of $35.00 (see Chart B). On Chart A, we drew simple percentage moves of gold plotted to each other, for a very simplistic attempt at Fibonacci interrelationships. That was disasterous! We have shown Fibonacci time progression in days, weeks, months, and years for your benefit (see Chart C).

Fibonacci Progression Time And Price Analysis

The Golden Ratio Applied

Chart A

Fibonacci Ratio or Series = 1.618 or 0.618

Fibonacci Count Series; 1, 2, 3, 5, 8, 13, 21, 34, 55, 89, etc.

Commodity Quote-Graphics   TQ-20/20

Fibonacci Price Analysis

Chart B

Fibonacci Multiples of the $35.00 - 36 Year Controlled
U.S. Government Dollar Fixed Price

U.S. Gold Price Per Ounce Per Dollar

A. $19.39/troy ounce (480 grains) Act of April 1792, one dollar = 23-3/4 grains.

B. $20.67/troy ounce Act of 1837, one dollar = 23-2/9 grains.

C. $35.00/troy ounce Order of 1934, one dollar = 13-5/7 grains.

    Ironically, $35.00 is 69.3% above the $20.67 fixed level, arbitrarily picked by President Franklin D. Roosevelt but reasonably close to a 62% ratio increase.

C x   2 = $70.00   1972's August High - $69.00

C x   3 = $105.00   1973's Intermediate High - $125.00 (poor)
                                     1973's Intermediate Low - $90.00 (poor)
                                     1976's Major Low - $99.00

C x   5 = $175.00   1978's Intermediate Low - $183.00
                                     1974's Orthodox High - $180.00 in March, 3% variance from the multiple.

          *

C x   8 = $280.00   1985's Major Low - $282.00
                                     1982's Major Low - $296.00

C x   13 = $455.00   1980's Panic Selloff Low - $453.00
                                     1981's Intermediate Low - $452.00

C x   21 = $735.00   1980's Orthodox High - $732.00

          **

C x   34 = $1,190.00

C x   55 = $1,925.00

C x   89 = $3,115.00

C x   144 = $5,040.00

C x   233 = $8,155.00

* The major 1974 high of $196.00 was 10.1 x A, but only 5.6 x C.

**Absolute recent high for free gold in U.S. dollars (since the 1776-81 War for Independence) was $873.00, exactly 25 x $35.00 (C).

Fibonacci Time Progression Table

Chart C

A	B/C		D/E	F/G
Day	Weeks		Months	Year
	(Rounded Off/Exact)		(30.33 Days/Mo.)	
1				
2				
3				
5				
8	1	(1.14)		
13	2	(1.85)		
21	3	(3.00)		
34	5	(4.86)		
55	8	(7.85)	2	
89	13	(12.71)	3	
144	21	(20.57)	5	
233	33	(33.29)	8	
377	54	(53.86)	12	1
610	87	(87.14)	20.5	1.7
987	141	(141.00)	33.2	2.7
1,597	228	(228.14)	52.6	4.4
2,584	377	(369.14)	85	7.2
4,181	597	(597.29)	138	12
6,765	966	(966.43)	223	19
10,946	1,564	(1,563.71)	361	30
17,711	2,530	(2,530.14)	584	49
28,656	4,094	(4,093.71)	945	79
46,365	6,624	(6,623.57)	1,529	127
75,019	10,717	(10,717.00)	2,474	206
121,380	17,340	(17,340.00)*	4,002	333

*2% Error From Daily Progression

Fifty Percent Retracement Rule

The 50% retracement concept was made popular by Dow and Hamilton in their stock market observations at the turn of the century. It is sufficiently utilized by professionals to warrant particular mention. (See Percentage Retracement Analysis.)

More recently, the 50% retracement has been made popular by Edward D. Dobson in his book, The Trading Rule That Can Make You Rich, published in 1979. In his book, Mr. Dobson refers to his having *read* of the 50% retracement being a prime rule of Gann, Pugh, Gold, etc., but he never really *accepted or learned* the rule. Mr. Dobson also recommends using a 66% level close-only stop protection as a back-up rule. This negates larger price swings that may occur, forcing traders out of their positions when their closely placed stops are touched off, only to see the primary trend resume.

When Dow and Hamilton published their commentary, it was in reference to their observations of the then popular Axe-Houghton Index of common stocks. Dow developed the concept of having sub-indexes to better show underlying money flows. A hundred years ago in a daily newspaper, Dow's price analysis of individual stocks, industry groupings and the three famous stock averages contained the 50% rule throughout his commentary. Today, we call these indexes the Dow Jones Industrial, Utility and Transportation Averages.

Studying the Percentage Retracement Analysis section will give you a selection of the numerous different percentages that did occur in gold's past decade. Some retracements did have 50% (±1%) which is quite remarkable for major swings within a dynamic market. Unfortunately, not all moves maintained consistent 50% retracement reactions. That is the primary fact which withholds favoring this approach over most others. Its occurance fluctuates within different markets. The 50% retracement rule appears to be most applicable for markets having a balanced trading group of floor brokers, commercials, and public investors.

Formation and High-Low Analysis

The following data is interpreted as events occured. The chart is best reviewed by placing a sheet of paper over the entire chart and moving it slowly to the right to each letter, then reading the explanation given.

All prices shown are for "free" gold quoted in U.S. dollars, which is un-official or unpegged by the U.S. Treasury. Gold's official price had been pegged at $20.67 per troy ounce in the United States for over 150 years. During the Civil War, gold's price in the free market rose to $60, and over $8,000 in the war for independence.

It should be explained that with a pegged price for gold, that price becomes either a floor or a ceiling, depending on changes in worldwide supply and demand. For example, if freely traded gold is priced in Europe at U.S.$250 per ounce, the pegged price of U.S.$500 then becomes a floor. The U.S. government will sell dollars in an effort to support the pegged $500 level overseas and buy gold in the process. Conversely, an upmove on the part of the free market to U.S. $600, will draw all excess gold to that market and force the U.S. government to sell gold to depress the free market price. The pegged price of U.S.$500 then becomes a ceiling.

This price fluctuation has caused tremendous physical movement of gold and silver in the U.S.' history, due to a fixed price mentality. Most traders of physical and gold futures are European, Middle Eastern, or Far Eastern.

A.   December 1974/January 1975. The last day in December, gold hits a high of $199 both in cash and spot futures prices and then drops sharply. This is the second major high since 1969 when free gold in Europe rallied over $43 from the pegged U.S. price of $35. December 31, 1974 is the first day allowing U.S. citizens to freely trade gold bullion in over 40 years. Drawing trendlines off previous highs, $199 when connected to the $43 high in 1969, creates the top side of a long term bull channel. For the past 4-1/2 years, prices have climbed within this channel.

B.   May - September 1975. This is the first support wave of a down correction for the prior 4-1/2 year bull move (1969 - 1974). Many advisory firms bought here thinking it was **the** blowoff of the correction. In September (in line with the 18 week cycle) the lows of four months are violated to the downside continuing the long term bear reaction.

C.   June - July 1976. This collapse puts spot futures at $99.90 and cash at $101. These prices become the lows for the six year cycle (last prior low was $35 in 1970), as prices rally solidly for the next few weeks. The exact low is on June 21, 1976, the day of the summer solistace.

D.   August - September 1976. Significant down trendlines of 8 to 13 weeks are violated to the upside. This bullish action makes C, the $99 low in June, the second major low point from which to draw a trendline back to the $35 low in 1970. The bottom of the long term trend channel can now be defined.

E.   July - November 1978.   Prices move above the prior high of $199 in July. The bull move is in full force.   Prices hit $250 in October, a 150% increase of the $100 low in 28 months.   The U.S. dollar is being sold heavily by foreign investors in the process of accumulating gold.   On October 31, 1978, President Carter's "trick or treat" speech to defend the dollar causes gold, precious metals, and foreign currencies to reverse sharply for four weeks.   The prior dumping trend of all U.S. debt instruments halts.

F.   November 1978/March 1979.   The spot price of gold sells off to $196 just after Thanksgiving and immediately rallies at a sharper rate than previously. The bull pattern is in force again with more of the public coming in droves. January 1979 gold prices touch higher than the October 1978 high of $250 and a $30 reaction is heavily bought by everyone during a three month consolidation.

G.   Mid 1979.   The gold price clears $300 - a psychological and news reportable level that creates panic buying by numerous people who are reading the four different gold gurus' books on hard asset investing.   These books actually make the New York Times 10 Best Sellers List simultaneously; a record for anything of a financial nature.   The gold price rate of climb becomes geometrically compounded - a technical phenomenon.   This means prices increase at a geometric rate progression creating a perfect channel when plotted onto a semi-log scale chart.   Now viewed, the price of gold will be at infinity within two years.

H.   August - September 1979.   Gold prices run $100 higher than prior highs; mainly on sympathetic buying from silver investors and traders.   Heavy commercial hedgers who are in silver short positions buy gold as a speculative hedge to their losses in those positions, as hedge money becomes scarcer from banks.

I.   January 1980.   Prices shoot straight up for all metals traded at the Commodity Exchange of New York (COMEX).   Sympathetic moves are made in other metals contracts in Chicago, London, Winnipeg - wherever rare metals are traded.   The spot high comes on January 21, 1980 when the COMEX changes the rules of trading and tops out the silver move, collapsing gold prices in the "bloodletting".   Silver longs are, in effect, ordered to liquidate.   Gold, platinum, and copper prices move in conjunction with silver and collapse in sympathy.   It is argued that the top is "manmade", "exchange induced", and "artificial".   The top price for spot gold created after 8:00 a.m. Monday, January 21, 1980, is $877, as the panic on the part of the shorts continues.   Trading is closed by exchange officials for an hour.   On reopening, prices collapse due to the "long liquidation only" order.

J.   June 1980.   By the end of March, a 50% retracement of the bull move (1976 - 1980 price range of $99 to $877) to approximately $482 is made in eight weeks after the rule change.   Prices then go into a $100 sideways consolidation.   Once again, prices move higher to resume their bull pattern; this time with the lows of March and May connected by up trendlines to the early 1979 lows, creating a less demanding rate of price gain.

K.   September 1980. A high of $732 creates a 62% price retracement from the $482 low and $877 high. A new perfect Fibonacci retracement of a grand move. Prices immediately soften, creating the belief that this is another high.

L.   December 1980/January 1981. Prices violate the 8 to 13 week up trendlines to the downside thus ending a four year bull move. Even though the high prices in September were lower than in January 1980 by $250, this is the real top in high-low trendline analysis. Gold share prices make their absolute highs in September 1980, confirming this fact. With a lower high at K, however, the new intermediate downtrend is now established with a trendline off those highs.

M.   July 1981. Prices drop to $400 exactly opposite the seasonal mid-year moves of the prior three years. This pattern in combination with the down trendlines from the two 1980 highs reinforces the intermediate bear trend.

N.   June 1982. A major low develops June 21st at $300, touching the long term up trendline going back to 1970 and 1976. The overall long term bull channel is still intact if prices turn to the upside. However, the intermediate trend is still down.

O.   July - September 1982. Gold's price moves sharply up as the Penn-Square Bank failure occurs. By September, prices hit $500 an ounce, but backed and filled to trade in the $400 - $450 area.

P.   February 1983. Gold hits $515 after a total 8 month rally from the June 1982 low of $300. This is exactly a 50% rally of the K to N drop of $432 ($732 less $300) or $216. December 1982 and January 1983 see the Kuwaiti stock market panic collapse create a forced gold selling spree from the Middle East to raise funds. Oil prices are also lowered by OPEC to maintain gross revenues; compounding selling forces. Prices drop over $100 or 20% in **8 days**.

Q.   September 1983. Prices bounce off the $400 level for seven months until September when prices erode through that support level.

R.   1984. Support at $340 from the 1982 trading area gives gold a six week rally to $410, only to find that one time support has now become resistance to any upside move.

S.   June 1984. A total rally of $70 from the $340 level is still extremely weak compared to the drop from $515. Prices erode downward into the high $300 range until June. The Continental Illinois National Bank has the biggest bank run in all history, requiring support from the federal government to keep credit markets from possible collapse.

T.   July 1984. Gold resumes its downtrend in July by going through the primarily long term up trendline that goes back to 1970, which touches $35, $99, and $300. The 5-1/2 year major cycles has turned into a bear trend.

U.   February 1985.   A new multi-year low of $283 is seen in February, suggesting new yearly lows to come as 1982's $300 low is breached.   A complete lack of volume lends credence to this being an exhaustion blowoff and not a continuing move.

V.   July 1985.   Gold's price rallies and moves above the 8 to 13 week trendlines in July in sympathy with up moving foreign currencies, as the U.S. dollar plummets. $346 is touched briefly and then gold falls to the $325 area. The next few months will tell whether or not this move will carry for years, or was merely the start of a long term sideways consolidation.

Both $345 and $410 levels have to be violated to the upside to turn the long term trend up again.   A confirmed move through the $315, $295, and $283 levels will decisively turn the sideways pattern down.

Note: All reversal patterns can be for either top or bottom situations.

Formation and High-Low Analysis

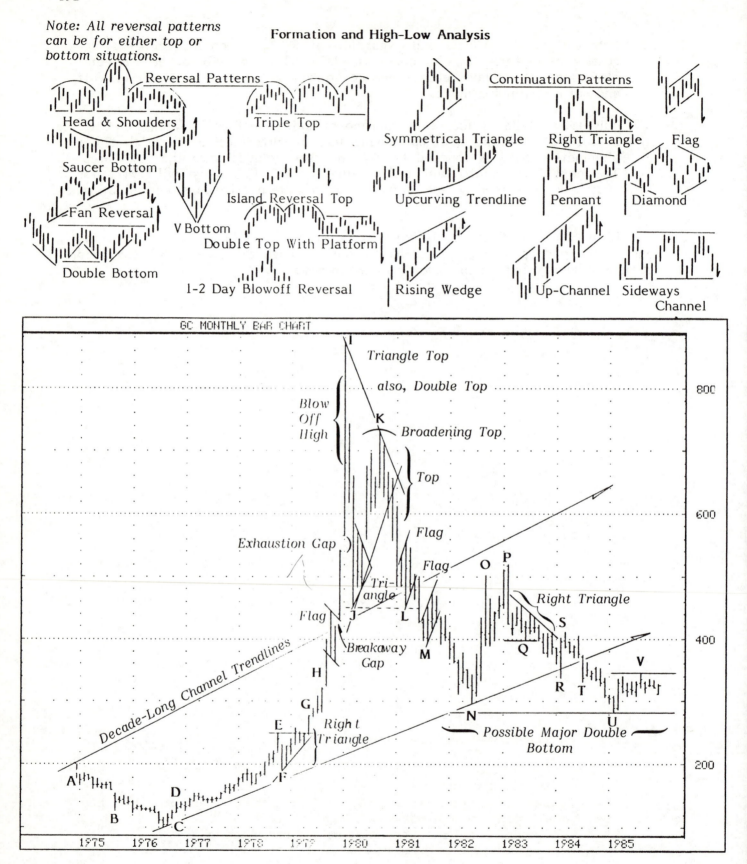

Reversal Patterns

Head & Shoulders

Saucer Bottom

Fan Reversal

Double Bottom

Triple Top

V Bottom

Island Reversal Top

Double Top With Platform

1-2 Day Blowoff Reversal

Continuation Patterns

Symmetrical Triangle

Upcurving Trendline

Rising Wedge

Right Triangle

Pennant

Up-Channel

Flag

Diamond

Sideways Channel

GC MONTHLY BAR CHART

Triangle Top

also, Double Top

Blow Off High

Broadening Top

Top

Exhaustion Gap

Flag

Flag

Right Triangle

Flag

Tri-angle

Breakaway Gap

Decade-Long Channel Trendlines

Right Triangle

Possible Major Double Bottom

800

600

400

200

1975 1976 1977 1978 1979 1980 1981 1982 1983 1984 1985

Formation and High-Low Analysis

Formation Analysis

A. —
B. Confirms "A" as a major top of the prior 3-1/2 year upmove.
C. —
D. Confirms "C" as a major bottom of the prior 18 months' downmove. Long term channel trendlines can now be drawn off the 1971 and 1976 lows, as well as off the 1969 and 1974 highs.
E. —
F. Flat-topped Right Triangle: Usually an intermediate consolidation pattern with the eventual breakout occurring in the original direction of price trend (80+% reliability).
G. Prices move and stay above the up channel. Usually a sign of a very strong trend.
H. A Run-away Uptrend: Usually the sign of an exceptionally strong trending market.

— A Flag Formation: A short term consolidation sometimes considered a half-way counting tool. In this case, the top of "H" ($440) minus "C" ($99) equals $341. When added to the bottom of the flag ($360), a minimum objective of roughly $700 is projected.
I. Blow-off High: Fast running market, turning on one day to a fast collapsing market.

— Exhaustion Gap: Rarely seen on monthly charts; indicative of a forced situation commonly seen in running markets.
J. Equilateral Triangle Consolidation: Occurring after the collapse in prices from the blow-off high, prices break out to the upside.
K. Broadening Top: Prices keep stabbing higher in a rounding or arching pattern indicating a slowing of the rate of climb and imminent turn possible.
L. Confirms "I" and "K" as major high points; a double top with steeply down sloping trendlines.

— Up-leaning Flag: Bearish continuation pattern. If considered a half-way counting formation, projection from "K"'s top ($732) to the bottom of the flag ($450) gives a count of $282, when taken off of the high ($560) projects a bottom of $278.
M. Up-leaning Flag: Bearish continuation pattern.
N. Price collapse reaches down to decade long uptrend line drawn back to 1971, touching $297, and then turning up.
O. Sharp Upmove: Confirms "N" as a major bottom.
P. Collapse.
Q. Flat Bottomed Right Triangle: Flat or shelf support develops on the bottom. "P" is confirmed as an intermediate top.
R. Prices bounce off decade-long up trendline.
S. —
T. Confirms "R" as not being the bottom as prices make new lows and stay below the decade-long trendline. Very bearish pattern.
U. February lows take out 1982 lows by $15, then rallies, suggesting the possibility of a major double bottom. Count is from "P" ($520) to "U" ($285) for a $235 potential move above "P" if it ever breaks on up.

Edwards, Robert D. and John Magee. Technical Analysis of Stock Trends. 5th ed., John Magee, Springfield, MA., 1966.

Forty-Five Degree Angle Analysis

This approach is derived from simple trendline analysis. It is used to project appproximate future support and resistance areas. Using graph paper, (paper ruled into small squares of equal size) lines are drawn down from highs and up from lows at 45° angles.

In most consolidations, prices oscillate between overhanging supply and underlying demand until they break out. There is also a tendency for prices to narrow from the first high and low to form triangles, pennants, closing consolidations, etc. When either buying or selling becomes predominate, prices edge through support or resistance levels. The 45° lines give some traders an indication as to which force will be predominate.

With graph paper, it is easier to draw or visually imagine diagonal lines from high or low points. When prices move through the angles, the trend of prices is broken.

Interestingly, the heavy use of 45° angles originally came from floor traders who had learned the point and figure method for interday trading. (See Point and Figure Analysis.) When floor traders utilize bar charts for position trading, they continue to visualize the 45° angles they are accustomed to. However, different chart services use different price scales. As the angle methodology is set, but the price scale can be changed, the 45° angle support or resistance lines appear arbitrary and not a measure of actual price/time activity.

On our long term gold chart, we applied all the 45° angles we could, to see how reliable they are. The intersecting of the future prices by the 45° angles is very poor for support or resistance determination. The number of times the 45° angles were useful did not compensate for the greater number of times they weren't.

Forty-Five Degree Angle Analysis

45° Angle Lines

Bar Plots

Forty-five degree lines are drawn off lows to project support.

Forty-five degree lines are drawn off highs to project resistance.

The above is true in bullish markets as far as support and resistance are concerned. In bearish markets, the opposite is true for support and resistance.

GC MONTHLY BAR CHART

Commodity Quote-Graphics   TQ-20/20

W. D. Gann Time and Price Analysis

William D. Gann was a stock and commodity "operator" (major trader) who traded markets from 1902 until his death in 1955. His business was that of retail broker and eventually full time speculator. A dedicated researcher of numerical series, angles, time sequences, advanced time periodicity and even astrology, his work has succeeded him to almost become a cult among systems followers. Commodity brokers going to work in the early hours in Chicago lugging artist-type large portfolios are known by others as Gann methodology followers. The usual cynical remark by some is that Gann followers create a natural bull market in lumber futures because of all the trees needed to make their large chart paper.

Gann spent years in intensive study of mathematics as it related to price movement. His studies led him to state throughout his writings that "price is a function of time and that when time runs out, a change of trend occurs in the market." Because of the depth to which he developed his extensive theories and applications of mathematics to price analysis, we can only present brief comments on some of his approaches.

Most discussed and understood of Gann's price mathematics are:

1) Anniversary Dates
2) 180° Turn Dates
3) Squaring Price and Time
4) Master Price & Time (MP & T) Calculator
5) Natural Degrees and Dates of Occurance
6) Master Number Chart - For Yearly Projections
7) Geometric Angle Form Charts
8) The Octagon Chart - Projecting Support and Resistance Levels
9) Time Rules - "Law of Vibration"
10) Natural Resistance Levels

Anniversary dates of trend changing major tops and bottoms are important to market analysts because they repeat themselves in changing trend. Gann referred to it as time "vibration" that has a tendency to reverse the current prevailing trend on the same date, (give or take a day) besides repeating in a pattern of every 2 years, 5 years, etc. Dates also tend to cluster at certain times within the months such as the 3rd through the 6th, the 20th and 21st, etc.

Turn dates are a corollary to anniversary dates as Gann modified time in the same manner he modified price. From the date of a major trend reversing high or low, he divided time into eighths and thirds. The 1/3 and 2/3's time point (121 day and 242 day) and midpoint (182 day) were the most important for support or resistance to develop at. Support or resistance in time translates to a change in the prevailing trend. This approach creates the possibility of extremely positive ratios in the reward/risk area. The reason being is that this approach enables the user to project within 1 to 3 days when the end of a market swing may occur and the start of a new price swing in the opposite direction.

Perhaps the most esoteric and advanced of Gann's hypotheses is his squaring of price and time. Both price movement (price range between high and low) as well as major high and low prices were used as geometic functions of time. When an amount of time passes that is equal to the price range, price and time become "squared" or equal. This then reverses the trend.

For example, if a price range is 100 units from high to low, you calculate 100 days from the last reversal price which gives you a potential date in the future which should "square" time. That squaring of time then calls for a change in trend. In addition, the same price can be "squared" in weeks on a weekly chart, and in months on a monthly chart, and in some cases, for years on yearly charts. He postulated this squaring effect and used it in real trading with successful results. Gann believed every current price swing, minor, intermediate and major, is the result of continuous squaring and resquaring of both price ranges and significant highs and lows from past actions.

Once disciples of his work begin to comprehend the basics, they must make sure their relative balance of price scale to time scale is proportionate, as his was. This forced the relationships he developed to hold more true.

In the squaring of price to time, he developed what is called master price and time calculators (MP & T). One was developed on the circle of 360° to time, very close to the earth's 365-1/4 day yearly cycle, exhibiting certain constant angles and time periodicities for squaring. Gann called these time rules. Because of his concentration in grain and cotton trading he used the MP & T wheel primarily for agricultural commodities.

Main time periods Gann found when trend changes occur are: March 21st, June 21st, September 22nd, and December 21st. June 21st is 91 days and 90° on the wheel from March 21st; a 3 month "hard" aspect, as they say in astrology. September 22nd is 182 days and 180° from March 21st; December 21st is 273 days and 270°. When the year and circle completes again on March 21st, it is at both 360° on one cycle and at 0° for a new cycle — an anniversary date.

Other periodic trend change dates are a constant 15 day cycle starting from March 21st (the vernal equinox) and continuing throughout the year. This is on the basis of 30° and 15° divisions of the 360° circle, considered by Gann to be based on a 12 (÷ 2) division of the circle and year's divisions. A 9-fold division of the circle and year results in a 45° and 22-1/2° (360° ÷ 9 ÷ 2) series of divisions. The first series appear in 15° increments as 0° = March 21st, 15° = April 6th, 30° = April 20th, 45° = May 6th, 60° = May 21st, etc. The 22-1/2° incremental series is 0° = March 21st, 22-1/2° = April 12th, 45° = May 5th, 67-1/2° = May 27th, etc. You can easily see why this approach is favored and more readily accepted by traders who are mathematically inclined.

Referring back to the MP & T calculators, some are overlays of fixed time and price divisions, often called Gann "squares". While Gann used different overlays of his "calculators", he stated that he favored both the 90 and the 144 unit calculators especially for weekly and monthly price charts. For grains and cotton, the circular calculator called the Gann wheel was favored (see Example A). The trine angles, 120° or 4 months from the 0° starting point are positive

158

periods. The squared heavy angles, 90°, 270° and especially 180° are basically negative. If a major high or low does occur on a date other than March 21st, the user rotates the 0° mark to that date and begins listing future dates of potential trend reversals. An interior Gann square on an octagon chart of 9 printed on the wheel is also included for price series projections. One-seventh of a year is 52 days, and usually a fatal time point which often marks a trend change.

Other master charts Gann developed were the "Master 12 Chart", "The New York Stock Exchange Permanent Chart", "The Master 9 Chart", "6 Squares of 9", "The Master 360", and "The Square of the Circle".

Geometric angle form charts or angle analysis applies Gann's natural resistance rules from the division of price moves into segments of angles. Again, eighths, thirds, etc. Since the right angle or 90° is a primary division of a circle, Gann applied his divisions to that angle to obtain fractions that seem to follow natural law in explaining support and resistance. Dividing 90° by 3 and then by squared ratio angles, he developed 9 major angles to use in his geometric angle analysis.

The most constant and important angle is the 1 x 1 time/price relationship or 45° angle plotted from major lows upward or major highs downward. The 2 x 1 time/price angle, either 63-3/4° or 26-1/4° from the major price point is the next important angle. The 1 x 4 (75° or 15°) and 1 x 8 (82-1/2° or 7-1/2°) are next in importance. The 1 x 3 angles (71-1/4° or 18-3/4°) are very important and best used on longer term time charts (weekly and monthly plot).

For a good application of Gann's angle analysis to gold, see Chart B for a graphic application. In general, interpretation is very simple. In a bullish move, prices "ride" these upward trendlines. When prices break below an up trendline, they usually drop down to the next level and ride that angle trend for awhile. In a bullish move when prices stay above the 45° angle, it is in a strong position and indicates higher prices. If the 45° angle is broken and prices go below it, the trend has probably begun to change. The above is true for a bear market by applying the rules in reverse.

Two rules dominate all angle interpretation. When prices break under an angle, it indicates a decline to the next angle. The angles on long term charts are greater in value than those on daily or shorter time periods.

The next type of price series that Gann developed was a price spiral, also called a Gann square or an octagon chart. Taking a major low price and starting up (or major high and starting down) a price series can be derived that has cardinal cross points and fixed cross points in a price series that are significant for future price resistance levels (top or bottom). Using an article by Anthony G. Herbst as our guide, he took $20 for the major low in gold, which was gold's fixed price for almost 175 years. Adding $5 increments for each progression, a complete move around an inner circle or spiral develops a magnitude increase in price increases (see Chart C). By visually comparing all major high and low prices and then seeing where they come on this Gann octagon, we can see that the fixed-2 to fixed-3 (F2 - F3) axis has almost all significant price levels. We can't say why except that for a table having 400 numbers, it is very fascinating to see almost all major turn points for this market on one axis.

We plotted all of the numbers on the F2 - F3 axis onto our gold chart and then compared all major highs and lows to gold going back to 1969. A high majority of the numbers were hit within a few percentage points. Most tended to be important highs. One, the $620 level was completely skipped over being neither a major high or low. The most unique feature, this could have been scaled into a chart in the 1920's when gold was fixed at $20.67 for decades.

A student of Gann published an article in 1980 giving an interesting geometric construction called a pythagorean cube. Divided into 16 divisions on both the horizontal and vertical axis, Gann's angles are shown eminating from all corners. Combinations of numbers when multiplied together create numerical price series that are used by Gann. Where the angle lines intersect, the whole numbers closest to those intersections are drawn in (see Chart E). While not precisely located, it helps to define the natural divisions of a price move. It does imply Gann's concept of the culminating high as a by-product of a commodity's (or stock's) low.

We could not adequately sum up the essence of W. D. Gann's teachings due mainly to his depth and quantity of research he did. His commodity trading course was offered for $5,000 in the early 1950's. (He died in 1955.) To put this in perspective, a new house cost $12,000 to $15,000 at that time. All his papers, charts, books, etc., were purchased by Billy Jones of Lambert-Gann Publications in Pomeroy, Washington, and is currently offered in course format at one-tenth the former cost.

Chart A

The Gann Wheel

The diagram below explains the various components of the GANN WHEEL. The Instruction Guide further clarifies the importance of each component and the concept behind its application in the use of the WHEEL.

Courtesy: Wheels of Gann, Inc.,
P. O. Box 281,
Fort Atkinson, WI. 53538

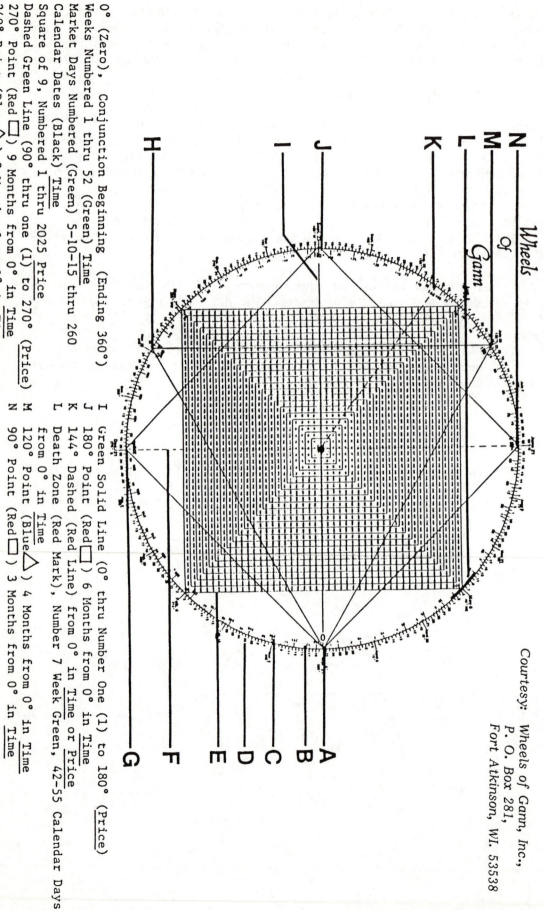

Wheels Of Gann

A 0° (Zero), Conjunction Beginning (Ending 360°)

B Weeks Numbered 1 thru 52 (Green) Time

C Market Days Numbered (Green) 5-10-15 thru 260

D Calendar Dates (Black) Time

E Square of 9, Numbered 1 thru 2025 Price

F Dashed Green Line (90° thru one (1) to 270° (Price)

G 270° Point (Red □) 9 Months from 0° in Time

H 240° Point (Blue△) 8 Months from 0° in Time

I Green Solid Line (0° thru Number One (1) to 180° (Price)

J 180° Point (Red □) 6 Months from 0° in Time

K 144° Dashed (Red Line) from 0° in Time or Price

L Death Zone (Red Mark), Number 7 Week Green, 42-55 Calendar Days from 0° in Time

M 120° Point (Blue△) 4 Months from 0° in Time

N 90° Point (Red □) 3 Months from 0° in Time

W. D. Gann Angle Analysis

Chart B

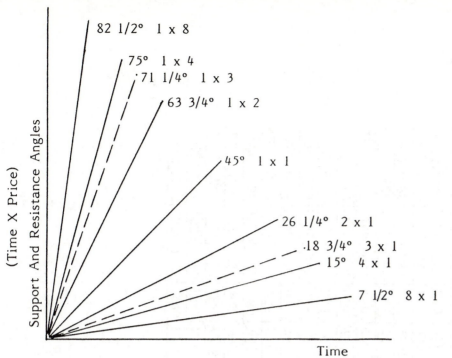

82 1/2° 1 x 8

75° 1 x 4
71 1/4° 1 x 3
63 3/4° 1 x 2

45° 1 x 1

26 1/4° 2 x 1
18 3/4° 3 x 1
15° 4 x 1

7 1/2° 8 x 1

(Time X Price)

Support And Resistance Angles

Time

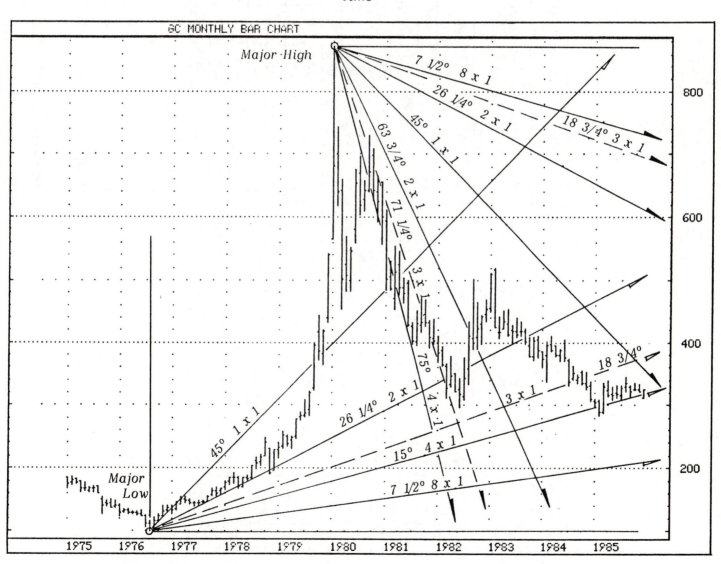

GC MONTHLY BAR CHART

Major High

7 1/2° 8 x 1
26 1/4° 2 x 1
18 3/4° 3 x 1

63 3/4° 2 x 1
45° 1 x 1
71 1/4°
3 x 1
75°
4 x 1
18 3/4°
3 x 1

45° 1 x 1
26 1/4° 2 x 1
15° 4 x 1
7 1/2° 8 x 1

Major
Low

1975 1976 1977 1978 1979 1980 1981 1982 1983 1984 1985

800

600

400

200

Commodity Quote-Graphics   TQ-20/20

W. D. Gann Cardinal Square Chart Analysis

Chart C

F 1   C 1   F 3

1920	1925	1930	1935	1940	1945	1950	1955	1960	1965	1970	1975	1980	1985	1990	1995	2000	2005	2010	2015
1915	1550	1555	1560	1565	1570	1575	1580	1585	1590	1595	1600	1605	1610	1615	1620	1625	1630	1635	1640
1910	1545	1220	1225	1230	1235	1240	1245	1250	1255	1260	1265	1270	1275	1280	1285	1290	1295	1300	1645
1905	1540	1215	930	935	940	945	950	955	960	965	970	975	980	985	990	995	1000	1305	1650
1900	1535	1210	925	680	685	690	695	700	705	710	715	720	725	730	735	740	1005	1310	1655
1895	1530	1205	920	675	470	475	480	485	490	495	500	505	510	515	520	745	1010	1315	1660
1890	1525	1200	915	670	465	300	305	310	315	320	325	330	335	340	525	750	1015	1320	1665
1885	1520	1195	910	665	460	295	170	175	180	185	190	195	200	345	530	755	1020	1325	1670
1880	1515	1190	905	660	455	290	165	80	85	90	95	100	205	350	535	760	1025	1330	1675
1875	1510	1185	900	655	450	285	160	75	30	35	40	105	210	355	540	765	1030	1335	1680
1870	1505	1180	895	650	445	280	155	70	25	20	45	110	215	360	545	770	1035	1340	1685
1865	1500	1175	890	645	440	275	150	65	60	55	50	115	220	365	550	775	1040	1345	1690
1860	1495	1170	885	640	435	270	145	140	135	130	125	120	225	370	555	780	1045	1350	1695
1855	1490	1165	880	635	430	265	260	255	250	245	240	235	230	375	560	785	1050	1355	1700
1850	1485	1160	875	630	425	420	415	410	405	400	395	390	385	380	565	790	1055	1360	1705
1845	1480	1155	870	625	620	615	610	605	600	595	590	585	580	575	570	795	1060	1365	1710
1840	1475	1150	865	860	855	850	845	840	835	830	825	820	815	810	805	800	1065	1370	1715
1835	1470	1145	1140	1135	1130	1125	1120	1115	1110	1105	1100	1095	1090	1085	1080	1075	1070	1375	1720
1830	1465	1460	1455	1450	1445	1440	1435	1430	1425	1420	1415	1410	1405	1400	1395	1390	1385	1380	1725
1825	1820	1815	1810	1805	1800	1795	1790	1785	1780	1775	1770	1765	1760	1755	1750	1745	1740	1735	1730

(End of Cycle)

F 2   C 2   F 4

C 3   C 4

W. D. Gann Cardinal Square Prices
Chart D

Cardinal Square - Fixed Axis	Major Price High/Low		% Variance
(Assumed Base) 20	$20.67	Fixed Price	
40	42.22 (1970)	Fixed	5.5
	45.00 (1969)	High	12.5
60	69.00 (1972)	Minor High	15.0
100	99.70 (1976)	Low	0.3
140	127.00 (1973)	Minor High	9.3
	129.00 (1974)	High	7.9
200	199.50 (1974)	High	0.2
260	249.40 (1978)	Minor High	4.1
340	345.80 (1985)	Minor High	1.7
420	453.00 (1980)	Panic Low	7.9
	397.00 (1981)	Minor Low	5.5
520	515.00 (1983)	High	1.0
620	—	Missed	—
740	729.00 (1980)	High	1.5
860	873.00 (1980)	High	1.5

Commodity Quote-Graphics TQ-20/20

W. D. Gann Angle Analysis

Chart E

A Pythagorean Cube On A Square Of 16

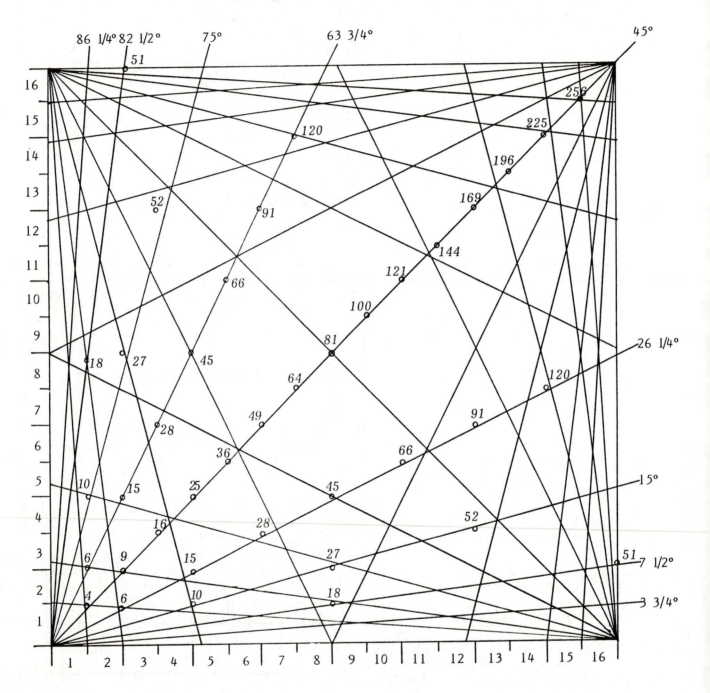

Source: Steffgen, Kent H. "Simplifying Gann to square one." Commodities, Dec. 1980, pp. 37-39.

W. D. Gann Time and Price Analysis Bibliography

Gann, W. D. "Speculation, A Profitable Profession." 1910.
 Truth of the Stock Tape. 1923.
 The Tunnel Through the Air. 1927.
 Wall Street Stock Selector. 1930.
 New Stock Trend Detector. 1935.
 How to Make Profits in Commodities. 1942.
 45 Years in Wall Street. 1949.
 How to Make Profits in Puts and Calls. 1949.

Herbst, Anthony F. "A Modified Gann Square for Gold." Commodities, May
 1980, p. 37.

Kahn, Phyllis. "Getting the Most Out of Gann Angles." Monterey, CA: 1984.
 Gann Angles Newsletter. Monterey, CA: Gann World Publishing, April
  1985.
 "Applying Gann to Interest Rate Futures." Commodities, Aug. 1980,
  pp. 58-62.

W. D. Gann Technical Review. Pomeroy, WA: Lambert-Gann Publications,
 Aug./Sept. 1984.

Steffgen, Kent H. "Simplifying Gann to Square One." Commodities. Dec. 1980,
 pp. 38-39.

"Gann Tools"

"Opportunity Angles" Tool: A right triangle with all major angles used by Gann. Available from K.C.B.T., Marketing Department, 4800 Main St., Suite 303, Kansas City, Mo. 64112, 1-800-821-KCBT. ($3.95)

"The Gann Wheel" Tool: A double circle slide rule with a square of 9 in the center. Available from Wheels of Gann, Inc., P. O. Box 281, Fort Atkinson, Wi. 53538, 414-563-2860. ($864.00)

Harahus Pentagon Analysis

Harahus expounded the use of a regular pentagon not as a high/low projection tool, but as a correction measurement tool. Lines connecting corners of a pentagon (both diagonals and sides) are supposed to be support or resistance to price moves. Harahus draws arcs from significant highs (in the example, point B) with 38%, 50% and 62% measures as price reaction areas.

Using strictly mathematics to determine projected price moves or areas of significant trend reversals is an esoteric art. Esoteric in that the analyst must be mathematically inclined, have a precise mechanical mind, and yet be imaginative in his application to price patterns.

Using an established major low (point A) and major high (point B) for gold, a diagonal line can be drawn between the two extreme prices. You can then fully construct a pentagon using a compass and a ruler. Since the sides are always 0.618 of the diagonal (see Fibonacci Analysis) all three unknown points can be drawn through bisection. Lines drawn vertically up or down from the points indicate where important price levels or reversal points should be. For gold it is most revealing.

Point A - $99   Primary 5-1/2 year cycle low.

Point B - $873   Primary 5-1/2 year cycle high.

Diagonal AB   1.618 of each side of a pentagon drawn from points A and B using a compass. All sides of a pentagon are equal in length and are 0.618 times the length of any diagonal.

Results

Point C   Is over the December 1974/January 1975 5-1/2 year prior cyclical high ($199).

Point D   Is over the July/August 1984 trend change to the downside through the 12-year uptrendline ($335).

Point E   In July 1982 directly under gold's new 5-1/2 year cyclical low and trend resversal to the upside ($298).

In the 1969 - 1974 - 1976 bull/bear cycle, this retracement analysis fitted Fibonacci numbers (61.8%) almost exactly. In the past decade, however, Fibonacci percent retracements have not been as applicable, as prices have ignored all those reversal counts. Either gold has entered a primary bear market or most of the mathematical elements of a pentagon have only chance relationship to price movement.

Harahus Pentagon Analysis

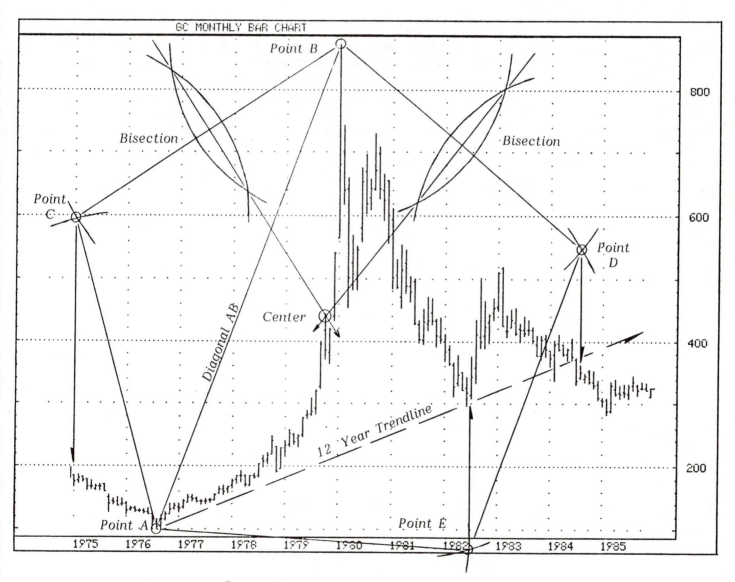

Commodity Quote-Graphics   TQ-20/20

*"Those who cannot remember the past
are condemned to repeat it."*
---Santayana

January Annual Syndrome Analysis

January Syndrome; Annual Trend Bias. As January goes for gold prices, so goes the whole year.
64 % Positive Signs (7 out of 11 years.)
36 % Interim Reversals (4 out of 11 years.)
Note; Almost All Reversals Occurred Mid-Year.

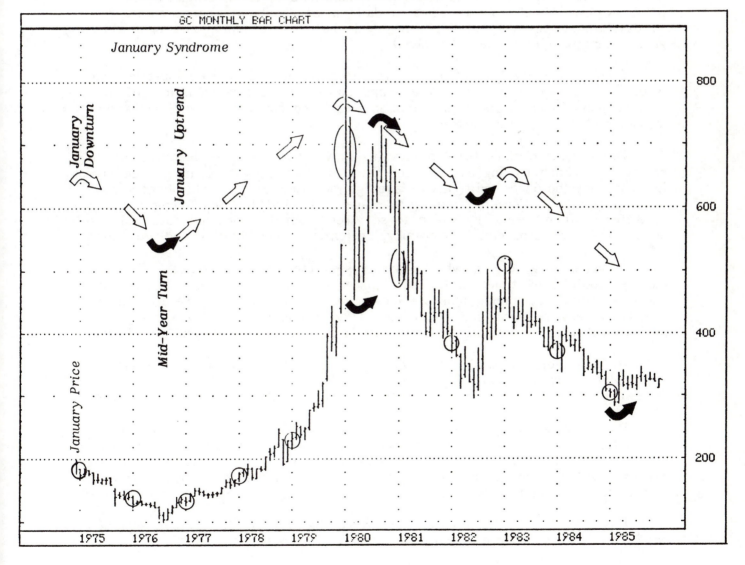

Commodity Quote-Graphics   TQ-20/20

Moving Average Analysis

A moving average is the adjustment of erratic or extreme price data into a stabler, smoother line, thereby better showing trend. The manner in which price data is smoothed, adjusted and plotted depends on what type of moving average is wanted. The length of time used will determine the frequency and rapidity of signals. The longer time span used; the fewer the signals generated.

Any moving average is merely a sequence of price data that can be restructured from the actual price movements to the desired trend.

The best time span can be chosen to eliminate extreme price fluctuations by observing the cyclical high and low prices. The average can then be calculated and plotted. When the plotted moving average reflects an almost flat line, the calculation can be repeated for additional data to eliminate extreme price swings. Usually short cycles in daily price charts of approximately 8 to 15 days' length are part of a greater cycle harmonic of 3, 4, or even 5 times greater length. (See Cycle Harmonics.)

Each commodity has its own characteristics, therefore, each must be analyzed for the type of moving average applicable. Various combinations of floor traders, public speculators, commercial interests and commodity fund participants influence each commodity differently.

The analyst decides how to plot his moving averages — leading, current or lagging. Each moving average generates its own signal. Future price projections may be made with above average accuracy once cycle lengths have been calculated. Centered moving averages are used for developing channels of different time periods by which to see trends better. Original data can also be modified by exponential smoothing, weighting, accumulating, ad infinitum.

A signal is generated when price crosses the moving average. This too can be modified by time lag (called skip) or other types of delay in reversing one's position. Combining multiple moving averages can also generate delayed signals thereby reducing the frequency of erroneous signals. One commodity professional uses six moving averages for trend interpretation and positioning.

The main disadvantages of moving averages are that they are mechanical, (nonthinking) always positioning long or short, (never neutral) and position in "sideways" markets long near the high or short near the low (trading patterns).

The main advantages of moving averages are that they are mechanical, (non-anticipatory) always in a directional mode, (long or short; not neutral) and are best used for catching intermediate to major trend moves. Moving averages will position you in the direction of a major move, but moving averages will never catch the high or low.

This is essentially the greatest advantage that any moving average approach has over any individual's judgment — discipline.

Comparison of Different Moving Average Combinations

Utilizing our now familiar decade-long monthly bar chart of gold, we will show different interpretations of two moving average combinations, on the following pages.

Moving average Chart A is an 8 month moving average and a 16 month moving average (1:2 ratio). These moving averages' main characteristics are shorter time periods and more responsiveness to the raw price data.

Shorter term moving averages appeal to the professional, more aggressive trader who is closer to the market. Signals given are less reliable but risk generated is less, as exit signals are closer to the moving average price; therefore less costly per trade when wrong.

The same type of general buy/sell signal generation and probability of trend change can be obtained from daily or weekly bar chart interpretation.

Price penetration of the 8 month moving average at points A, B, C, D, and E show the possibility of significant reversals, but no follow through. Some of these points had monthly closes (the last Friday of the last week of the month) that appeared significant but failed to reverse. The same points A through E plotted against a longer moving average (Chart B) show an entirely different set of signals and reliability.

Moving average Chart B shows a 13 month moving average and a 39 month moving average (1:3 ratio). These moving averages' main characteristics are longer term averages and much smoother, slower trends, with very few signals generated.

Seasoned investors can use this combination of moving averages with confidence that very few signals given will be erroneous. In general, financial benefits of moving averages are greater when compared to other interpretative systems. This is due to the objectivity of the mechanics of moving averages.

The 13 bar moving average (approximately 56 weeks) gives amazingly few erroneous signals with almost no price moves through it, unless prices continued to reverse.

The signal generated became significant only when prices penetrated the 13 bar moving average at the close of the month. When this occurs, prices tend to remain in the new trend for at least 12 consecutive months.

The 39 month moving average eliminates annual and seasonal effects. This is due to this moving average's length being greater than the seasonal and annual effects of 12 months. The angle of the 39 month moving average should tend to parallel the long term trend.

Multiple Moving Averages

Chart A

Using the relatively short term 8 month average, the following points have been determined:

False Penetration Points - A, B, C, D and E.
Real Penetration Points - F, G, H, I and J.

8 Month Moving Average - Fast
16 Month Moving Average - Slow   1:2 Ratio

Commodity Quote-Graphics   TQ-20/20

Multiple Moving Averages

Chart B

Using the 13 month average as signal generator, along with monthly closes, the following points have been determined:

Real Penetration Points - A, B, C, D and E.

13 Month Moving Average - Fast
39 Month Moving Average - Slow

1:3 Ratio

Commodity Quote-Graphics   TQ-20/20

Glossary of Moving Averages and Moving Averages Terminology

Accumulated: Adds new data to a price sequence without discarding prior data stored usually at the beginning of a contract and continued through expiration of a futures contract. Hence data is accumulative.

Arithmetic Mean: Each piece of data has an equal effect in the sequence. Extreme values tend to be more reflected in the totals compared to other moving averages.

Band: An area above and below a moving average usually defined as a percentage or set amount.

Centered: The average is plotted in the center of the timespan covered. This is used best for channeling of price action to better visualize trends.

Crossing: When the price crosses the moving average, a trading signal is given.

Exponential Smoothing: Essentially a weighted moving average with new data continually added, no data dropped, and all old data reduced by a constant percentage.

Filter: Used usually with multiple moving averages; once a crossing occurs, the signal given is filtered by a confirming average.

Geometric: Presenting all moving average data on a percentage or comparable basis (i.e. 10 is to 20 as 40 is to 80). Primarily used for ratios or rates of change in price analysis.

Harmonic Mean: Time weighted average, non-biased towards higher or lower values.

Intraday: Signals generated by price trading through a price average during the day, usually not needing a close of that day's action to create a signal.

Lag Plot: The average is plotted continually ahead of the most recent data by a set amount to better conform to the price pattern.

Lead Plot: The average is plotted continually ahead of the most recent data by a set amount to allow for time delay.

M.P.T.D.I. (Major Price Trend Directional Indicator): R. J. Taylor's original published system from the early 1970's. it is a weighted moving average with variable price bands adjusted for daily price ranges or volatility.

Multiple Averages: Usually two or three moving averages with a neutral position signal generated when the very short term crosses over the second or intermediate average. R. Donchian's 5 and 20 day moving averages is probably the most famous two average system.

Simple Average: A simple total of a number of prices divided by that number.

Skip: Usually a delay in reversing positions to allow for spurious signals created at the signal point.

Weighted: Average is adjusted for some variable (price, time, quantity, etc.) and biased toward that chosen as the significant element. Usually the most recent data is favored as traders attempt to predict the near future.

Moving Average Bibliography

Computerized Trading Techniques - 1982.   Merrill Lynch Commodities, 1982.

"Daily Commodity Computer Trend Analyzer". New York: Commodity Research Bureau, 1969 through 1981.

Davis, R.E. and C. C. Thiel, Jr. A Computer Analysis of the Moving Average Applied to Commodity Futures Trading. West Lafayette, IN: Ouiatenon Managment Co., 1971.

Donchian, Richard D. "Donchian 5 and 20 Day Moving Averages." Commodities Magazine, Dec. 1974.

Dunn, Dennis D. and Edwin F. Hargitt. Trader's Notebook. Lafayette, IN: Dunn & Hargitt's Financial Services, 1970.

Hurst, J.M. The Profit Magic of Stock Transaction Timing. Prentice-Hall, Inc., 1970.

Kaufman, P.J. Commodity Trading Systems and Methods. New York: John Wiley & Sons, 1978.

Waters, James and L. Williams. "Measuring Marketing Momentum." Commodities Magazine, Oct. 1972, p. 13.

Option Analysis

Option analysis is more correctly stated as being a means of investment always having a limited life as its main characteristic. An option is a legal contract giving someone the right but not the obligation to buy or to sell an asset. In commodity options, they are standardized as to price level increments and time of duration or life. While most approaches in this guide are merely systematic or analytical methods applied to a single market, options are a variation of the underlying financial instrument that can be applied in different ways.

The futures contract is an instrument used to monitor the cash market. Futures are more extended in time, more liquid than cash markets, and most importantly, have a total value of a set quantity valued by the cash market and short term interest rate cost-of-carry as future price valuations.

Options on the underlying futures however are a by-product with one essential difference. They are an asset with a market value, called a premium, that has a tendency to become worthless over time. In finance this is termed a wasting asset. Intrinsic and extrinsic value constitute the market price of an option. Time decay is the main variable interrelating all kinds of option trading — outright and spread.

One obvious advantage of option trading is to initiate positions in a commodity when market prices are quiet. Because the maximum loss is the cost of the option itself, no stops are needed and you have unlimited potential gain in one direction. A major investor can establish a sizeable position knowing what his maximum cost is up front with the choice of converting his positions into the underlying futures once evidence of a major move appears. He knows if prices stay within the trading range, he could lose up to 100% of his purchase price due to the time decay effect inherent in a wasting asset.

If prices move in the expected direction, the possibility of gain is a multiple of the base cost. A return of five times cost is not unusual. A thousand or even two thousand percent return has been made by some investors. In the 1970's cocoa, sugar, and silver had such grandiose moves that American option firms which had sold options naked were caught and wiped out financially due to their exposure.

Aggressive option traders who usually trade only for a few days or weeks prefer option spread strategies. They hedge their trading with options positioned opposite to their primary profit expectation. While reducing risk, they reduce profits, but greatly increase the probability of their trading goals occurring. At last count, over 24 spread strategies have been developed with puts, calls, combinations, (puts and calls combined) synthetic positions and writing for premium income. Income is made from an understanding of the price decay effect on option values by writing or selling options with an opposing position on the physical underlying asset.

For making money by the writing or selling options as an adjunct to owning the underlying asset, some means must be used to value what an option premium is worth. Mathematical models have been proposed, with one, the Black-Sholes model most popular in determining fair market value. Professor Black's model for a call premium is:

$$C = e^{-rt} [UN(d_1) - EN(d_2)]$$

$$d_1 = [In(U/E) + (sd^2 t)/2]/sd \sqrt{t}$$

$$d_2 = [In(U/E) - (sd^2 t)/2]/sd \sqrt{t}$$

C = call premium
E = exercise price
t = term to option
   expiration (in years)

U = underlying futures price
r = short-term interest rate
sd = market volatility (standard deviation of market returns on annualized basis)

N = refers to normal cumulative probability distribution
In = the natural log of the term

e = 2.7183 (base of the natural logarithm)

$$P = -e^{-rt}[UN(-d_1) - EN(-d_2)]$$

Another benefit of option trading is the larger positions that are possible. In precious metals for example, gold option contract limits at the COMEX in New York were increased to 4,000 from 2,000 contracts in 1984.

In March 1985, three individual floor traders were caught short, each having sold the 4,000 contract limit of calls naked in an attempt to earn the premium when gold futures rallied $9.00 one day and $36.00 the next. The magnitude of having sold short 12,000 calls to earn those premiums was a $54,000,000.00 loss in two days. Their equity and their member clearing firm, Volume Investors Corp., was essentially wiped out. All customers' segregated funds and excess margin were frozen by the exchange when it was closed and put into receivership. All this in just over two day's time.

Interestingly, for all that equity which was lost, other traders made it with no risk beyond the actual purchase price of their calls. The 340 June gold calls went from around $1.00 to $16.00 in two days; a 1,500% return. You have to know the mathematics of options and option spreads to trade to your advantage. Option markets are a zero-sum game. For every dollar that goes into the market, the same amount comes out.

In the history of regulated futures trading, options have always been the underdog. At times with no champion to come to options' aid, they have been banned, declared illegal, taxed excessively and even over-regulated by two federal commissions at one time.

Originally called privileges, options on grain contacts were traded from the mid-1800's forward in Chicago. They were banned after being blamed for the falling markets after the Civil War, also around 1885, and 1933-36.

When commodity prices went up, speculators invariably would buy options. Option writers (sellers) would have to buy the underlying futures to hedge the risk incurred from originally selling the option. When markets turned and dropped, the option writers knew option buyers would not exercise as most options became worthless. Writers knew that most of their long physical positions would not be called away, and proceeded to liquidate positions during falling markets. Pegged as sellers in falling markets, option writers (mostly floor traders of exchanges) became marked as targets to blame for the falling markets in the first place.

Option writers became net commodity sellers, which in the 1800's equated their actions to bear pool activities. While bear pools were not illegal at that time, they did have a negative association, as the public was almost always on the bull side. The press usually sided with the bullish public, who at the end of a collapsed market were usuallly turned into steers.

In the 1860's Civil War, excessive money inflation affecting commodity prices was created by the Union greenback paper currency. Prices moved up (in Union currency terms) through 1864 and then collapsed. It became apparent the North was decisively winning and peace was near. In 1865, the Chicago Board of Trade ruled "privileges" (options) were not recognized as a business transaction and thus were forbidden. The collapsing commodity market, along with gold collapsing from over $200 per ounce, had the usual disgruntled bulls who overstayed their positions and lost heavily. Jay Gould's infamous 1869 attempted squeeze on gold failed due to dropping price levels.

Twenty years later, the Illinois Supreme Court actually declared grain options illegal. This came after a speculative binge on railroad stocks in the 1870's and early 1880's. Commodity prices moved up in general with the railroad bull market and collapsed in tandem. Options were blamed once again.

A few decades later, options were declared legal and allowed to trade. In the 1910 to 1920 period, unbridled credit expansion in the form of paper money created a worldwide inflation that pushed commodity price levels to unbelievable heights by 1921.

All bull markets collapse due to overextended credit. The 1921 recession drop in the U.S. (called the "Silk Shirt Recession" because it happened so fast laborers were still buying silk shirts after it was over) was no exception. In 1921, the Futures Trading Act imposed a 20¢ per bushel tax on privileges to effectively stop their use. In 1926, the U.S. Supreme Court ruled the tax unconstitutional.

In the 1930's, stock markets collapsed pushing commodity prices down to rock bottom levels. The low in U.S. stocks occured right after the final wave of bank collapses in mid-1932. In 1933, the Commodity Exchange Act banned options on all grains, butter, eggs, flaxseed, and potatoes. In 1940, the remaining commodities traded on exchanges had their options banned.

The pattern is unmistakably repetitive. 1970 forward saw the reinstatement of options, mostly precious metals and international softs traded on London exchanges in pound sterling in metric sized lots. Several bucket shops were exposed during the 1970's for improperly selling options with fraudulent schemes, thereby holding new option development to a crawl.

In July 1979, the C.F.T.C. approved a three year pilot options trading program for gold, sugar, and GNMA futures.

Having been fully proven and accepted, exchange listed put and call options are now traded daily in the hundreds of thousands. Standardized time and price increments are the unique features that were created by the Chicago floor trade crowd.

By mid-1985, there were five different options on gold active on exchanges to our knowledge. They are:

Gold	Options On	Size (In Ounces)
Amex Commodities Corp.	Physical	100
COMEX (Commodity Exchange Inc.)	Futures	100
IOCC (International Options Clearing Corp.)	Physical	10
MIDAM (Mid-America Commodity Exchange)	Futures	33.2
WCE (Winnepeg Commodity Exchange)	Futures	20

Option strategies involve over 24 combinations which are listed in the Option Glossary. Books have been written extensively on option strategies, as there are numerous details such as market bias, profit and loss potential, time decay, and premium costs. We have only attempted to present an overview on options as a tool giving you a basic understanding; not a concise in-depth study.

For a sample chart which would best present current gold options, we have reproduced the daily plot February 1986 option series on Chart A. Gold maintained a sideways pattern for the time period covered in the example; August through November of 1985. Because of the overall neutral price pattern at that time, both puts and calls showed the time decay effect with all price series eroding toward zero value.

It is important to exhibit a trending futures market to visualize how options would look. Chart B shows two different bullish markets and the effect on their put and call options. Stock index futures and T-Bond futures both enjoyed robust bullish markets during September through November 1985. Both of their call option charts have erratic but distinct uptrends present. The put option charts on both futures show opposite bear patterns concurrently. The time decay effect that exists in all put and call options were present in these series. They were not noticeable due to the inherent leverage involved in option price trends when the underlying asset trends strongly.

180

Glossary of Options and Option Terminology

AG-Options: Agricultural options listed on exchanges, such as corn, wheat, and live cattle, in contrast to financial futures options or metals options.

Assignment: The conversion of an option position into the underlying futures contract at the exercise price.   For the writer of a call, a short futures position; and for the writer of a put, a long futures position.

At or Near-the-Money-Option: An option with a strike price at or near the underlying futures price.

Bear Call Spread: Buy one call at the money and sell one call in the money, each with the same date.   This spread, like the bear put spread, has predetermined profit and loss.

Bear Put Spread: Buy one put at the money and sell one put in the money, each having the same expiration date.

Beta: The relationship between the movement of an individual stock to that of the overall stock market.

Black, Professor: The creator of an option mathematical pricing formula model designed to value options.   Black-Scholes Model.

Box: (See Conversion).

Bought the Spread: (Also Debit)   Paid money out to buy a spread.

Breakeven Point: The futures price at which a given option strategy becomes zero.

Broken-wing Condor Spread: A condor spread with one "wing" or outside option extended so as to be unequal or unbalanced.

Bull Call Spread: A long call with a lower strike price and a short call with a higher strike price, both with the same date.

Bull Put Spread: A long put with a lower strike price and a short put with a higher strike price, each with the same expiration date.

Butterfly Spread: A variable spread with one additional option.   That is, a balanced spread (equal number of puts and calls) with two of one kind of option in the middle, and opposing options on each side.   Simply stated, a combination bull spread and bear spread with three strike prices.   If the center options are calls and the outer options puts, it is a short butterfly.   If the opposite formation is created, it is a long butterfly.

Buyer: (Also Holder).   The person who purchases an option; can be either a put or a long.

Calendar Spread: (Also Time Spread.) (See Horizontal Spread.)

Call Option: An option that gives the purchaser the right but not the obligation to exercise or receive a long futures contract at the strike price.

Call Ratio Spread: Buying calls with a lower strike price and selling a greater number of calls with a higher strike price against that position (unequal ratio level) for gain in a stagnant market.

Call Ratio Backspread (Spread): Selling calls with a lower strike price and buying a larger number of calls with a higher strike price. This spread is lopsided with an unlimited potential to the upside.

C.F.T.C.: Commodity Futures Trading Commission.

Class of Options: All call or put options exercisable for the same underlying futures contract which expire on the same date.

Class of Trade: Three categories of spread approaches; directional, locked trade and precisional.

Closing Purchase Transaction: (Also Offset Transaction.) A holder of a short option position liquidates the position by a purchase.

Closing Sale Transaction: (Also Offset Transaction.) The holder of a long option liquidates it by a sell transaction.

Combination: A strategy involving purchase or sale of both puts and calls.

Condor: A spread having at least two calls and two puts with a wide profit area between the two center options. Also referred to as a "super butterfly".

Contract Month: Of an option, corresponds to the delivery month (contract) of the underlying futures.

Conversion: A trading technique involving purchasing the underlying futures contract, selling a related call, and buying a corresponding put.

Covered Long Option: A granted (sold) option that is matched against an opposite futures position held by the option grantor (seller) in the underlying futures contract.

Covered Short: The sale of a put option against a short futures position.

Credits: Establishing a spread where the value of the option sold exceeds the value of the option bought resulting in a credit to the account.

Currency Options: Options on listed exchanges on standardized foreign currency contracts.

Cycle: The months in which options expire, which parallel the underlying futures contracts. Actual expiration of the option usually takes place during the month before the futures contract expires.

Daily Price Limits: For options — none.

Debits: Doing a spread where the value of the option purchased exceeds the value of the option sold.

Decay: The loss in market value of an option or option spread over time.

Deep-Out-of-the-Money Option: An option with a strike price significantly away from the current price of the underlying futures contract.

Delivery (Date): The process and time at which funds and the physical commodity change hands upon expiration of a futures contract.

Delta: The ratio of the change in the option's value divided by the change in the price of the underlying futures contract.

Delta Neutral Strategy: A spread trade that reduces directional bias; the position holder is indifferent to the underlying contract's price move up or down.

Diagonal Spread: Buying and selling of calls or puts that differ in strike price and expiration date.

Exchange Traded Futures Option: An option contract on an underlying futures contract, both of which are traded on an exchange designated as contract markets by the C.F.T.C.

Exercise (Notice): Also called the conversion of a long call or long put option into the corresponding long or short underlying futures contract at the strike (exercise) price.

Exercise Price: (See Strike Price.)

Expiration Date: The final date on which an option that has not been offset or exercised expires.

Extrinsic Value: (See Time Value.)

Financial Futures Options: Options on standardized financial instruments, such as treasury bonds, Eurodollars, GNMA's, etc., on listed exchanges.

Gamma: A mathematical derivative of delta that tells you when to adjust the delta by adjusting the number of contracts held.

Grantor: (Also Writer, Seller.) One who grants or sells an option, said to have a short option position, obligated to perform on the option contract if exercised by the purchaser.

Guts: A spread done with puts and calls in the money and the future contract midway between strike prices.

Haircut: (Used mainly in stock options.) Special margin rates for floor traders.

Historical Volatility: The range of price fluctuation over a sample period of time used as a measuring guide. Sample periods are 30 days, 90 days, and 180 days.

Horizontal Spread: Buying and selling of puts or calls that have the same strike price but different expriation dates. Usually the time value of the spread will decay more rapidly diuring the last few weeks of its life than the first few weeks.

Implied Volatility: The volatility of the futures implied by the options market.

In-The-Money Option: An option that has the underlying futures price above the call option strike price (if a call) or underlying futures price below the put option strike price (if a put).

Intrinsic Value: The amount an option is in-the-money, or the difference between the underlying futures contract price and the strike price.

Last Day and Hour of Trading: The last day for trading or offsetting a position. The last exact time can be different than regular trading hours.

Leverage: To get a proportionately larger return for each dollar invested.

Limited Risk: Outright option buyers can never lose more than the initial cost of the option.

London Commodity Option Market: Non-regulated options dealt in for various commodities having no set or unified time class, usually for a specified period of time (i.e. 90 days) from the date of purchase at standard price increments. Both groups, London agricultural and metal options were guaranteed by either an overseeing London exchange or listed member thereof. Went into disfavor in the 1970's due to improper marketing by a few American bucket shop organizations selling naked options at excessive price markups to investors, often not paying off investors. The C.F.T.C. regulates American commodity options on underlying futures contracts.

Long Call: The purchase of a call option with the right to exercise but not the obligation to buy the underlying futures contract at a set price anytime prior to expiration.

Long Put: The purchase of a put option with the right to exercise but not the obligation to sell the underlying futures contract at a specified price anytime prior to expiration.

Margin Requirement: Money posted in commodities trading only. Option buyers pay full price to purchase options and do not post margin since their risk is limited to the premium paid.

Married Put: (Used in stock options). The put and the underlying stock identified on the holder's records as intended to be exercised, usually acquired on the same day.

Metals Options: Options on the standard listed exchanges that trade metals futures.

Money Spread: (Also Price Spread.) (See Vertical Spread.)

Month Traded: That time series of an option that is standardized to conform to the underlying futures.

Naked Call Writing: (Also Uncovered Call Writing and Short Call.)   Selling a call without having the underlying futures contract sold if assigned.

Naked Option: Any uncovered option owned by a writer who does not have the underlying commodity or security.

Naked Put Writing: (Also Uncovered Put Writing and Short Put.)   Selling a put without having the underlying futures contract bought if assigned.

Neutral Approach: The strategy an investor employs when it is thought that the price trend is sideways.

Neutral Covered Long: Selling call options against a long futures contract.

Neutral Covered Short: Selling put options against a short futures contract.

Offset: The closing out of an existing position by making an opposite trade of the same option position.

Option: (Also Wasting Asset.)   A contract involving a buyer and a seller to the right but not the obligation to either buy or sell an underlying futures contract.   Can also be stock, bonds, real estate, or any tangible or non-tangible asset.

Option Class: All option contracts of the same type, puts or calls, covering the same underlying futures contract.

Option Pricing Model: (See Professor Black.)   Mathematical pricing formula used to calculate the fair market value of an option premium.   Famous models currently used are: Black-Scholes and Cox's Constant Elasticity of Variance.

Option Series: All options of the same class having the same strike price and expiration date.

Option Type: A put or a call.

Out-of-the-Money Option: An option strike price that is above (call) the underlying futures or below (put) same.

Parity: The point at which the premium of an option is exactly equal to its intrinsic value.

Position Limits: The maximum numer of options allowed per holder to reduce the undue influence of control over a market.

Premium: (Also Quotes.)   The total price of an option, consisting of intrinsic and extrinsic value.

Price Spread: The purchase and sale or two options covering the same futures contract with the same expiration dates but different exercise prices.

Privileges: An early form of agricultural option, no longer traded.

Purchase Price: The total actual cost paid for an option, including commissions and fees.

Put Option: An option that gives the purchaser the right, but not the obligation, to receive a short futures contract at the strike price.

Put Ratio: An uneven spread buying puts with a higher strike price and selling a greater number of puts with a lower strike price.

Put Ratio Backspread: A bearish uneven spread selling puts with a higher strike price and buying a greater number of puts with a lower strike price.

Reverse Conversion: A trading technique involving selling the underlying futures, purchasing a related call and selling a corresponding put.

Risk/Reward Ratio: The potential loss compared to potential gain in a strategy, expressed as a ratio.

Settlement Premium: The settlement price of an option as of the daily close.

Short: The establishing of a position by selling first in the hope of a price decline.

Short Box: (See Conversion.)

Short Call: (See Grantor.)

Short Put: Selling a put option for a premium, with the obligation only if assigned to buy the underlying futures at a specific price.

Sold the Spread: (See Credits.)

Spreading: Being long one or more options of a given class and concurrently maintaining a position as writer of one or more options of a different series within the same class, all to reduce the risk of an outright position.

Stock Index Options: Options on a stock index futures that are designed to follow specific listed indexes but not convert into them.

Straddle (Long): A combination of buying an equal number of put and call options with the same strike price and expiration date. This is usually when the underlying futures are near the strike price.

Straddle (Short): A spread consisting of the sale of both puts and calls having the same strike price and expiration date. The hoped for result is to earn the premium when volatility declines.

Strangle (Long): Purchasing both puts and calls having different strike prices with a common expiration date.

Strangle (Short): This spread involves the sale of both puts and calls having different strike prices but a common expiration date.

Strap: (Old stock option term.) A combination of two calls and one put with the same strike price.

Strike Price: (Also Exercise Price.) The specified price at which the purchaser of an option may acquire the underlying future contract upon exercise.

Strike Price Interval: (Also Increment.) The point of dollar amount difference between various option strike prices.

Strip: (Old stock option term.) A combination of two puts and one call with the same strike price.

Synthetic Long Put: Selling a futures contract short and buying a call, establishing a set upside risk. Essentially the same as a put option.

Synthetic Long Call: Buying a futures contract and buying a put; equivalent to being long a call option.

Ticker Symbol: Standardized listing for identifying a put or call on a particular futures commodity contract (i.e. New York gold is OG).

```
          (Month )  (Call-D)  (Last 2 )
OG        (       )  ( or  )  ( Price )
          (Symbol)  (Put-Q )  (Digits )
```

Time Decay: The erosion of price by the time factor in an option usually more noticable when the underlying futures contract stagnates.

Time Premium: (Also Risk Premium.) The additional value of the option due to the volatility of the market and the time remaining.

Time Spreads: (Also Call Spreading, Calendar Spreads.) (See Horizontal Spreads.)

Time Value: The market value of an option minus the intrinsic value.

Trading Hours: The different exchanges' determined hours for option trading usually set to parallel the trading hours of the underlying futures contracts.

Trading Limits: The maximum number of option positions a single speculator may own.

Uncovered Call Writing: (See Naked Call Writing.)

Uncovered Put Writing: (See Naked Put Writing.)

Uncovered Option: (Also Naked Option.) An option that is written (granted) with the writer having no opposite or covered position.

Variable Spread: Spreads in which the number of options purchased is different from the number of options sold.

Vertical Spread: The buying and selling of calls or puts that share the same expiration date but have different strike prices.

Volatility: A measure of the market' instability usually by price measurement.

Volatility Spread: An option spread designed to catch excessive price swings. Exactly the opposite expectation than that of stagnant market spreads where profit occurs mainly due to the time decay effect on prices of options.

Writer: (See Grantor.)

Writing Calls: Mainly done by institutions; the selling of call options to earn additional premium income with the possibility of being exercised anytime.

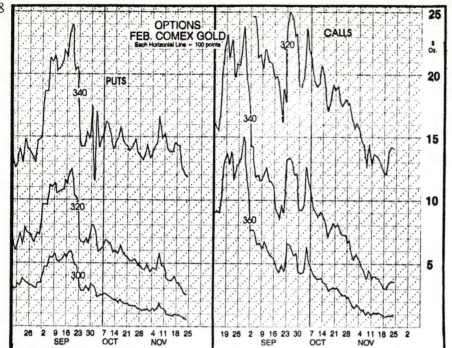

Option Analysis

Comex Gold Options
Chart A

Trading or sideways markets
in futures showing the erosion
in both put and call options.

Option Charts Reprinted
From:
Commodity Price Charts
219 Parkade, Cedar Falls, Ia. 50613

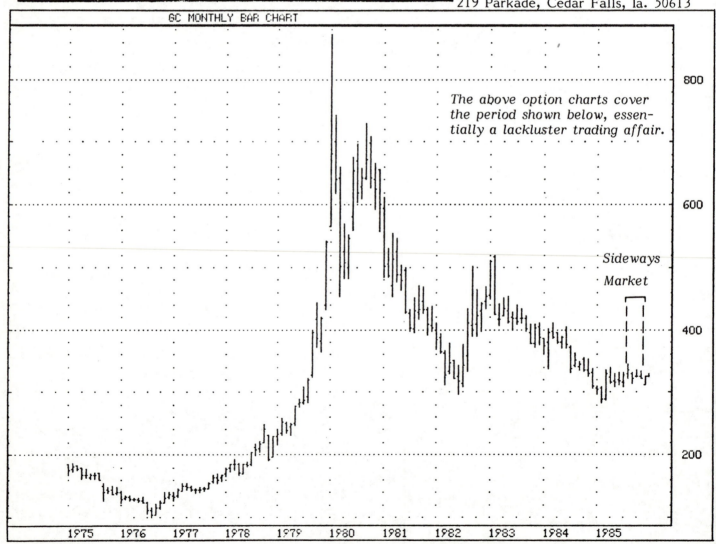

*The above option charts cover
the period shown below, essentially a lackluster trading affair.*

Sideways

Market

Option Analysis

Underlying bullish futures patterns, put and call patterns shown
for comparison purposes.

S & P Stock Index Options

T-Bond Options

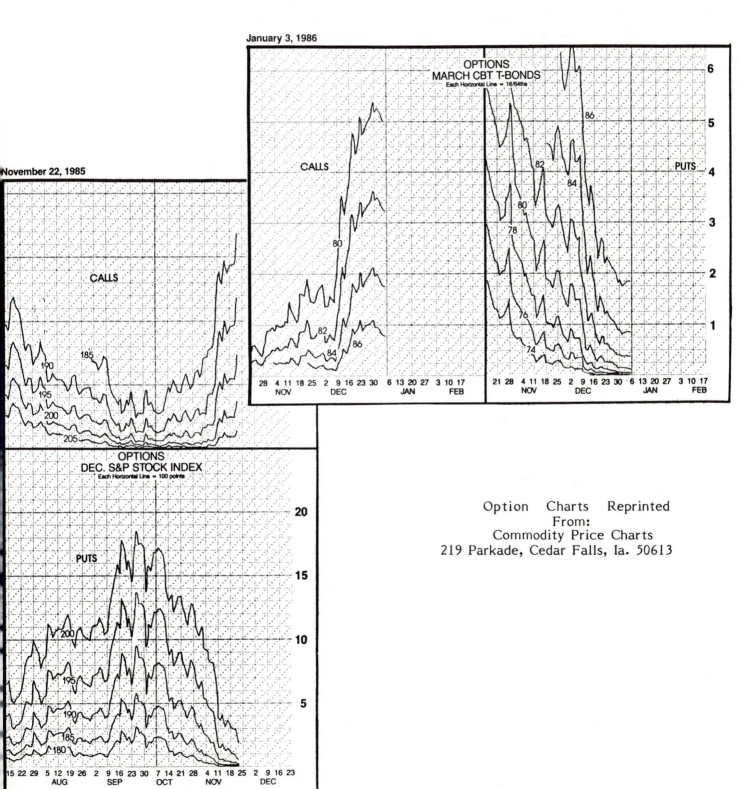

January 3, 1986

OPTIONS
MARCH CBT T-BONDS
Each Horizontal Line = 16/64ths

CALLS

PUTS

November 22, 1985

CALLS

OPTIONS
DEC. S&P STOCK INDEX
Each Horizontal Line = 100 points

PUTS

Option Charts Reprinted
From:
Commodity Price Charts
219 Parkade, Cedar Falls, Ia. 50613

Options Bibliography

Abbot, Susan. "Options Expanding Rapidly to Reach Global Audience." Futures, Apr. 1985, pp. 48-50.

Becker, H. Phillip and William H. Degler. "Nineteen Strategies and When To Use Them." Futures, June 1984, pp. 46-51.

"Options on Soybean Futures - Fundamentals, Pricing & Applications." Chicago: Chicago Board of Trade, 1984.

The Chicago Board Options Exchange - Reference Manual. Minneapolis, MN: Golle & Holmes Corp., 1977.

"Options on Currency Futures: A Strategy Guide." Chicago: Chicago Mercantile Exchange, 1985.

Robb, Richard G. "The Black-Scholes Model and Common Sense." Intermarket July, 1985, pp. 49-51.

Szala, Ginger. "How COMEX Firm's Failure is Shaking Up the Industry." Futures, May 1985, pp. 64, 66, 68, 70.

Zieg, Kermit C. Jr. Ph.D. and S. H. Zieg. Commodity Options. Larchmont, NY: Investors Intelligence, Inc., 1974.

Oscillator Analysis

(Also: Velocity, Rate of Change, Momentum, and Dual Oscillator Analysis)

The oscillator is the difference between the actual price of a commodity and one or more moving averages. It shows the value of price as a plus or minus difference plotted against the moving average as a straight line. In effect, an oscillator detrends prices and defines cycles. It can be smoothed out by a moving average to reduce choppiness. There can be multiple oscillators or moving averages of oscillators on the same graph.

The oscillator is used primarily to show price trends' rate of change, often called momentum. Normally, most markets do not have drastic changes in overall price levels. There are usually enough buyers and sellers of both a commercial and speculative nature to balance one another to keep prices fluctuating closely together. The oscillator shows the normal range of price fluctuation in trending markets and can be used in a countertrend fashion for short term trading.

When applied to daily plot charts, shorter term cycles appear on oscillator graphs more readily. If a 10 day oscillator showed several waves averaging 32 days in length, we could then program a 32 day oscillator. That cycle would tend to disappear and other cycles may appear. By process of trial and error, you can develop the ideal oscillator with the greatest significance at the time of analysis, showing where prices become overbought or oversold. In effect, you are developing a tool to show which cycles exist and how to trade with them.

In Chart A, we used a 14 bar (month) directional oscillator to show long term price changes plotted relative to our familiar gold chart. You can see on the oscillator chart, price changes going from very bearish levels of -30 (1976) up to positive levels by the third quarter of 1977. Constantly increasing in its bullishness, the oscillator kept in tandem with actual prices including the fourth quarter 1978 correction. The oscillator plot continued to increase in its rate of bullishness up to the absolute price high of January 1980. A close inspection of the 1980 trend change to down and collapse through 1985 showed the oscillator essentially mirroring the price moves. A simple interpretation is to go with the oscillator in its direction and change when it changes. A divergence of the two presents a warning of possible trend reversal.

Oscillators can be averaged to smooth out erratic moves. Two or more oscillators can be plotted as "fast" and "slow" plots for simple crossover trading plans (i.e. 5 and 20 day oscillator differences). Oscillators can be weighted by time, volume, price or daily close price changes. In Chart B the oscillator plot from April through September 1980 was flat, whereas actual prices clearly showed a resumption of the bull trend. When the rate of change slows in a primary trending market, this almost always preceeds a reversal. This quality is one of the unique properties that momentum displays.

In Chart C, we have shown a 3 and 10 bar difference plot against a 5 and 12 bar difference plot to show a multiple "fast/slow" oscillator against the gold price. The application of multiple oscillators is endless especially with 4 variables to choose from as well as monthly, weekly, daily, hourly, etc. time frames to plot against. An encyclopaedia of experimental results can be worked out with computers just on this one general approach. Quickness of turn, time cycles favored, market thinness, type of market, commission costs and slippage, and trending or trading market conditions all combine to make 100 ideal systems for 100 different traders.

Oscillators applied to daily or shorter time charts tend to show repetitive cycles well. Therefore, in congested markets short term traders lean toward overbought/oversold oscillator interpretations. Long term traders use oscillators as a tool to show divergence from trend when momentum changes. It is the experience and patience of each individual that determines his leanings and eventual return on equity.

The main disadvantage of oscillators is that they perform differently in congestion areas than in trending phases. When prices leave a sideways pattern, the magnitude of oscillator fluctuation expands greatly. This usually overwhelms the short term trader who believes prices will stay in the prior bracketed trading range. It is this forced re-thinking that affects both the usage and judgment of oscillators.

Some of the better known long term oscillators and detrended price series used for gold by advisory services today are:

Aden Analysis: 45 and 65 week (10 and 15 month)
Bank Credit Analyst: 13 and 26 week (3 and 6 month)
Pring Market Review: 40 week and 14 month (9 and 14 month)

We believe there is no ideal combination of oscillators to use. However, the cycle analysis elsewhere in this book shows that the 19 week cycle (approximately 5 months) and the 48-52 week cycle (11 to 12 months) are most significant for gold price data. This is roughly a 2-1/2X ratio of cycles, close to the noted 3X ratio that appears to have strong harmonics in multiple cycle studies.

Oscillator Analysis

Chart A

Commodity Quote-Graphics TQ-20/20

Oscillator Analysis

Chart B

Commodity Quote-Graphics   TQ-20/20

Oscillator Analysis

Chart C

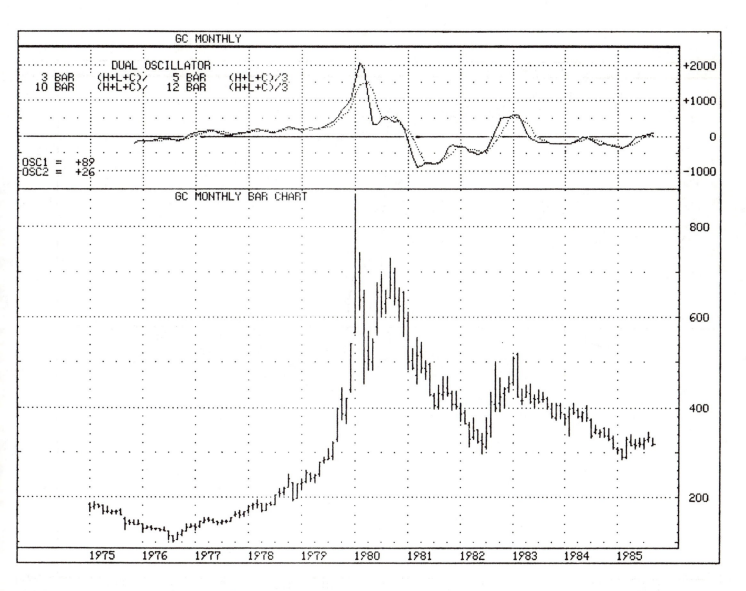

Commodity Quote-Graphics   TQ-20/20

Oscillator Analysis

Chart D

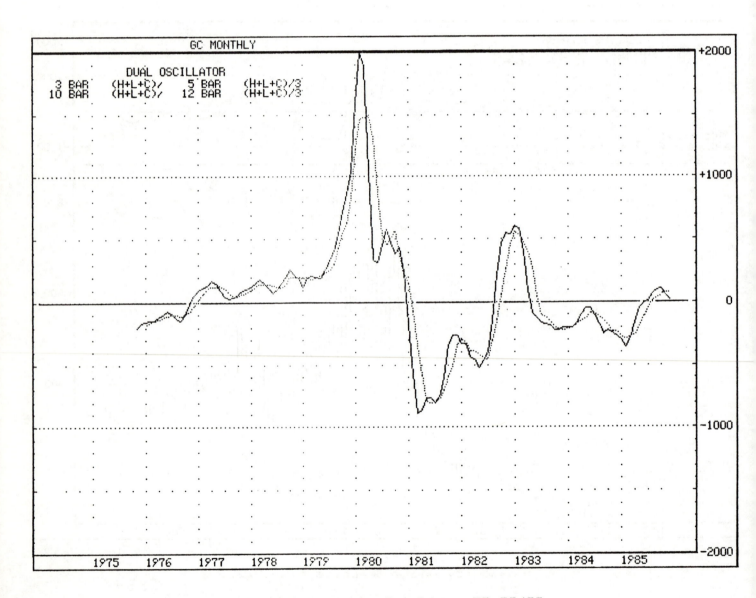

Commodity Quote-Graphics   TQ-20/20

Parabolic Analysis

Parabolic Analysis is more correctly termed a system approach. This is due to the protective stop/reversal signal being generated automatically. On the other hand, an analysis merely provides a methodology of analyzing price, volume, and open interest data. It gives the user multiple ways of looking at the market requiring interpretation.

Parabolic approach measures past volatility using two variables — trading ranges and price acceleration (rate of change). In this approach, you are always in either a long or short position; never neutral. The trailing stop is always double your level of contracts that you can afford to systematically trade. Once prices violate your stop order, your position is automatically reversed. A new reversal stop is entered, again double your normal trading level, at the parabolic signal price in the opposite direction.

We used this approach on our computer with the monthly plot gold chart. We could not effectively utilize the results because of the few signals generated. Extreme volatility from 1979 forward distorted calculations and generated a single position for 4 years missing extreme price swings.

Because we believe it important to present a meaningful chart representative of an approach or analysis, we used a weekly plot chart of gold covering April 1983 through December 1985. This generated a total of eleven signals overall (or 10 reversal signals). For 2 of the 3 years covered, prices were in a definite decline with the third year sideways. The turning or reversal points are indicated by small circles drawn at the weekly reversal levels where the parabolic stop order was touched.

Traders who favor this system lean toward having their protective reversal stop close in to their initial position. This continually reduces risk or potential loss. There are times when whipsaws will occur because prices swing counter to the primary trend, run stop orders, (see point A) then reverse back toward the original direction, as though by homing instinct (see point B). In the meantime, two trades have been generated; one on the whipsaw when prices ran stop orders in the countertrending move, and the next trade when prices reversed and hit the newly entered stop. Your position would be right back where you originally were, but after two trades generated, commissions charged, and probably a small loss. See points A and B on the chart for an example of whipsaw as seen by hindsight.

A minor note on the ability of traders to analyze past market behavior. Many claim to have the ability of 20/20 hindsight. We say ours is 40/40. Of course, foresight is another matter.

Parabolic Analysis

○ Price Penetration Reversal Points

Parallel Channel Line Analysis

This analysis involves the construction of numerous parallel trendlines as another way of determining support and resistance areas. Usually this analysis is applied to a mature commodity, such as gold. By mature, we mean a commodity which has experienced two or possibly three bull and bear cycles thus making its followers very experienced with numerous moods and nuances. New futures contracts do not have this history of investor emotion influencing prices and are, therefore, more erratic. After gold's "ascent to heaven" and subsequent collapse, gold investors experienced every extreme emotion possible. This experience factor may be the cause of this parallel effect of price movement.

By hindsight, trendlines are drawn either off the intermediate lows (A & B on Chart A) or the intermediate highs (C & D on Chart B). A network of parallel trendlines can be drawn which for no apparent reason hit many support and resistance points, as well as highs and lows. In gold's case, there are two angles of trendlines involved — 39° off the lows and 45° off the highs. Prices apparently vascillate downward in a series of channels or lanes, much like cars on a multilane highway, taking the easiest flow rate. Whether this is a valid approach of a real phenomenon or just a random coincidence, we cannot say. We have not come across any in-depth original work on this analysis.

How prices behave when they violate support or resistance or violate a trendline usually confirms a trend reversal. Only through numerous experiences can you judge accordingly. We will let you judge which of the two graphic examples given is more valid — parallels visually fitted off gold's intermediate highs or lows.

This approach is known by other names such as parallel lines, channel lines, roadway lines, and Andrew's pitchfork lines.

Parallel Channel Line Analysis
Chart A

—— Channel Lines

O   Starting Point, Visually Fitted   *Note: Angle is 39° off the horizontal*

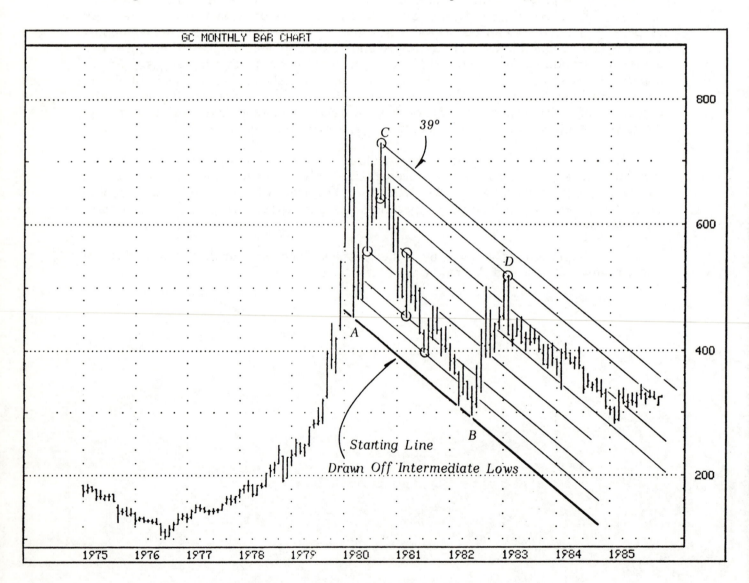

Commodity Quote-Graphics   TQ-20/20

Parallel Channel Line Analysis

Chart B

—— Channel Lines

O   Starting Point, Visually Fitted

Note: Angle is 45° off the horizontal

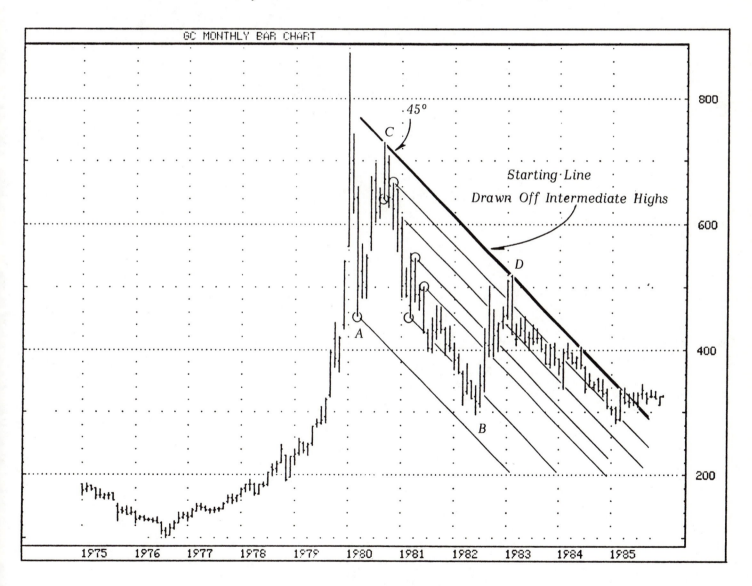

Commodity Quote-Graphics   TQ-20/20

"Everytime history repeats itself, the price goes up."
---Anonymous

Percentage Retracement Analysis

Usually market prices do not continually trend in one direction. They normally retrace their moves, then resume their primary trend usually in a cyclical pattern. Many traders try to catch this reaction; not give away equity gained; and perhaps reverse position to participate in the reaction.

Used mainly by technically inclined aggressive traders, retracement calculations are useful, as they give traders a second chance to participate in major moves. Certain percentage measurements seem to occur more frequently than others. There are two groups of numbers that are currently accepted as being most "in vogue" or best for today's markets.

Most Frequently Used:

25% Standard One Quarter	50% Standard One Half
33% Standard One-Third	60% Standard Three-Fifths
40% Standard Two-Fifths	75% Standard Three Quarters

Second Most Referred To:

38.2% Fibonacci Retracement   61.8% Fibonacci Retracement

In the following table, we calculated standard divisions of 100% for easy reference.

We illustrated the major percentage retracements on our now all too familiar gold chart. Please note the different percentages of all reactions for moves that are considered part of larger moves. In our opinion, there is no consistency in using any single percentage or group of percentages. If we were asked to make a selection, we would use 40%, 50% and 60% retracement percentages without favoring any. Over 60%, prices tend to keep on going, making a retracement become a reversal.

All mathematical retracements come from standard divisions into 100%.

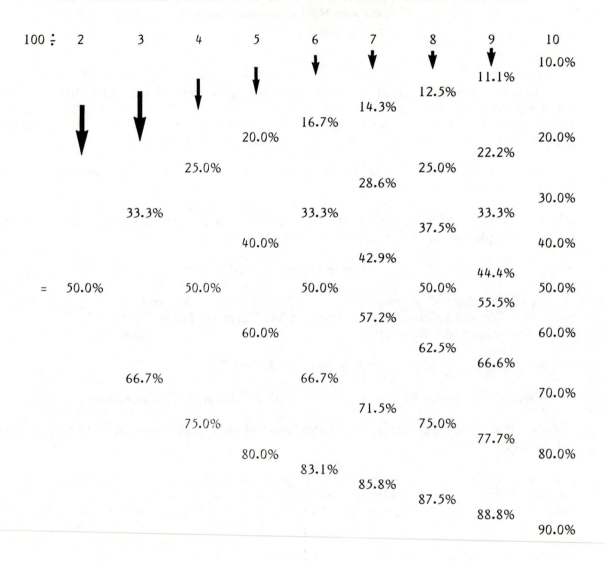

100 ÷	2	3	4	5	6	7	8	9	10
									10.0%
							12.5%	11.1%	
						14.3%			
				20.0%	16.7%				20.0%
			25.0%				25.0%	22.2%	
						28.6%			30.0%
		33.3%		33.3%			33.3%		
			40.0%			37.5%			40.0%
						42.9%		44.4%	
=	50.0%		50.0%		50.0%		50.0%		50.0%
						57.2%		55.5%	
			60.0%				62.5%		60.0%
		66.7%		66.7%				66.6%	
						71.5%			70.0%
		75.0%				75.0%		77.7%	
			80.0%						80.0%
				83.1%		85.8%			
							87.5%		
								88.8%	
									90.0%

Percentage Retracement Analysis

Chart A

A = $ (   )   Full Wave

$\dfrac{(\quad)\%}{\$ (\quad)}$ Percentage Of Move, Dollar Amount

O   Points from which counts are taken.

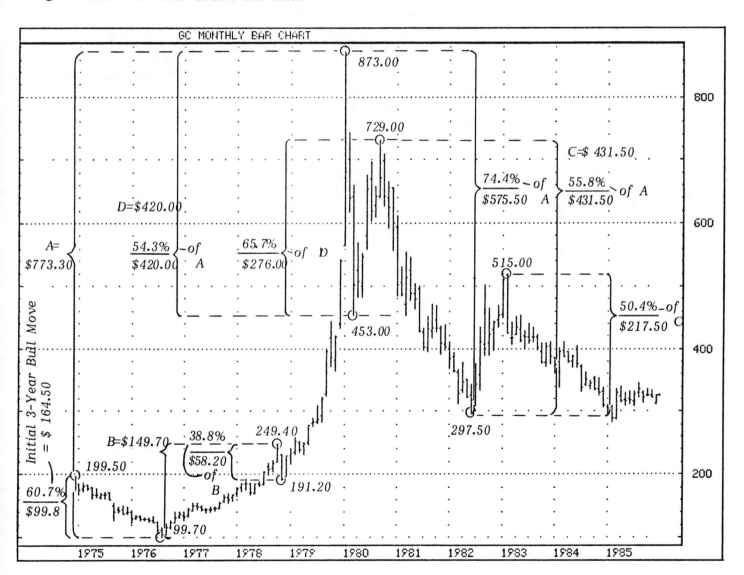

Commodity Quote-Graphics   TQ-20/20

Percentage Retracement Analysis

Chart B

Many technicians use standard percentages of a price movement to project how far prices may retrace without turning into a reversal. This allows them to enter into a new position with a very close stop order as risk insurance. On chart B, we showed gold's main bullish move ($873 less $99, or $774) as a straight line AB. Simple percentages can now be used with reduced risk to project reaction downmoves.

The most important factor of this approach is determining when a major high has been made. Using the pattern of a blowoff action with volume and price verification, you can immediately calculate the amount prices can drop and still be considered bullish. Using Fibonacci percentage retracements (see Fibonacci Analysis) and the most commonly used halfway (50%) retracement, multiply 38.2%, 50.0%, and 61.8% by the total range covered. Subtract these retracements and you have a choice of price support levels that should hold. Retracement lines are drawn as flat support levels into the future from where you began to anticipate a downmove.

By March, 8 to 10 weeks after the January 21st blowoff high, prices had dropped to the $457 level. Prices then rebounded to consolidate and, coincidentally, held mostly at the projected 50% ($486) level before resuming their uptrend. Therefore, to technicians this action completed a normal, though vicious, 50% reaction, enabling the bull market to continue.

After a rally to over $700, prices proceeded to collapse through line C (38.2%) in December 1980; line D (50%) in June 1981; and finally line E (61.8%) in January 1982. This approach technically suggests that rallies should now be sold. It is reasoned the long term trend has turned bearish as material support failed to arrest the downslide where probability dictates most markets should have held.

To show the most common percentage retracements, we decided to use Fibonnaci numbers, as well as the commonly used halfway point. You can calculate 40%, 50%, and 60% retracement levels and be reasonably close to real support in a majority of markets most of the time.

Percentage Retracement Analysis

Chart B

Percentage Retracement Lines - Fibonacci Counts; C and E. AB = $ 774 range.

Line C = 38.2 % of AB or $ 296. AB less $ 296 = $ 577.
Line D = 50.0 % of AB or $ 387. AB less $ 387 = $ 486.
Line E = 61.8 % of AB or $ 478. AB less $ 478 = $ 395.

Point & Figure Analysis

Point and figure (P & F) is actually a charting approach having two distinctive features. It has a unique system of price counting to project price objectives and a distinctive form of price plotting that ignores time progression. We believe this is a refined version of swing charting (see Swing Chart Analysis) which has a proven history of use over hundreds of years. P & F charting shows price moves up or down by X's and O's respectively in columns on graph paper. Time is not portrayed on the bottom scale as is usual with bar charts. The fluctuation of prices within any range is what is important to a P & F user.

Point and figure is used extensively by traders on exchange floors. This form of charting clearly shows support and resistance levels on a price scale that the user determines is best for his needs. Whatever price monitoring detail the trader uses determines his minimum price increment (called a box) and the minimum amount needed before a price trend is reversed. The cost of doing business for a floor trader is usually less than the minimum price fluctuation on most markets.

Speculators who are not members tend to be position traders. They want clearly defined buy or sell signals with as few false breakouts as possible. Therefore, some P & F users plot prices only from the daily close price action. This tends to reflect more meaningful trends when compared to all intraday price swings that occasionally give false signals.

As prices have a tendency to trade predominately within well defined support and resistance levels, the number of times that prices run up and down develop what is called "count". Count is the projected magnitude of price move when prices leave a trading range in either direction. The more prices back and fill, the bigger the trending move after a breakout. All kinds of different trading range formations have this count developed within their structure. The key in P & F charting is accurately locating proper breakout points. In bullish markets, it is one box above a prior high, at the defined top level. In bearish markets, it is a one box move through a prior low price.

The two most common methods of counting to establish the extent of an advance or decline are the vertical method and the count method.

The vertical method employs measuring the height of the trading range added onto the breakout point, which then gives a reasonable objective most of the time.

The count method uses the length of the sideways or horizontal range, again added to the breakout point determining an objective. Since objectives are not achieved 100% of the time, experienced users of P & F counting usually take 80% of the count for a minimum move that has a higher reliability of occurring.

Formations derived from P & F charting are similar to regular bar chart formations. They fall into the two general categories of reversal patterns and continuation or consolidation patterns. At times, price channels are observed in P & F charts when they aren't noticed in regular bar charts. The P & F condensing effect on prices sometimes changes price patterns.

Trendlines in P & F charting are drawn at 45° angle plots off of significant highs and lows. While they can be drawn off of highs to other highs, they seem to have less reliability than the 45° angles. In any event, support and resistance levels are what stand out most in P & F price analysis.

The primary advantages are threefold in point and figure charting. First, only price movement is considered in plotting. Time is not considered at all. The technician considerably reduces his time needed to follow a quantity of these charts. Secondly, the consolidations or trading ranges give better count or potential price moves. The greater the sideways move, the more extensive the eventual breakout tends to be. Third, minor price moves can be eliminated at the choice of the technician. This is done when the minimum box size and reversal size is picked. It also saves money in trading by determining more correct breakouts, price determination and, in the long run, more reliable signals.

Our graph example is the gold bar chart converted into a P & F chart from 1970 forward. Box size or the minimum price fluctuation considered for this long term chart was $10. A major problem of P & F is the minimum box size usefulness. A $10 box at $150 gold is 7% of total value. A $10 box at $750 gold was barely over 1% of total value, and considering how prices were moving at $750, merely a sneezing motion of a well-to-do established floor trader. However, ten dollars at the $150 level in 1974 took weeks to achieve. Experienced traders use small base semi-log scale charts to reduce unreliable percentage distortion.

The minimum number of boxes needed to reverse trend was three boxes or $30 worth. Therefore, this chart is defined as a $10 x 30 P & F chart. Experience shows most market scales are best shown as a three box minimum needed to reverse. Any larger number of boxes would have considerably condensed price action. The ratio of a three box reversal best presents the proper P & F chart. This seems to hold at most levels on the risk tolerance scale.

Again, referring to long term gold prices, we started at 1970 for our chart. In the course of 16 years, there were ten buy and sell signals generated by this approach. The arrows point to specific price boxes which gave the signals. We showed a "B" or "S" inside each box to give the direction.

Because of the simplicity of P & F charts and its need for price data only, it can be applied to illiquid, unorganized markets not found on exchanges. Examples are over-the-counter stock not volume quoted, coin prices, antiques, old cars, diamonds, etc. They fall ideally into P & F chart structure and signal interpretation. Very liquid, organized exchanges such as stocks, bonds, and commodities can use this form of charting just as well.

Point & Figure Analysis

➤ Reversal Signal $10 x 30 Gold Chart

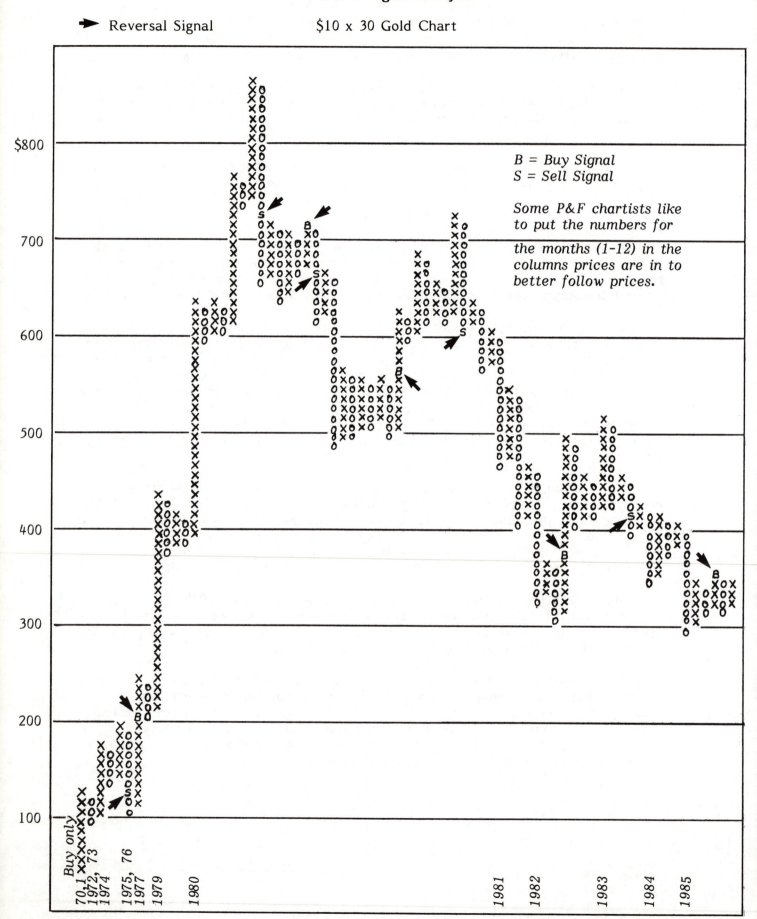

B = Buy Signal
S = Sell Signal

*Some P&F chartists like
to put the numbers for
the months (1-12) in the
columns prices are in to
better follow prices.*

Years under the price action when plotted.

Point & Figure Analysis Bibliography

Cohen, A. W. The Chartcraft Method of Point & Figure Trading. Larchmont, NY: Chartcraft, Inc., 1967.

Henfrey, Tony. "Inflation, Interest Rates and the Outlook for Gold." On Gold. pp. 169 - 183. DeKalb, IL: Waterleaf Press, 1982.

Thiel, Charles C., Jr., Ph.D. and Robert E. Davis, Ph.D. Point and Figure Commodity Trading: A Computer Evaluation. West Lafayette, IN: Dunn & Hargitt, 1970.

Wheelan, Alexander H. Study Helps in Point and Figure Technique. New York: Morgan, Rogers & Roberts, Inc., 1954.

Price Box Congestion Analysis

This approach comes from the observation that prices seemingly move in a staircase fashion during a primary trend.

Initially, prices climb consecutively higher (in a bull trend for example) in a constantly trending fashion. Then, prices usually pause to consolidate price gains, in a lateral or downward action. Often prices will come down to touch prior highs attained in the previous upmove. We call this action a box congestion pattern; with the high and low becoming the top and bottom of a box.

Drawing horizontal lines off the top and bottom of price moves creates a staircase effect of boxes, each one progressively higher than the one before.

A move of prices through the top side of the box congestion ends the box formation; usually shown by drawing a vertical line up from the lower horizontal line at the breakout time.

When prices fall back sharply into a defined box area just after having broken out, the odds are that a reversal of trend will follow. In the following gold chart, we noted four areas of trend reversal by using this method.

The range of price congestion is too wide to be effectively used for getting in or out of positions near highs or lows. Shorter term charts, such as daily and weekly plot, are better suited for that task. The overall advantage of this analysis is that fewer decisions have to be made; which appeals to the position investor.

Price Box Congestion Analysis

GC MONTHLY BAR CHART

Reversal

Reversal

Reversal

Reversal

800

600

400

200

1975 1976 1977 1978 1979 1980 1981 1982 1983 1984 1985

Commodity Quote-Graphics   TQ-20/20

"Man can climb to the highest summits,
but he cannot dwell there long."
---George Bernard Shaw

Psychological Crowd Profile Analysis

Crowd psychology is the study of strong emotions dominating individual reason, thereby changing that individual's value system. Philosophically, it can be said that one's ability to maintain independent ideas and an objective analysis of the market is subjugated by the mesmerizing influence and intensity of the crowd. Economic influences are changes of minimum contract requirements fluctuating with both the price levels and volatility of the market. For example, different extremes of activity, squeeze situations, limit moves, and closed trading sessions combine to affect the mentality and behavior of customers of brokerage houses. In the last stages of a bull market, it has been observed that investors become gamblers — those who have more money than expertise.

Essentially, there are three stages to a psychological crowd profile and the crowd's gradual changes in attitude, emotion and economic situation.

THE THREE PSYCHOLOGICAL STAGES ARE MANIA, BUBBLE, AND PANIC.

The Bull Phase

Hope becomes greed. This is the mania portion of crowd activity. Hearsay is taken as gospel and hope changes to religious obsession, mainly due to the constant effects of communication with other investors, traders, brokers, printed and visual media as well as self hypnosis. We have shown these emotions and attitudes at different stages on our long term gold chart (Chart A).

Initial Margin Required:

$450

Initially, there is very little interest in the market as traders and investors doubt prices are going anywhere. Comments such as "it won't improve", "look where it came down from", and "some days it just doesn't trade" can be heard. Margin requirements for gold are $450 per contract which has a total value of $10,000. (See Chart B for a chronology of margin requirements. Compare Charts A and B for an economic intensity level coinciding to emotional levels.)

As prices drop, there is no interest by the investing public, floor traders, or retail brokers who normally tell stories to incite interest. The lack of floor traders in the pit gives rise to "it's a shotgun market". (You can fire a shotgun across the pit without hitting anyone.) The perennially optimistic public just isn't buying.

Fear dominates reason. Everyone is afraid to buy as prices may drop further. No one can envision a trend change by looking at charts of price activity and prior highs.

$700

Gold's price has moved up slightly, but caution is the key word. "Just because it's moved up in price doesn't mean it will continue." Token buying is taking place. With gold at $200/ounce the total contract value is now $20,000. The margin required is now $700 per contract, or 3-1/2% of total value. However, most traders would rather trade corn (5% margin) or cattle (6% margin) where there is "more return for the money". This illogic is shown by traders not looking at the percentage of margin required, but at the dollar amount required (i.e. corn, $350; cattle, $500).

Rumors begin to appear in the media. Credibility is strained as radical stories appear creating new situations that may affect prices. The number of times the President has died, been shot, or had a heart attack, is not as great as the number of times Paul Adolf Volker (Chairman of the Federal Reserve Bank) has resigned, retired, or had *his* heart attack. You have to experience first-hand a rumor in action involving large groups of people and their money, to appreciate the distortion of people's judgment. Political events — "always a fun happening" — and strange opinions of economic experts add to the anxiety of a rumor and the resultant price response.

Opinions overwhelm fact! Information such as supply and demand is now interpreted in the direction of the market's trend. This is especially true when talking to commission houses and bullion dealers. As a result, slanted opinions dominate the financial media. When negative facts are released, they tend to be ignored.

$1,000   The crisis atmosphere begins when any good news regarding the bullish trend is exaggerated, then causing hysteria. This is best described as economic anxiety; crisis thinking in its simpliest form.

Confidence is king. Due to consistently higher prices, the majority of speculators are fully confident of continuing bullish action. Their inexperience in other dynamic bull/bear markets shows by their accumulated irrational actions. An experienced minority, however, are patient; fearful of sharp reactions or a vicious collapse when prices compound as they are now doing.

$1,500   Optimism prevails. Statements such as "this is what should happen" and "it is good for all" are the logic of the day. All includes anyone who can only see one side, have little market experience, and cannot envision a downturn because this is gold - king of hard assets.

$2,000   Instant wealth occurs. Compared to bank accounts, bonds collapsing, industrial stocks dropping, etc., real wealth accrues to participants in a manner never before experienced in the gold market. Psychologically, mental processes become "heady" as individuals contemplate uses for this new found gain.

Buying madness ensues. For every long position in the futures market, there is a short position. In major bull markets, commercial hedgers, in order to offset possible equity loss, have significant short positions equal to their physical inventory. Bullion dealers and some speculators also maintain short positions. As prices rise sharply creating margin demands by exchange clearing house rules, these groups must add additional funds to cover their market losses as they occur. At this stage of the market, their action is to frenziedly buy back their losing short positions. The profitable longs are now easily adding on additional long positions with the accrued profits, watching their equity numbers increase at a geometrically compounded rate. This is what causes curvilinear bullish patterns.

$2,500   <u>No danger of loss.</u>   At this stage, the market mentality actually becomes dangerous or destructive. It denies the possibility of any move to the downside — sideways, on a perpetually new high plateau perhaps, but not back down. Market participants start to believe it can't happen to them and they deserve their new found wealth. Actually, this becomes a selfdefeating prophecy. For those who believe it can't happen, their disbelief creates bigger losses when prices collapse because they wait longer to sell, turning the selling into a panic.

$3,000   <u>Buying panic</u> occurs. "Buy before there isn't any more." The rate of buying increases exponentially against the poor shorts who are trying to get out of their losing positions at an arithmetic rate of selling. At this phase, much higher projected prices are heard and believed.

$4,000   <u>"Old standards do not apply today."</u> When statements like this are heard, the top is imminent. Be it crude oil in 1979, go-go stocks in 1968, uranium stocks in 1956, defense stocks in 1945, gold mining stocks in 1937, growth and utility trusts in 1929, etc., all markets fluctuate! Even when the government closes markets, black markets continue to fluctuate up and down in their place. For every bull market, there is a bear market. In hyperinflationary bull markets (destruction of the currency) there is a hyper-deflation afterwards as currency values disappear, the middle class is wiped out, and all paper investments are wiped out. The standards of supply and demand will always apply.

$8,000   <u>Everyone shows interest.</u> The bull market is the talk at social gatherings, at special events, on news programs, and within all other unrelated market areas in investment firms. Related businesses, such as coin dealers, are handling business that is 10 to 20 times normal levels. Establishment publications, magazines, investment dailies, and periodicals, not to mention the specialized pro-gold investment letters, present major articles explaining the complete story of what has happened and their projections as to what is to come. Margin requirements per contract are now $8,000 to $10,000 at some investment firms; other firms won't allow any new positions. Technically, no new positions means margin prices are at infinity. Silver contract margins go to $25,000 and then $60,000 per contract.

This is, of course . . .

The Top

Euphoria! All values are now distorted; there are no negatives — only positives. New market participants have only "little" profits (hundreds of percent) compared to old market participants who have made fortunes (thousands of percent profits). Media articles start out with, "Did you know that your secretary had a greater return this year with her earrings than all of your regular investments?" Traders are spending money in a manner indicative of kings and rock stars. Orders for large, wealthy homes, flashy status cars, jewelry too heavy to wear, etc., become commonplace.

This second stage is the <u>BUBBLE</u>.

A <u>selling panic</u> ensues. The bubble pops and emotional values and price levels begin to retrace their very recent upmove to the downside. The 1976 to 1980 gold bull market was not a singular thing. Silver, platinum, palladium and other rare metals, as well as other hard assets all moved up in sympathy. January 21, 1980 saw the Commodity Exchange of New York economically forced to change the contractual provisions of a futures contract to stop the silver price climb. Silver collapsed dragging down gold. Because of the sisterhood of precious metals, gold drops from its $873 spot high to $453. All longs tend to be position holders, not short term in their beliefs. All short holders (remember for every long there must be a short) are primarily day traders, floor traders, and a very few well-to-do commercial short hedgers and large speculators. All the position traders who bought can now sell their positions to a very select group — themselves. Margin requirements are so high that no one wants to or can add onto their position. Some investment houses refuse new positions, especially in silver. Prices collapse. Longs want out. In six weeks, gold drops $400 due to forced liquidation of overextended margin traders. This is exactly the same pattern as late September/October 1929; too many amateur margin traders long in an unbalanced holding ability market. In 1929, American stocks lost 50% of their total value with margin requirements of 10%. The margin traders were the first to go.

<u>Confidence and confusion</u> reign. After the initial financial bomb hits and the latecomers wiped out, only the diehards remain along with old traders (those who started more than six months ago). They still have a profit or are monetarily ahead on balance. In the midst and confusion of this six week drop in prices, not one inherent thing has changed. The belief persists that it will come back. In the physical gold bull market, the actual holding of the asset is in weak hands, but is a convert to the greater fool theory. That is, when it gets back up to where I bought it (or where my equity was the greatest) I'm going to sell it (to the next fool).

<u>$3,000</u>   <u>Prosperity</u> reigns. Now that gold has moved back up into the high reaches again, doubts about selling re-enter the novice's mind. "After all, it still is the ultimate investment." "What are my choices?" "Where else can I place my investment money if I get out now?" "Nowhere, I'll stay with my position."

This has got to be . . .

The Bear Phase

<u>Fear changes to despair</u>! All values and attitudes are that these high prices, these times and all that they will bring, are the norm. This is the big mistake. If current market participants had experienced a total bull and bear market before, they would know better.

Technically, the bear side is the <u>PANIC</u>.

$2,000   <u>Caution</u> is again the key word. When prices first drop, most don't believe it will continue. Ignoring the trend being opposite their position and their shrinking profit, the only thought is caution. As the price drops and volatility shrinks, the exchange reduces margin requirements to help pick up trading activity. This is the beginning of the primary major downtrend. A great many investors and long traders are finally wiped out during this phase.

<u>Lost wealth</u> abounds in commission houses, investors' actions, and all business related activity. Orders for wealthy houses, cars, etc., are cancelled and rescinded en masse. A sure sign of reduced activity is lower exchange membership prices. Tied directly to trading activity, the reduced quantity of public orders or "paper" in the pits is perhaps the best reflection of reduced investing interest in this market.

<u>Doubt and worry</u> pervade all thought. Experts can't explain what happened when prices dropped. As a matter of fact, they couldn't explain why prices rose as much as they did, but that period of bullishness has been reduced to a memory as self preservation places survival above greed. This is the main thought of long term investors.

$1,500   <u>Anxiety</u> appears in many forms. Erratic behavior and irrational statements begin to be common. Some traders have become destitute from their acts of greed. Others actually accomplish developing a negative net worth, go bankrupt, and because of the daily settling practice of futures trading, drag down some brokerage firms in the process. Explanations from investment advisors for the magnitude and reasons for the drop become exaggerated and extreme.

The crowd's dominant emotion is <u>fear</u>. Little hope and projections for lower prices proliferate some two years after the high. Prices start trending up out of nowhere and for no apparent reason. Long term investors have feelings of despair and little hope for any major turnaround. Some economic signs reinforce prior bullish attitudes, but are directly opposite the recent price collapse.

$2,500   <u>Confidence</u> returns quickly to traders, mainly due to prices climbing at a strong rate in an intermediate rally. Since the improved (bullish) market is appreciating at close to the original bullish rate of climb, expectations are for it to continue. This becomes a false hope. More importantly, this is the third major up-thrust during this bullish wave, increasing belief that this move will continue.

$2,000   <u>Panic</u> ensues in the next downturn in prices. Not only have investors been financially beaten enough to remember the last two downturns, but in their effort to exit their favored long side, so many sell stops are bunched together that gold loses 25% of its total value in 8 days. This doesn't damage investor egos; it destroys them. Selling panic is just what it sounds like, a one sided market with almost all sellers and no buyers.

$1,500 Facts begin to re-establish themselves. More objective commentary from investment publications develop, trying to cover all viewpoints. Conclusions, however, lean toward the bear side.

Pessimism evolves as a natural result of a lackluster market with little profit for investors. The normally bullish public who buy rallies are continually beaten, demoralized, and pessimistic. Only the professionals trading with short time goals and smaller profit margins make any money. Total numbers in this market shrink to a fraction of the bubble top horde.

No interest, no media hype, almost no investment pundits touting the stories they touted on the bull side of the price mountain. Little or no talk as all interest migrates to markets that move.

Lack of confidence is the exact opposite when almost all had complete confidence in the trend, in the future, in the object of the bull move, etc. Reverse process.

Despair is the underlying crowd emotion; a chronic doubt of the market's ability to maintain a bullish trend for any length of time.

Fear - doubt - no interest. Another horde of novice investors please.

Next cycle . . .

Psychological Crowd Profile Analysis

The financial and emotional bubble effect of a
complete bull and bear market.

Chart A

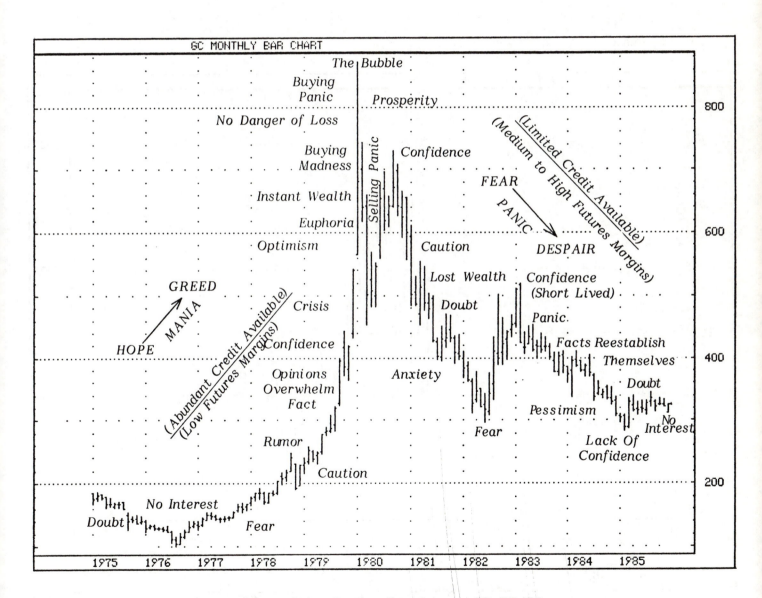

Commodity Quote-Graphics   TQ-20/20

Psychological Crowd Profile Analysis

Gold Comex Futures Margins
Per Contract

Chart B

E = Estimate

Commodity Quote-Graphics TQ-20/20

Courtesy: Commodity Exchange of New York.

Relative Strength Index (R.S.I.)

The R.S.I. illustrates the percentage of increase of the total price movement from each bar to bar. The first R.S.I. chart is shown above the gold price for comparison.

$$R.S.I. = 100 \ \frac{\textit{Sum of Daily Upticks or Up Average}}{\textit{Sum of Daily Downticks + Sum of Daily Upticks or Down Average + Up Average}}$$

To calculate R.S.I., two smoothed averages are calculated. The first moving average shows the average of the net changes in the upward direction. As you calculate from left to right on the bar chart, if the new price is higher than the previous bar, then subtract the previous bar's price from the current bar's price. You then add this difference into the smoothed average for up prices.

A similar process is used to figure the down average, except that the current price would be subtracted from the previous price to maintain a positive number.

Once the desired number of bars is determined for moving averages' length, the numbers are plugged into the above equation. While there are variations of this formula in use today, the results should show the same pattern or results.

An expanded scale R.S.I. is shown separately on the second chart. More detail and a greater depth of understanding can be achieved through the expanded scale.

This analysis was developed by Welles Wilder and can be more thoroughly studied in his book, *New Concepts in Technical Trading Systems.*

Relativè Strength Index (R. S. I.)

The R.S.I. shown is computed for 26 days, which best relates to the 28 to 35 day trading cycle prevalent in most futures. A common interpretation is to use the R.S.I. as an overbought/oversold indicator. On a scale of 0 to 100, at levels above 75 to 80 R.S.I., (overbought) prices tend to reverse to the downside. At low levels, 25 to 20 R.S.I., (oversold) prices tend to reverse to the upside.

Commodity Quote-Graphics   TQ-20/20

Relative Strength Index (R. S. I.)

Expanded Scale

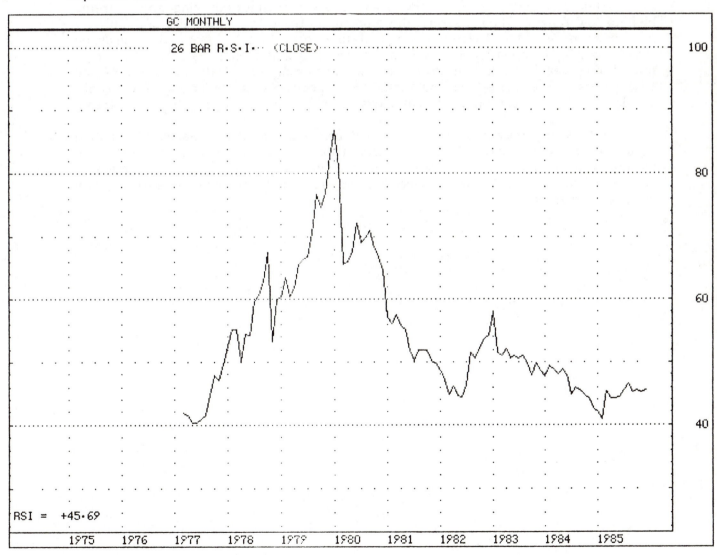

RSI = +45.69

Commodity Quote-Graphics   TQ-20/20

Speed Resistance Line Analysis

This approach attempts to establish trendlines after an intermediate price move has temporarily run its course. Also known simply as "speedlines", their usage is to try to determine how much prices will pullback in a trending market before resuming their primary trend. Since prices rarely move straight up or down, they tend to back and fill. The purpose of speed resistance lines is to help estimate how far prices may retreat before resuming their next trending move.

After a move has occurred, draw a vertical line covering the extreme high to low range. Then measure the amount of the price movement and multiply by 33% and 66% (or divide the vertical line into thirds). Mark the thirds on the measuring (vertical) line. Now draw two diagonal trendlines from the initial low through each mark you drew on the measuring (vertical) line — 33% and 66% points. These are your 33% and 66% speed resistance lines. These lines should provide support on price pullbacks from the direction of the major trend.

While speed resistance lines are used primarily on daily charts, we applied them to our gold chart. From our observation, either the 33% or the 66% line is equally applicable. If the price scale is changed, the angles are not affected, as the formulated angles are a byproduct of price and not absolute angles drawn using a protractor.

Speed Resistance Line Analysis

A Starting Price
B Extreme Price
c 66% Speedline
d 33% Speedline

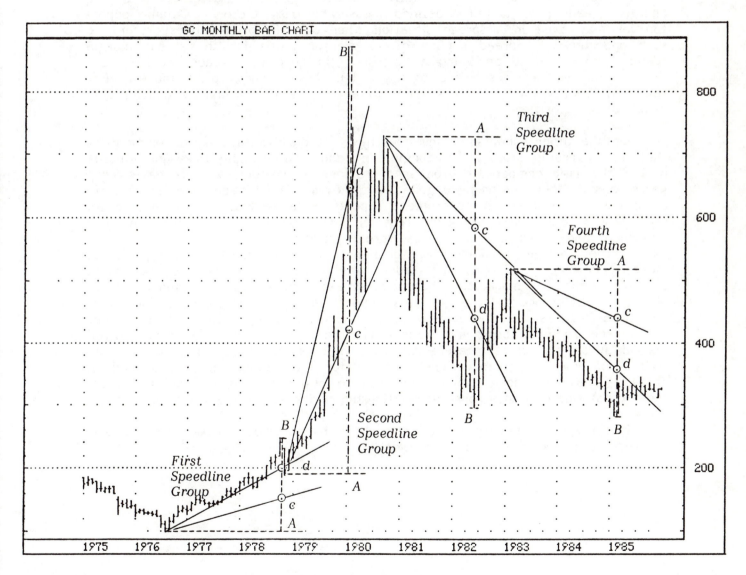

Spread Analysis

Spreading is the putting on of multiple positions in a simultaneous manner to reduce risk. The positions can encompass two or more months, either cash or futures, within one or between any number of commodities. Normally positions are in opposition to each other (buy vs. sell).

There are many advantages to spreading. By being simultaneously long and short, the speculator has some degree of protection from violent and surprising price moves. Most months in commodities are linked together in their fluctuation by interrelated economic or money flow associations. Spread trends tend to be of longer duration mainly because they essentially reflect primary relationships rather than the outright value. Outside influences do not distort the internal price differences as readily as outright prices are affected. Carrying charge spreads have a fairly defined measurable risk factor. Trading opportunities may exist in a spread situation when outright price moves present no such opportunity. Spread trading offers greater profit for the spread margin required compared to an outright position. In general, spreads require much less margin, yet are responsive to major bullish or bearish price moves. For small traders, spreading enables them to enter markets ordinarily unaffordable in an outright position.

On the other hand, spreading does have its disadvantages. In commodities that are not readily storable and fungible, spreads can be highly risky and actually double the risk compared to outright trading. Livestock spreads have "crop years" and certain months have gone limit moves against each other in opposite directions in response to government reports — a very dangerous occurance, especially on small spread margin requirements. Because of its normally slow movement and unique characteristics, spread trading appeals to certain personalities. The average outright trader does not have the ability to gauge spread moves accordingly. Spread stop orders used to limit risk are not permitted on most commodity markets. Therefore, spreads are liquidated by market order or a price difference order only. This requires more patience, greater judgment, and more finances than the average public speculator has. Because of the lower margin requirements, beginning traders use the dollar amount of spread initial margin as an equivalent measure of risk, which is incorrect. Therefore, overtrading becomes the number one problem for most beginning spread traders. Spread differences move slowly compared to outright position trading. Also, they do not fluctuate in a constant relationship to the spot price swings.

In our spread glossary, we tried to show the numerous spread combinations, yet keep definitions brief and to the point.

Gold/Silver Ratio

The gold/silver ratio is perhaps the most famous of all metal spreads due to excessive publicity during the 1972-82 commodity boom period. This ratio is the number of troy ounces of silver than can be bought by one troy ounce of gold. Hard asset advisors, pro-gold newsletters, N.Y. based metal dealers and major investment houses commented on this ratio by giving trading advice.

Armed with historical facts and distortions, analysts could easily research information on American monetary history that included our de facto bimetallic money standard that existed for over 150 years. Few people would believe that the U.S. gold standard was not adopted until the Currency Act of 1900. Before that time, the U.S. dollar was a silver denominated currency.

The U.S. dollar silver price was set in the Monetary Act of 1792 by Alexander Hamilton at $1.29/oz. Because of our parity of the U.S. silver dollar to the British pound (the Ł valued out at U.S.$4.86) the rate of exchange value between currencies was equivalent to 84-1/2 shillings per gold ounce or U.S.$20.67 per gold ounce. The ratio of dollars per gold ounce became 16 times the silver value of $1.29/oz, based on the defined legal silver dollar of 0.77 troy ounces.

In 1803, after the 1790 French Revolution and devastating hyper-inflation, Emperor Napoleon ordered set uniform coinage standards. The twenty government Latin European Monetary Union (L.M.U.) patterned their uniform standards for coinage after the French in 1862. The ratio of silver to gold was set by the L.M.U. at 15.5 to 1, close to the United States' 16 to 1 implied ratio.

In ancient history, as well as America's more recent entry into coin money, the ratio has been noted at: 25:1 (Rome 300 B.C. - silver denarius to gold denarius); 6:1 (Babylon 1900 B.C.); 8:1 (England 1100 A.D. - silver marks to gold marks); 100:1 (United States 1930's); and 15.5 (Europe 1860's). Historically there is no set ratio.

The use of the gold/silver ratio has been to formulate an average of the ratio for recent years, then develop an overbought-oversold approach to its interpretation. A monthly plot of the gold/silver ratio is presented against the monthly bar price of gold (see Chart A). The average ratio for the free price markets of the two metals (silver 1967 onward and gold 1971 onward) for about ten years turned out to be roughly 30 times (30x). Taking a best fit analysis and applying it on the scale, the best range was from 25x to 35x. Below 25x, gold was too scarce compared to silver and should be bought. Above 35x, silver became too scarce in comparison to gold and should be bought. The opposite metal at these extremes should either be sold against what was bought to reduce risk or just stayed away from. The shaded portions of the ratio are these periods of the ratio being in extreme areas. Please note the apparent cycle length of 3 to 4 years (top to top) developing in the ratio. This cycle is completely independent of anything showing in the outright gold price.

To fully understand these inter-commodity price swings, we recommend reading Cloyde P. Howard's article "The Gold/Silver Price Ratio - A Trading Strategy." He recommends an average ratio of 34 to 1 with swap areas above 39 for silver and below 29 for gold. The reason being is that there are benefits of a strategy without needing market sophistication. From January 1973 through May of 1980, a good 7 years' analysis concluded with prices at their highest level overall. A $6,500 purchase of gold in 1973 simply held would have been worth $51,650. Switching back and forth on a swapping technique with his specific rules, the ending value would have been $227,800+. Three major things that could go wrong according to Mr. Howard are: the basic ratio could change; government interference or control; and the government could stop inflating the currency.

We have not kept up to date on how Mr. Howard's approach fared with the change in the ratio's ranges since 1980 (32x to around 60x recently) or the 4 year drop in the rate of retail price inflation and producer price deflation through 1985. Mr. Howard can be reached at Dept. 107, P. O. Box 8277, Fountain Valley, California 92708.

Gold/Platinum/Silver

The W. W. Turner Index System has been well publicized in the numismatic media for over a decade. In essence, historic ratios of the three precious metals' price values are put onto an index chart and then onto a price chart. Mr. Turner devised this approach to allow plotting and comparison of the three main precious metals through the ratios he calculates. "When these ratios get badly out of balance, as compared with their accepted norms, then a genuine speculative opportunity exists." His research extends over 60 years, evidencing wide swings in their ratios, but interestingly always returning to their norm.

Mr. Turner uses moving averages of three time periods to get a norm value for the three metals. The ratios used in the moving averages are biased to favor the most recent price experience. These ratios are: 1/3 for the year just past; 1/3 for the past three years; and 1/3 for the past ten years. He then averages the three totals to get his "norm" ratio plotted onto a triangle schematic. This Ratio Analysis (see Chart B) gives investors visual evidence with which to spread the weakest against the strongest metal or trade in their favorite metal outright, having an idea of what is overbought or oversold at all times. Another procedure is switching to the lowest value metal as it compares to the others to benefit from its return to a normal relationship, as well as any outright appreciation.

A second chart Mr. Turner uses is his Price Chart (see Chart C). All three metals are plotted onto indexes and then put onto a semi-log scale (to the base 2) price chart. This price chart is more familiar, except the overlay effect can be shifted depending on where you base your index for each metal. This would modify the results.

More information can be obtained directly from Mr. W. W. Turner, P. O. Box 387, Leesburg, Florida 32748.

Platinum/Gold

The next most familiar gold spread is the platinum/gold spread which we have shown by computer plot (see Chart D). The net difference between the two metals is shown by dollar amount, not a ratio scale basis. Prior to the 1971 deregulation of gold's price by the U.S. Treasury, platinum had sold at a premium of 100 to 200% above gold's fixed $35 price. After a few years of allowing gold to fluctuate freely, the two metals traded closer to each other in price due to normal supply and demand forces.

By studying the platinum/gold chart it can be seen that platinum over the past decade has fluctuated sharply above and below gold in sympathy to speculation and industrial demand. When the economy was slow and speculation at low levels, platinum was at a discount to gold by as much as $100 per ounce. At 1980's high activity level, platinum reached a premium of $250 over gold. When prices of the two metals are near parity, it is usually in the middle portion of a cyclic move. Platinum is more dynamic and responsive to an increase in activity. Since platinum is scarcer than gold for physical availability, this implies a more responsive price action to prevailing market forces.

Gold/T-Bond

The next spread to be presented is the gold/T-bond spread (see Chart E). Adjustments to the scale had to be made in order to show correct comparisons. It can be seen that when gold is compared to long term 30 year treasury bond prices (or the inverse of long term interest rates) the difference had been in a constant downtrend since 1980. One can almost consider this chart an ideal representation for monitoring inflation or deflation trends. When inflation is trending up, gold is going up relative to bonds going down (or long term interest rates going up) and vice versa.

Cost of Carry Spread

Rarely used because of its computational difficulty, apparent low profitability, and sophistication, yet a low risk approach, trading the cost of carry spread is the final example we found worthwhile to comment on. Because of the huge above ground stocks of gold, the nearby or spot price never goes to a premium to the deferred months.

In a gold bull market where prices are rising, deferred months appreciate more than the nearby months. This is due to the fact that as the total value increases, assuming carrying charges remain the same, the cost of carry will also increase over that time period. To benefit, you would buy the deferred and then sell the nearby months, for a twelve month spread difference as far out as it can be placed on the gold futures market.

In a gold bear market where prices drop, the exact opposite is true. The deferred months drop much more than the nearby months. If outright prices halve in price, the carrying charge will also halve over a 12 month spread difference.

The part of the carrying charge that doesn't stay static is interest rates — the cost of money. In a gold bull market, interest rates usually (but not necessarily) increase. Therefore, if outright prices double, the net difference of a 12 month spread may more than double due to increasing interest rates. In the bear market, interest rates generally contract and reduce the net difference of the spread accordingly.

There are three advantages to using the spread method for trading as opposed to outright trading. They are reduced risk, lower margin requirements, and easier implementation. Where this approach does not work is in a sideways trading affair where spread differences can do very little for a long period of time. Patience is the building block in this approach that becomes the cornerstone, level guide, and support, for all else above.

Because of the great degree of discounting in commissions today, this approach is more profitable now than at anytime in the past. Commissions are the biggest measurable cost factor in carrying charge spread trading.

In essence, the factors affecting the carrying charge spread are shown below as a nine variable matrix.

Spread Factors
Gold Price

Interest Rates	D. Up	E. Steady	F. Down
A. Up	*Bull*	*Bull*	*Varies*
B. Steady	*Bull*	*Varies*	*Bear*
C. Down	*Varies*	*Bear*	*Bear*

Bull
Buy Far / Sell Near

Bear
Buy Near / Sell Far

Combination A-D is most profitable for a pure bull market action, putting on a buy deferred/sell nearby spread. Combination C-F is most profitable for a pure bear market doing just the reverse.

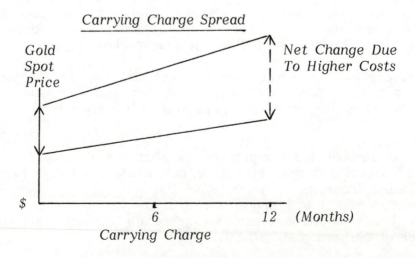

Carrying Charge Spread

Gold Spot Price — Net Change Due To Higher Costs

$ 6   12 (Months)

Carrying Charge

Spread Analysis

Gold / Silver Ratio

Chart A

Note: The Highest Level The Ratio Was At Was 100:1 in 1939.

Note: The 3 to 4 Year Cycle Of The Gold / Silver Ratio Shows The Following.
Tops: A, B. C and D. Bottoms: E, F and G.

Ratio: The Number Of Ounces Of Silver That One Ounce Of Gold Will Buy.

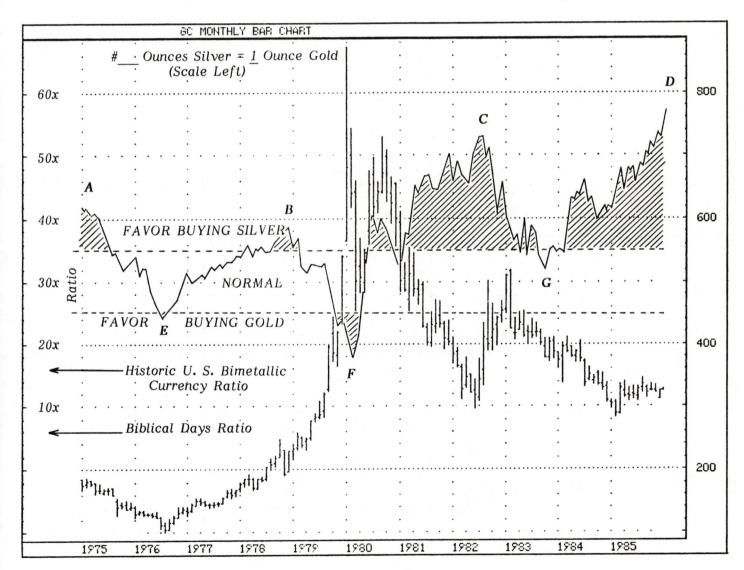

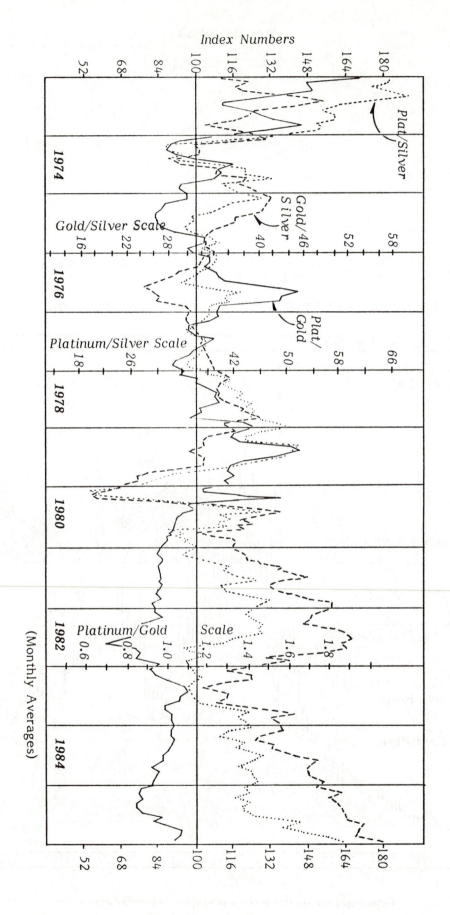

Spread Analysis

W. W. Turner Index System

Price Ratio

Chart B

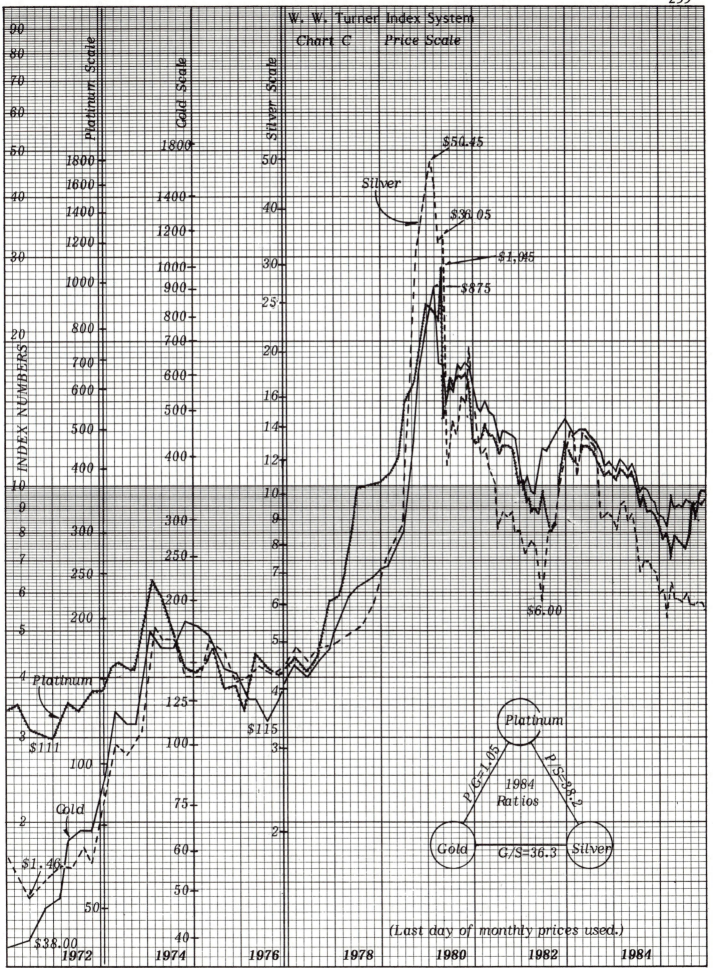

(Last day of monthly prices used.)

Spread Analysis

Platimun / Gold Spread

Chart D

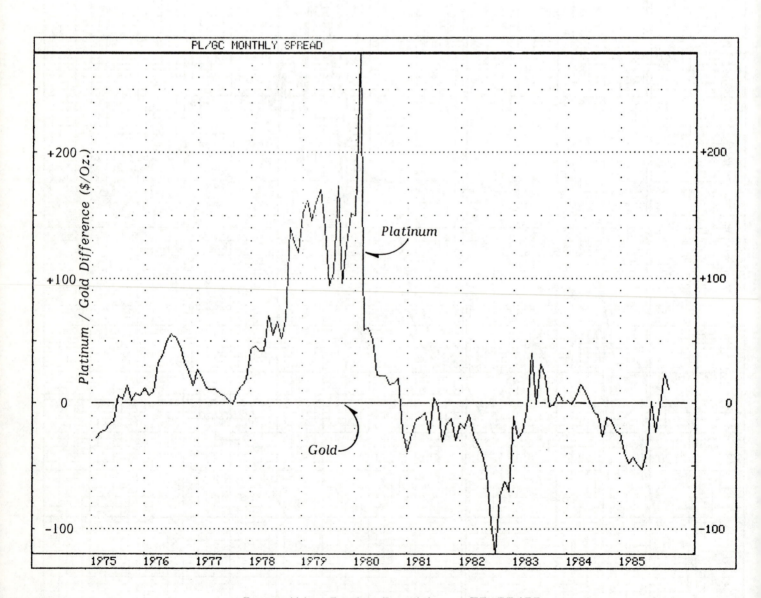

PL/GC MONTHLY SPREAD

Platinum

Gold

Commodity Quote-Graphics   TQ-20/20

Spread Analysis

Gold / T-Bond Spread

Chart E

10 Oz. Gold to 1 Bond, Par Value

1976 10 Oz. Gold = $ 1,000
1976 1 Bond, Par = $ 1,000

Commodity Quote-Graphics   TQ-20/20

Glossary of Spreads and Spread Terminology

To understand the unique world of spreading, a thorough listing and description of every kind of spread follows. Examples of markets other than gold or the metals are shown.

Animal/By-product Spread: Using a live animal contract and one of its slaughter by-products (i.e. Live Hogs/Pork Belly). A short lived contract called boneless beef (used for hamburger) naturally would have been spread against the live cattle contract.

Arbitrage: Simultaneous buying and selling of a similar item in two different markets in order to profit from a price discrepancy. Numerous metal arbitrage possibilities exist today [i.e. foreign versus domestic commodities (London Copper/New York Copper; 5 Winnipeg Gold/Chicago Gold; Sydney Gold/New York Gold) and domestic versus domestic commodities (Chicago Silver/New York Silver)].

Back Spread: Buy the back month, sell the near month.

Backwardation: Premium on the nearby months; also called an inverted market.

Bastard Hedge: Using a substitute for what should be a regular hedge.

Bear Spread: (See Back Spread). Used in gold during bullish markets.

Bull Spread: Buy the near month, sell the back month. For use in gold during bearish markets.

Butterfly Spread: A three legged combination that reduces price risk to a minimum including carrying charge risks. Usually a [buy 1 - sell 2 - buy 1] or a [sell 1 - buy 2 - sell 1] spread structure, this spread gained excessive use by investors moving taxable trades from one year to the next. Its usage has dropped since the I.R.S. closed that loophole. Both in 1978 and 1979, silver butterfly spread users were devastated when the nearby month got completely out of line for carrying charge price structure.

Carrying Charge Spread: (Also Contango - British.) The most basic spread structure, spot cash price plus increased monthly prices which include interest, insurance and handling. Can only be applied to storable commodities.

Cheap Spread: Small traders trying a low margin or cheaper method to trade a high margin requirement market.

Commodity Ratio Spread: (See Ratio Spread.)

Contango: (See Carrying Charge Spread.)

Cost of Production Spread: (Also Feed/Animal Spread.) Essentially used by commercial hedgers to hedge their cost of feed and sale of animals to insure costs and solidify gross sales revenue (i.e. Corn/Cattle and Corn/Hogs).

Cracking Spread: When refiners refine crude oil into its major by-products, heating oil and gasoline, they are "cracking" the crude oil.   The profit margin difference is the processing margin and can be traded either way. A trader puts on a crack spread when he anticipates the processing margin narrowing; he puts on a reverse crack when he anticipates the margin widening (i.e. Buy Crude Oil/Sell Heating Oil and Gasoline).

Crush Spread: (Also Processing Spread and By-Product Spread)   Buy soybeans and sell the two crush by-products (soybean oil and meal).   Because of weight differences, the correct ratio of contracts for this spread is 50,000 bushels of soybeans (10 contracts) equal to 12 soybean meal and 9 soybean oil contracts.   [Reverse Crush is just the opposite.]

Currency Spread: Buying a commodity in a weak monetary country and selling a commodity in a strong monetary country (i.e. Buy London Copper/Sell New York Copper; D-Mark/Japanese Yen; British Pound/Canadian Dollar; U.S. Dollar Index/Swiss Franc; ECU/U.S. Dollar Index).   Very difficult for American traders unless well versed in both currency histories and commodities.

Even Money Spread: Buying and selling two positions at the same price.

Exotic Spreads: (Actually Non-Spread Spreads)   Buying and selling two different commodities that are quasi-related but are never given spread margin considerations by the exchanges (i.e. New York Gold/Crude Oil).

Familiar Spreads: Another name for common or well publicized spreads.   Also, spreads used extensively by system books (i.e. Wheat/Corn; Gold/Silver; T-Bill/Eurodollar; London SIlver/2 New York SIlver).

Feed/Animal Spread: (See Cost of Production Spread.)

Forward Spread: (See Bull Spread.)

Hedge: (Also Basis Hedge, and Sell Hedge or Buy Hedge.)   In essence, a spread between a cash position and opposite position in futures.

Hidden Spread: (Also Chance Spread.)   When one has numerous outright positions, liquidating some of them may result in two outright positions falling into a preferential spread margin situation.   Usually this occurs by chance. Computers compute the lowest rate of margin requirements allowed by exchange clearing house rules to gain customer favor.

Historical Spread: (Also Historic Ratio Spread. See Ratio Spreads.)   A spread put on to establish a trading objective from historical research and relationships (i.e. Gold/Silver Ratio; Long Term Municipal Bond Index/T-Bond).

Income Tax Spread: (See Tax Straddles.)

Industrial Metal Spread: Spreads designed to play the difference between industrial metals as opposed to precious metals (i.e. Copper/Aluminum; London Copper/New York Copper; L.M.E. Lead/L.M.E. Tin; L.M.E. Zinc/L.M.E. Nickel).

Import/Export Spread: Buying and selling the same commodity in two different countries to profit from differences due to tariffs, import quotas, or levies (i.e. World Sugar #11/Domestic Sugar #12).

Inflation/Precious Metals Spread: Spreading the consumer price index to a precious metal for long term trend patterns (i.e. Consumer Price Index/COMEX Gold; Consumer Price Index/C.R.B. Futures Price Index - 27 commodities).

Inter-Commodity Spread: Buying and selling similar markets, usually adjusted for weight differences, that are similar but not exactly the same (i.e. 4 Live Hogs/3 Live Cattle (each totals 120,000 pounds). Gold/Crude Oil).

Inter-Crop Spread: In the same commodity, buying and selling two different crop months (i.e. July Corn/December Corn).

Inter-Delivery Spread: Buying and selling two different months of the same commodity. This is the most widely known spread (i.e. July Corn/September Corn).

Inter-Grain Spread: Buying and selling equal quantity of any two grain contracts (i.e. Corn/Oats).

Inter-Market Spread: (See Arbitrage and Inter-Commodity Spread.) Additional examples: New York Heating Oil/London Gasoil; S & P's OTC/NASDAQ 100 Index.

Interest Rate Spread: Buying and selling any two interest rate contracts to benefit from their yield and time structures (i.e. GNMA/T-Bond; T-Bill/T-Bond; T-Bill/Eurodollar; C.D./T-Bill).

Intra-Market Spread: (See Inter-Delivery Spread.)

Inverted Market Spread: (See Backwardation.) Front months are at a premium to the deferred months.

Leg, To Leg Into, Lifting a Leg: One side of a spread; a legged-in spread is merely doing one position of a spread first, then the other position minutes or days later. Lifting a leg is undoing one side at a time; taking a much greater degree of risk.

Limited Risk Spread: A spread designed to have minimal risk exposure, such as only carrying charge difference risk. Used mainly in tax straddle operations.

Margin Call Spread: Maintenance margin calls can be met by traders spreading against a losing positon to reduce the margin requirement and not be forced out of a position that they believe in. Creating a spread out of a single position.

Money Spread: Spreading two related products, not necessarily equal in size or price (i.e. Soybean Oil/Soybean Meal; GNMA/T-Bonds; Heating Oil/Crude Oil).

Narrowing: When forward contracts lose to the deferred months.

Pattern Spread: Based on yearly patterns, not necessarily seasonal, but designed to take advantage of usage and supply variations (i.e. Copper Seasonality).

Precious Metal Spread: Any combination of the four precious metals contracts platinum, gold, palladium, and silver. Silver has changed to an industrial metal, having been phased out as a circulating coin metal years ago (i.e. Gold/Platinum; Platinum/Palladium; Gold/Silver/Platinum; Gold/Silver). See "Supercharged Precious Metals Investing" by Cloyde P. Howard and "W. W. Turner Index System" by William W. Turner.

Premium Spread: (Also Bullish Spread.)   Nearby month reflects tightness of supply whenever it goes to a premium to the deferred month.

Price-Fixing Spreads: (See Hedge.) Cash to futures price fixing.

Processing Margin Spread: (See Crush Spread and Cracking Spread.)

Ratio Spread: (Also Historical Spread.)   (See Precious Metal Spread.)   Buying and selling two different related commodities on the basis of normal or historic relationships or ratios. Actually a form of dollar averaging two commodities by historical price/quantity switch methods.

Raw Material/By-Product Spread: (See Crush Spread.)   Buying and selling the base material and its resultant by-product(s) (i.e. Soybeans/Oil and Meal; Crude Oil/Heating Oil and Gasoline).

Raw Material/One Product Spread: Offsetting one side of the raw material with only one by-product (i.e. Crude Oil/Gasoline).

Reverse Crush Spread: The opposite of Crush Spread.

Seasonal Spread: Designed to benefit from seasonal trends from the growing and harvesting cycle influences.

Stock Market Spread: Any combination of different stock indexes (i.e. Standard and Poor Stock Index/Value Line Stock Index; TSE 300 Index/NYSE Index; London F.T. Stock Exchange 100 Index/S & P Index).

Straddle-Up Spread: Legging into a spread one position at a time.   Usually done by traders to lock in a loss.

Straddle: Old cotton market term for spread.

Suicide Spread: High risk, no trading plan approach for implementing a spread. Actually double risk exposure as either side could go against the trader.

Switch: Another term for spread.

Tax Straddle: (See Butterfly Spread.)   A spread put on expressly for shifting tax exposure from one year to the next.   Still allowed, but with many qualifications.

Three and Four Dimension Analysis: Name given to using spread differences to catch reversals in the market through monthly price spread divergence.

Unwinding: Usually liquidating a spread one side at a time.

Widening Spread: Nearby months widen in relation to the deferred months.

Spread Analysis Bibliography

Clifton, Frederick T. "Old and New Factors in Popular Commodity Spreads." 1973 Commodity Research Yearbook, pp. 41-47.

Crim, Elias. "Are Old Gold Ratios Still Holding Up?" Futures, Aug. 1985, p. 57.

Dobson, Edward. Commodity Spreads - A Historical Chart Perspective. Greenville, SC: 1974.

Greenberg, Stephen. °Commodity Spreads and Straddles." Guide to Commodity Price Forecasting, Commodity Research Bureau, 1965, pp. 213-229.

Howard, Cloyde P. "The Gold/Silver Price Ratio - A Trading Strategy." Gold Standard News.

Howard, Cloyde P. "Super Charged Precious Metals Investing." Gold Standard News, Vol. IV, No. 10, 1980.

Lipscomb, H. Alan. "Golden Leverage." On Gold. DeKalb, IL: Waterleaf Press, 1982, pp. 273-356.

A Guide to Trading Commodity Spreads. New York: Loeb Rhoades Hornblower.

Strauss, Simon D. "Gold and Silver As Stores of Value." Asarco, Inc., 1981.

Tiger, Phil. "The Limited Risk Spread." Commodities, Jan. 1977, pp. 28-29 & 48-51.

Turner, W. W. W. W. Turner Index System. Leesburg, FL.

Stochastic Analysis

Stochastic analysis was developed by the observation that price closes tend to lean in the direction of the overall trend. The method of interpreting the stochastic is by looking for overbought or oversold areas on the stochastic chart for divergence. This concept and mathematical process was orginally developed by market technician Dr. George Lane.

$$\% \ K = \frac{Current \ Close \ - \ Lowest \ Low}{Highest \ High \ - \ Lowest \ Low}$$

One first determines the number of bar plots or time periods to be used in the calculation. Because of the long term nature of the gold chart used throughout this study, we decided on ten bars' length or approximately 44 weeks.

Starting with the first ten bar total, find the extreme price range of that group. Then to determine the "Fast" % K, subtract the ten bars' low from the current close (last bar plot). Divide this amount by the ten bar price range; highest high less the lowest low. Continue for each successive bar plot, dropping the oldest one and adding the next newest bar figures.

The "Fast" % D is a 3 bar smoothed average of the % K. This tends to smooth the erratic "Fast" % K plots. Erratic price moves and % K plots on the stochastic chart respond more consistently in giving signals, turns, etc.

To interpret the % D and % K plot, there is one signal which can be a buy or sell, and that is divergence between the two, or when % K crosses the % D line. This is another oscillator type approach to market timing.

Stochastic Analysis

The stochastic is designed to measure prices within trading ranges of commodities, usually approximating 4 to 5 weeks' cycle length. Many futures have trading cycles of 14, 28, 56, and 112 days, with 28 days the most common. A frequently used stochastic is 10 days, which best tracks the current day's price level relative to the highest and lowest prices for the prior 10 trading days.

continued...

Commodity Quote-Graphics   TQ-20/20

Stochastic Analysis

The purpose of this measure will permit the stochastic to track cycles that vary by as much as 10 days either way, from an ideal 28 day cycle. The % K is a.3 day moving average of K. This creates a pure data plot (3 day moving average) and a smoother plot (3 day moving average) that eliminates some of the erratic movement of the first plot. The two plots together show the main trading cycles of the commodity being examined. Esentially, buy signals are generated when K rises above D; sell signals occur when K goes below D.

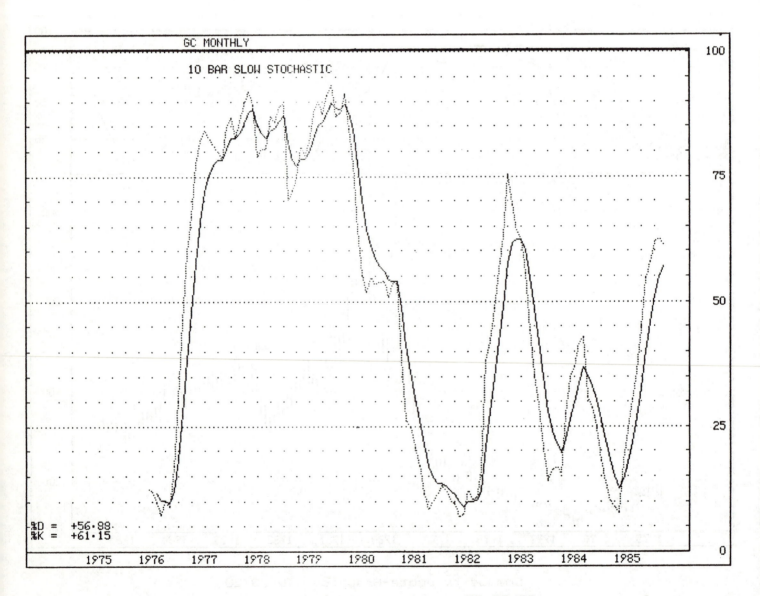

Commodity Quote-Graphics   TQ-20/20

*"Banking establishments are more dangerous
than standing armies."*
---Thomas Jefferson

Support & Resistance Analysis

When prices move up or down, they tend to congest between certain levels, more than others. At other price levels, trading moves dramatically between levels with little congestion for unknown reasons. Even more amazing is when prices retrace prior levels from years or even decades before. Seemingly the price action "remembers" these levels of activity and inactivity. How investors and speculators can act as a single entity, collectively "remembering" prior price trading levels is hard to explain. Major highs formed years ago in entirely different circumstances become what is called resistance as bull markets take contemporary price situations to those highs.

Reactions in bull markets usually stop at lower highs, thus providing support. A good example is gold's 1978 down reaction to the $190 area; exactly 1974's gold top. According to this form of analysis, support came right where it should.

The opposite holds true for bear markets. Prices on the way down meet resistance in prior congested price levels and support in the primary trend direction (down) when prices rally to prior lows. The knowledge of this action can be applied to very short term price charts as well.

In 1978 and 1979 bullish gold prices reached the $260 level, a high not seen since 1864 during the Civil War. For seven months, from October 1978 to April 1979, prices back and filled, but kept edging higher until resistance was overcome and new highs were made. Because of a lack of detailed price history and conversion into U.S. dollars, we cannot accurately project what levels of resistance will be encountered whenever gold moves into the stratosphere — $20,000 in 1781 when the continental dollar collapsed or $(infinity) in 1864 when the confederate dollar collapsed.

On the following chart, all major support and resistance points for gold are indicated by price and by parallel lines indicated to the right on the price scale. Any further bull market for gold will respect these significant price points. Major highs and lows from the 1975 through 1985 period will tend to effect price movements according to the rules expressed above.

Support & Resistance Analysis

Significant High and Low Price Levels (Support & Resistance) Basis Spot Gold

Commodity Quote-Graphics   TQ-20/20

Swing Chart Analysis

The swing chart is a simple price trending method. Like most older system approaches, it is basic, disciplined and unemotional. It has been traced as far back as 1700 A.D. to Japanese merchants using it in their rice trading.

Also known as the "Nehaba-Ashi" (Japanese) and the "Chang-Cheng Banfa" (Chinese, "Great Wall Method") the philosophical theme is to flow with the forces of nature. In other words, prices flow with the trend until the trend changes, then the method changes accordingly. It does not anticipate highs or lows, or when the market should turn. It is a trending approach with price the only consideration. Time, volume, or any other technical measure is not scaled in.

There are two elements of every swing method to be considered — the minimum amount of the swing to be plotted and the type and amount of penetration desired at turning points. Modifications to this analysis are endless and do substantially affect trading results. The main modifications made by traders are to the penetration rules, how they are implemented and whether there is a price or time lag in actually reversing.

The trader picks the minimum price plot size to reduce the number of price moves. This enables him to feel comfortable with the measurable risk, eliminating that price movement he feels is not applicable to his needs. This method becomes a linear plot, similar to the point and figure approach primarily used by floor traders. However, being a linear plot, it is identified as a continuous pattern, always flowing with the predominate trend.

To chart swing methods, you need to decide on a minimum price to be plotted. In our sample chart, we created a swing chart from our computer drawn monthly bar plot (see chart). We decided to use a $5/ounce minimum plot grid with major price grid lines at $100 increments. When we start to plot the price, one primary difference that doesn't appear in other analyses is a column representing the trend. When prices went through a prior low, we colored the line black to represent a downtrend. When prices went above a recent high, we colored it white to represent an uptrend. Time is not considered at all, similar to point and figure charting.

The main advantage to a conservative investor is apparent by the very small number of reversals shown in our long term swing chart. There are few whipsaws or changes in the primary direction. If you continually roll forward positions in the direction of the trend, this approach will enable you to catch the majority of any major trending move. It will not get you out near any top nor any bottom. When the price trend is dictated to reverse at a swing point by violating a prior high or low, it should not be considered just a price at which to close out a position. It is also used to reverse direction until the prior high or low is violated.

We could have used a daily or weekly chart for the example of this method, which is more familiar to most traders. Most people lean toward shorter time frames with smaller risk and more overall trades. Therefore, you should use close-only prices to make daily swings more meaningful. Studies of daily swing charts for gold have shown between 55% and 75% profitable trades with very large dollar totals.

For those commodities or securities identified as being choppy or erratic, we do not recommend this approach.

Swing charts when compared to moving averages show a noticable difference in performance results. In swing charting the protective stop/reversal order is usually placed just beyond the support point opposite the trend. Moving averages are normally bringing the protective stop order closer to where the current price is in order to "lock in" more of the price move for fear of losing profits. When prices vascillate as they often do, stops are sometimes touched off in a reaction, only to have prices turn back toward their primary trend. This creates a whipsaw or false move and reduces overall results. You learn to develop more patience using swing charting. Greater net profits can be gained compared to other trending systems.

Swing Chart Analysis

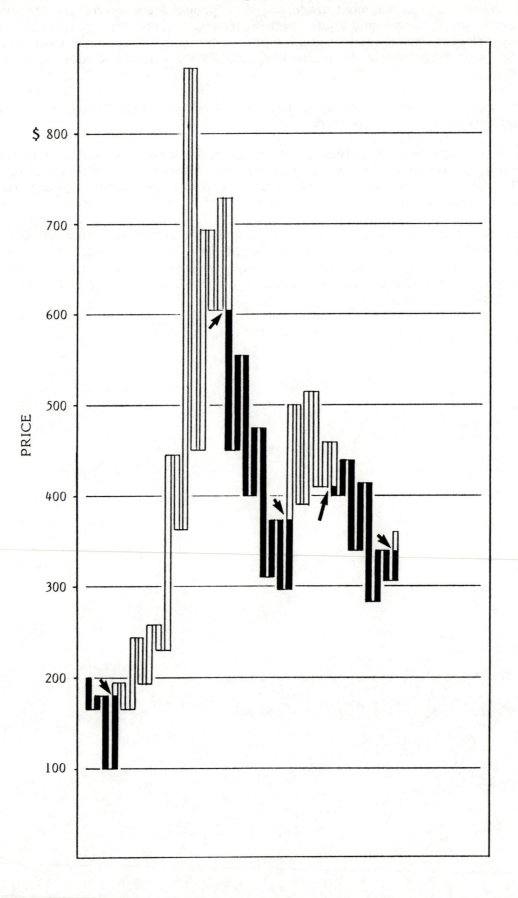

Swing Chart Analysis Bibliography

Donchian, Richard D. "Trend Following Methods in Commodity Price Analysis." Guide to Commodity Price Forecasting, Commodity Research Bureau, N.Y., 1965, pp. 48-60.

Libey, Donald R. "Chang Cheng Banfa: An Oriental Approach to Trading the Gold and Silver Markets." On Gold, DeKalb, IL: The Waterleaf Press, 1982, pp. 363-388.

Three and Four Dimensional Chart Analysis

This approach has been little publicized but is used in varying degrees by experienced traders and brokers to monitor money flows within the overall investing area. Developed by William Ohama in 1969, three dimensional charting is a divergence technique for catching market reversals. Price difference changes that develop between different months of the same commodity is called three dimensional and price difference changes of related commodities is called four dimensional. Both can lead to major trend changes.

The main logic Ohama uses is that large hedgers who spread extensively are major market forces in most commodities. They also do extensive non-hedging spreading (buying one month and selling another) for specific profit purposes. When they unwind major spreading, it shows in the month's differences and their price changes, usually at significant tops and bottoms.

While this analysis sounds original, a former client of mine learned an approach directly from Jessie Livermore. This approach utilizes the swing chart method which in essence is similar to Ohama's method. Livermore kept swing charts on every combination of contract price months of each commodity in which he heavily speculated. It was for the same purpose Ohama devised his three dimensional chart analysis — to catch major positions being put on or taken off in large fashion reflecting price trend changes. In Livermore's day, the major commodities traded were cotton and the grains, which are the basic carrying charge structured commodities. When these commodities leave their full carry price spread structure, a tight supply situation begins to appear.

How three and four dimensional analysis works is simple. For example, assume prices are in a strong up trending mode. A signal for a reversal occurs when new highs are touched by some months and other months of the same commodity fail to make simultaneous new highs. This is an obvious sign of new shorts being spread against established long positions. This divergence from bullishness indicates internal market weakness and a sign that sometime soon weak months could be sold short.

The reverse occurs when prices are in down trends. It is the internal composition or character of the market showing sophisticated or experienced money repositioning itself.

Because of numerous reasons why traders, brokers, hedgers, and investors spread, this is not a "sure fire" approach for spotting all reversals. Monthly contract prices are structured in most commodities to reflect the cost of carrying charges. When interest rates increase, price differences widen to reflect higher carrying charges. Some traders spread positions to move tax situations from one year into another. Other traders spread one commodity against another that usually have something in common; two metals on the same exchange, any two active pits on the same exchange, response to a change in short term interest rates, foreign currency sensitive markets, product and by-product markets, and finally simple arbitrage.

According to Ohama, comparison of separate commodities in interrelated markets is the fourth dimension to chart interpretation; again with monthly differentials as the leading signal. In the case of gold in 1979, in our opinion, the lead contract of silver literally pulled up the entire silver market, all silver arbitrage markets, gold and its parallel arbitrage markets, other precious metal futures markets, the base metal copper, and bullion coin markets. To a lesser degree, it also influenced money flows in foreign currencies, interest rate futures inversely, stock index futures, grain markets and some international softs. This was fourth dimensional analysis in extreme action, as suggested by Ohama.

At that time, I was an investment broker advising clients in active trading. Experience taught me that the spot price of New York's silver contract (the major liquid market commercial dealers use) was the key to the 1979/early 1980 price action. Floor brokers and traders in the grain pits at the CBOT could not trade normally due to the monstrous dollar amount changes occurring daily in the silver pits. When silver was originally around $6.00 an ounce, a margin requirement of $1,000 was adequate for price moves of 5¢ to 10¢ a day. This reflected $250 to $500 per contract value or 25% to 50% equity change on original margin. By November 1979, silver was around $18.00 an ounce and began moving 50¢ to $1.00 a day. This was $2,500 to $5,000 per contract value against a now higher initial margin of $5,000. In late December 1979, spot silver ran so fast, it locked all other months limit bid with no trading possible over an estimated two months — $5,000 a day equity change, plus or minus depending on whether you were long or short. In less than two months, total equity change was $200,000 per contract.

When the Commodity Exchange of New York (COMEX) changed the legal structure of the silver contract by calling for long liquidation only, silver's spot price collapsed, pulling all other months down in sympathy. All other commodities that had been influenced by silver's spot price month, sympathetically responded down immediately.

Gold basically follows the silver market for swings and reversals, due to their dual identity as precious metals. Actually, it is the tremendous quantity of literature espousing the gold/silver ratio or relationship in monetary history that implies an economic umbilical cord linking the two together. While this is actually incorrect, the important reality is that people believe it and make it so. With the two metals' trading pits at the COMEX adjacent to each other, traders could move readily between the two creating an economic siamese futures. Spread trading off of the gold/silver ratio charts occurs frequently, tying the two metals price action closer. One economist followed the gold/silver/platinum relationship for over 15 years with his investment methodology tying those 3 metals together in published form.

Using different months of different commodity contracts in a variety of combinations can give advance signs of major reversals, but not always. When markets change their nature and become lopsided or dominated by any one of the three main time-risk trading group categories (floor broker, public speculator and commercial hedger) market behavior patterns change altering the price fluctuation characteristics and reliability levels of past behavior patterns. What worked well 5 years prior may not even be worth remembering today. This is perhaps the most important point of Ohama's three and four dimensional chart analysis — know your market well.

Trendline Chart Analysis

Trendline analysis is perhaps the most basic of all technical approaches. Derived from stock traders doing simple analysis of daily stock charts; in essence it is simple trend determination by drawing trendlines off the highs or lows. Since most trends tend to run in straight lines, this method adapts itself to many moves well, especially when used in combination with rules from formation analysis.

Most important in drawing proper trendlines is using only significant highs or lows. Bullish trendlines are drawn off significant low points; bearish trendlines are drawn off significant high points. Only experience can best judge which of these prices are the most appropriate. Most markets respond well to this analysis in simple bull or bear trending patterns. However, about 20% of the time in major bull market tops or developing panic lows, prices begin to compound in geometric fashion making straight trendlines difficult to use.

The main advantage of straight trendlines is that once a trendline has been determined, prices will maintain that trend, touch it when prices dip for additional contact points, then continue in the same trendline.

Advocators of the random walk theory do not believe a multiple point trendline could exist. We refer to any chart service showing the 1928 - 1932 collapse of stock prices on an index basis plotted onto semi-log scale. The now famous Dow Jones Industrial Stock Index developed a distinctive down trendline eventually developing nine points touching.

Once a trendline has been determined, parallel trendlines can be drawn off price oscillations (i.e. a bullish uptrend drawn off two lows can have a parallel line drawn off of a significant high thus creating a bullish trend channel).

When prices violate a trendline, a trend reversal has occurred. The greater number of points on the trendline, the more important the reversal.

Finally, frequent violation of up/down trendlines in a generally static area defines a nontrending area or consolidation.

On the gold chart we plotted all significant trendlines, reversals and channel trendlines as they occured.

Trendline Chart Analysis

Trendlines Drawn In Sequence, A, B, Etc.

Commodity Quote-Graphics   TQ-20/20

"If two men had walked down Fifth Avenue a year ago — that would have been March 1933 — and one of them had a pint of wiskey in his pocket and the other had a hundred dollars in gold coin, the one with the wiskey would have been called a criminal and the one with the gold an honest citizen. If these two men, like Rip Van Winkle, slept for a year and again walked down Fifth Avenue, the man with the wiskey would be called an honest citizen and the one with the gold coin a criminal."
---Samuel Insull

Volume And Open Interest Analysis

In addition to price, there is other data obtainable directly from the market, less understood and, therefore, primarily used by the professional.

Volume is a barometer of trading activity and a measure of the intensity of supply and demand for certain periods. Open interest is purchase or sale commitments outstanding or unliquidated contracts. Open interest helps determine the character of the price moves.

Next to future prices, volume and open interest are the most widely disseminated statistics. Open interest should be shown on an adjusted seasonal basis to allow for annual influences.

Certain behavior patterns can be noted from empirical observations in revealing price trends. Generally, when volume moves with price in a direction, it tends to reinforce the nature and strength of the trend.

A set of four primary rules explains the essence of using volume for this area of analysis.

Rule One: In a major upmove, volume increases on rallies and declines on reactions.

Rule Two: When prices begin to develop reversal or topping tendencies, volume tends to decline and then increase sharply at the top, called the "upward blowoff".

Rule Three: In a major downmove, volume increases on drops in price, and then declines on rallies.

Rule Four: As prices drop toward a major low with bottoming tendencies, volume tends to dry up, and then increases sharply at the final "washout" or bottom. This is also called a "downside blowoff".

Open interest acts basically in the same manner. When prices are strongly trending up or down, and open interest expands more than what is seasonally normal, this is classified as technically strong or weak. When open interest contracts as prices are strongly trending up or down, the technical condition is counter-trending. That is, in an up market if the open interest contracts, the shorts are covering their positions causing the price rise. This is inherently an unsustainable condition and technically weak.

This analysis must be developed and learned to understand the variables within it because there are exceptions to these observations. In general, the most observable or distinctive action for gold are the two tops in January and September 1980 (see Chart A). Points A and B were definitely blowoffs of major price tops. It is interesting to note that prices made their absolute high in January 1980 (point A) but many technicians deem September as the real top (point B). It should also be noted that open interest reached higher levels at point B.

Volume and Open Interest Analysis

Twenty years ago, Joseph Granville, a stock market technician, conceived of utilizing price and volume together to analyze market trends, which is known as On Balance Volume (OBV). He theorized that volume's move precedes a price move when a trend begins.

In the stock arena, it is thought that smart money accumulates stock prior to a major upmove. Our concern is not whether this accumulation process is acutally the net cause of stock prices moving from one level to a higher level. Our concern is whether OBV can be used as a reliable indicator for price moves. Increased activity does show in increased volume, usually in the direction of price activity on the buy side. The reverse is true on the downside; supply overcomes demand in distribution and is apparent in OBV plots.

By simply creating a running total of volume figures, assigning a plus or minus to up or down days respectively, a net figure is derived. Essentially, a continuum of OBV can be plotted on a chart the same way that prices can be plotted. We used monthly figures computed as above to develop a long term gold OBV (see Chart C).

Interpretation is done by simple trend following rules applied to OBV along with comparison to the long term price chart of gold. In 1978, point A shows a bullish trend start to appear. OBV roughly parallels price action through January 1980; (point B) falls for two months; then reverses to continue rising to new highs. Point C, made in tandem with the September 1980 high for gold, is higher on OBV than the dynamic blowoff price high in January 1980 (point B). This is another confirmation to some technicians that September was the orthodox high in gold's cyclical price interpretation.

Prices collapsed into a bear market for two years on both the OBV chart as well as the price chart. Both charts' plots turned up after a low in June 1982 (point D) and both rallied to create a top in January 1983 (point E). A bear pattern reasserted itself from then on. In 1985, the OBV chart shows the distinctive February low, but then goes on to a new low in May 1985 (point F) contrary to the price chart. A rally in OBV action continued to show excessive strength in comparison to the price chart. Normal interpretation of this recent action suggests that point G is the high to watch. A move to the upside by OBV through point G suggests a bull market is at hand.

For long term implications, another observation is the low level of drop that point F had when compared to point D. It suggests a primary bear market is still at hand. Even if a 6 to 12 month rally occurs, the downtrend from C to E as drawn, would have to be violated to turn long term bullish.

It is our personal belief that this aproach is more applicable to weekly or daily data time periods with a smoothing constant applied, rather than long term.

Volume and Open Interest Analysis

We found information in our files relating to volume analysis published by Benjamin B. Crocker [Scientific Investment Research]. The information we have is 15 to 25 years old and we could not locate Mr. Crocker nor his firm to update this material. In following is a brief summary of his analysis.

Essentially, Mr. Crocker devised a "price versus volume" chart instead of using the customary price to time chart. This method (designated "P/V" Charting) graphically shows strength or weakness in how price fluctuates relative to volume. In the normal price to time chart, volume is customarily drawn on the bottom and left up to you to interpret volume in relation to price changes. On "P/V" charts, it is the circular motions or looping formations that imply what to expect in the way of a trend.

Two sample charts are drawn on Chart D. Sample one gives two stock "P/V" charts against two stock price/time charts. The top chart in sample one shows a clockwise motion giving a buy signal. The second chart shows a counter-clockwise motion giving a sell signal. In S.I.R.'s literature, an example was given of the Dow Jones Industrial Stock Average crash of 1962 (shown in sample two). Along with many sub-rules, the "P/V" chart was explained in detail with the final loop giving a buy signal within two weeks and 10% of the low. Other rules, too numerous to explain, gave exception refinements, i.e. when sell signals are given in bull trends and when buy signals are given in bear trends. The "3/10% rule" for diversification and probability analysis is another sample rule.

Because Mr. Crocker concentrated on stocks and then after a few years moved on to commodities, to our knowledge the work was unfinished and too unrefined to be implemented. Some portfolio work, computer "trend rating" guides and "special trending" analysis were developed.

"Speed trading" or aggressive trading with the most volatile commodities, using exponential moving averages, and an "average trend method" to help in differentiating between the market's trend mode or the whipsaw mode were also promoted.

Because of the nature of this overall "price versus volume" analysis, we believe it is more suitable for use with daily or weekly data. Because of the ability to do numerous calculations, a computer could even apply this approach for hourly or even shorter time periods.

Volume and Open Interest Analysis
Chart A

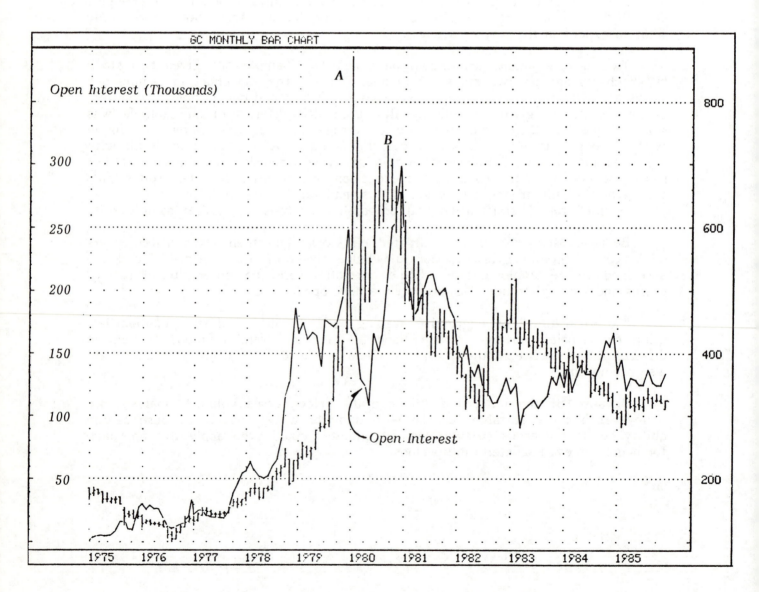

GC MONTHLY BAR CHART

Open Interest (Thousands)

A

B

Open Interest

Commodity Quote-Graphics   TQ-20/20

Courtesy; New York Commodity Exchange

Volume and Open Interest Analysis

Chart B

Commodity Quote-Graphics   TQ-20/20

Courtesy; New York Commodity Exchange

Volume And Open Interest Analysis

Chart C

On Balance Volume - Monthly Data

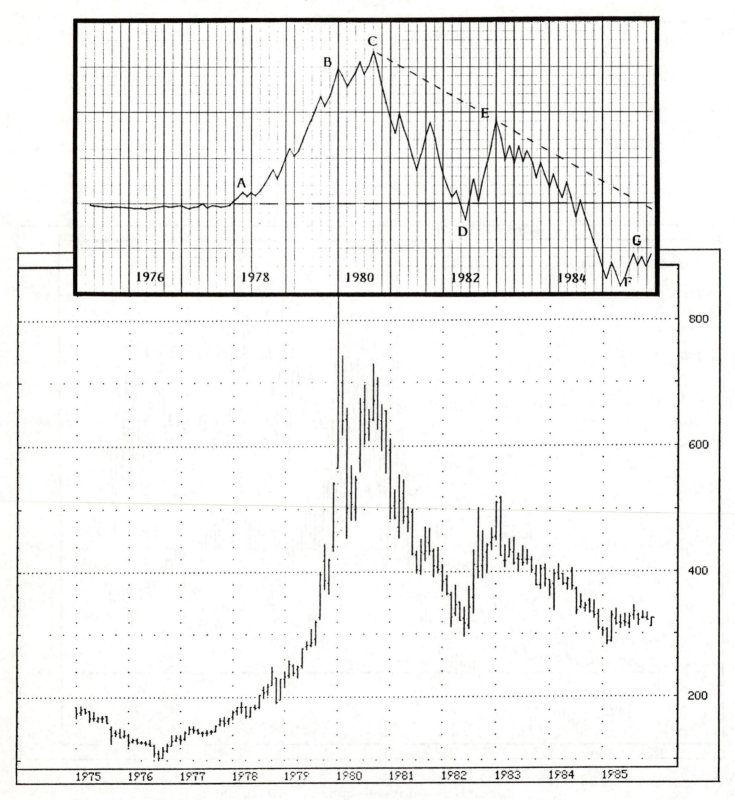

Commodity Quote-Graphics   TQ-20/20

Volume And Open Interest Analysis

Chart D

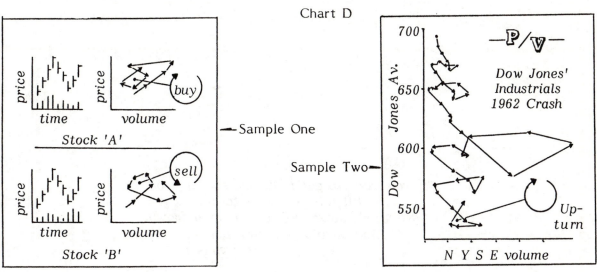

Commodity Quote-Graphics TQ-20/20

Courtesy: Scientific Investment Research.

"If you want to get rich, you son of a bitch,
I'll tell you what to do:
Never sit down with a tear or a frown,
And paddle your own canoe."
---Anonymous

PART V

Summary

Index

*"Panics, in some cases, have their uses;
they produce as much good as hurt."*
---Thomas Paine

Summary

The decision of which approach to use is a personal one. In the preceeding pages, we attempted to briefly present many diverse approaches and apply each approach to gold — the most controversial of all commodities. Whether you choose to use any of the approaches we presented — or none of them — is up to you. We did not attempt to "sell" you on any single method of predicting future price movement. No single method is 100% reliable. Most systems' reliability tends to fall around a two choice decision matrix, similar to that of flipping a coin — 40% to 60% reliable.

If you wish to study an analysis in greater depth, bibliographies were given after certain sections for this purpose. To thoroughly understand all the nuances of any particular analysis, we recommend more thorough research.

We may have omitted a few analyses, either as an oversight or by design. We chose to ignore those analyses which are merely clever rehashings of others.

If you have any questions or comments regarding this book or the futures markets, we welcome your correspondence. Please address all inquiries to Capital Futures Associates, Ltd., P. O. Box 2618, Chicago, Illinois 60690.

"There is nothing inherently wrong in effect with fiat money,
provided we get perfect authority and God-like intelligence for kings."
---Aristotle

Index

Consultation

As President of C.F.A., Ltd., a registered trading advisor, Mr. Schildgen is available for consultation and advice regarding your specific investments between 10:00 a.m. and 2:00 p.m. Central Standard Time.

An initial retainer based on a minimum number of hours is payable in advance. Thereafter, consultation will be billed on an hourly basis.

In order for Mr. Schildgen to give you <u>specific advice</u> tailored to your needs and current situation, a brief profile of your investments, equity situation, and liquidity would be appreciated. This is optional, however, it would enable Mr. Schildgen to provide you with advice based on your investment concerns.

If you are seeking advice concerning your trading account, method or approach, or Mr. Schildgen's specific opinion on the markets, a brief summary of your trades is requested. (Copies of monthly summaries are appropriate.)

For further details, please call or write Capital Futures Associates, Ltd., P. O. Box 2618, Chicago, Illinois 60690, (312) 274-9254.

ORDER FORM

Please send _____ copies of <u>Analytical Methods for Successful Speculation</u> at $49.95 each, plus $2.00 shipping costs. Illinois residents add 8% sales tax.

Enclose check or money order payable to Capital Futures Assoc., Ltd. No C.O.D., "bill me," or bank card orders accepted. Ship to:

Name_____

Company_____

Address_____

City_____State_____Zip_____

30 day return privilege.Enclose check or money order, this order form, and mail to:

CFA, Ltd.
P.O. Box 2618—Dept. A
Chicago, IL 60690

FOR ADDITIONAL COPIES, ATTACH CHECK TO ORDER FORM AND MAIL

ORDER FORM

Please send _____ copies of <u>Analytical Methods for Successful Speculation</u> at $49.95 each, plus $2.00 shipping costs. Illinois residents add 8% sales tax.

Enclose check or money order payable to Capital Futures Assoc., Ltd. No C.O.D., "bill me," or bank card orders accepted. Ship to:

Name_____

Company_____

Address_____

City_____State_____Zip_____

30 day return privilege.Enclose check or money order, this order form, and mail to:

CFA, Ltd.
P.O. Box 2618—Dept. A
Chicago, IL 60690

ORDER FORM

Please send _____ copies of <u>Analytical Methods for Successful Speculation</u> at $49.95 each, plus $2.00 shipping costs. Illinois residents add 8% sales tax.

Enclose check or money order payable to Capital Futures Assoc., Ltd. No C.O.D., "bill me," or bank card orders accepted. Ship to:

Name_____

Company_____

Address_____

City_____State_____Zip_____

30 day return privilege.Enclose check or money order, this order form, and mail to:

CFA, Ltd.
P.O. Box 2618—Dept. A
Chicago, IL 60690